THE AMAZING THEATRE

THE AMAZING
THEATRE

By

JAMES AGATE

BENJAMIN BLOM  New York/London

TO

ALFRED CHENHALLS, F.C.A.,

WHO CAN ACCOUNT FOR EVERYTHING
EXCEPT
THE AMAZING THEATRE

First Published 1939
Reissued 1969 by
Benjamin Blom, Inc., Bronx, New York 10452
and 56 Doughty Street, London, W.C. 1

Library of Congress Catalog Card Number 76-91307

Printed in the United States of America

Preface

On my bookshelves are the following books made up of reprinted dramatic criticisms:

> Henry Morley's *The Journal of a London Playgoer.* 1851–66.
>
> Dutton Cook's *Nights at the Play.* 1867–81.
>
> William Archer's *The Theatrical World.* 1893–97.
>
> Bernard Shaw's *Our Theatres in the Nineties.* 1895–98.
>
> Max Beerbohm's *Around Theatres.* 1898–1910.
>
> J. T. Grein's *Dramatic Criticism.* 1900–4.

From this the reader will perceive that I have no records of the years 1881–93. Some little time ago I received a letter from a daughter of Clement Scott asking if I would accept her father's scrap-book of *memoranda dramatica* : " The first cutting is from the *Morning Post* for December 30th, 1811—*Venice Preserved*, at Covent Garden Theatre. The last entry is dated 1833, and is a notice of Kean's *Othello*." This volume is now on a shelf specially built for it. It contains some six thousand articles, measures $15\frac{1}{2}$ by $11\frac{1}{2}$ by $5\frac{1}{2}$ inches, and weighs 16 pounds 10 ounces.

When I came back from the War of 1914–18 I discovered that no dramatic critic was reprinting or looked like reprinting his dramatic essays. And I determined that the years during which I practised should not go unrecorded. In other words, the dramatic critics of the future should not look to their shelves and draw a blank during that period. So I published a volume entitled *At Half-past Eight*, covering my work in the *Saturday Review* from 1920 to 1922. After that I published four volumes entitled *The Contemporary Theatre*, dealing with the years 1923 to 1926. An astonishing undergraduate, one Frank Whitworth, then turned himself into a publisher at Cambridge for the express purpose of publishing *Their Hour upon the Stage*, 1927–30. Since then I have published *First Nights*, 1930–34, and *More First Nights*, 1934–37. Nobody remembers now, and I have almost forgotten, that for seven years I broadcast fortnightly talks on the theatre, and of these I published the cream—if ' cream ' be the word !—in *My Theatre Talks*, 1925–32.

Seven publishers have been inveigled into issuing these books, and this inveigling I regard as a triumph. Anybody can write dramatic criticism; it takes a very clever fellow indeed to get it reprinted. I have never heard of anyone buying a volume of dramatic criticism, and I never go to a party without some one asking why I do not reprint my dramatic criticisms ! But I have attained my object. There will at least be on the shelves of the British Museum a record of plays produced in the London theatre from 1919 to 1939 —in other words, a more or less complete record of what would otherwise have been a total blank.

I have called the present collection *The Amazing Theatre*. That the drama should persist in spite of the cinema, broadcasting, television, dance music, lawn tennis, motoring, and the open hostility of the film-seduced Press—this dour resistance to mass attack, including the Storm Troops of General Indifference, strikes me as perhaps the most amazing thing in an astounding world.

The criticisms which compose this book appeared between June 1937 and July 1939 in the *Sunday Times*, to whose proprietors I am once again grateful for the courteous permission to reprint. I also wish to thank Alan Dent for his witty index and even wittier proof-correcting.

JAMES AGATE

September 1939

Contents

Two Victorias

VICTORIA REGINA. A play. By Laurence Housman. Lyric
Theatre, Monday, June 21, 1937.

FLOODLIGHT. A revue. By Beverley Nichols. Music by
Beverley Nichols. Saville Theatre, Wednesday, June
23, 1937.

[*June* 27, 1937]

MISS MITFORD, writing to a friend in Ireland in the week
of Queen Victoria's accession, devotes her letter to *The
Pickwick Papers*, the state of her geraniums, Harriet Mar-
tineau's new book on America, and the lack of elegance in
the letters of Charles Lamb. The letter ends : " If I had
time and room I could tell you fifty pretty stories of our
young Queen." But she doesn't. I wish I could burke this
play as beautifully as Miss Mitford burkes that drama. But
it is too late to write about Dickens and Lamb, I have no
geraniums, and my views on America will be found elsewhere.

My reason for funking Mr Gilbert Miller's London production of this play is that I have just seen the New York
one. The centre of the production over there is not a distant
star, but a blazing sun, and I am still so blinded by the
dazzling performance of Helen Hayes that I literally cannot
see that of Miss Pamela Stanley. On the first night the
mind's eye proved so much stronger than the physical one
that I found myself continually translating what I feel sure
is a very clever little performance into terms of remembered
magnificence. Off the stage Helen Hayes is plain, her
manner aloof, and she displays none of the dull coquetries
of sex. She has the " shy, fiery-eyed, school-marm " air of
Charlotte Brontë, and, talking to her, you feel that she has
that kind of mind. Having seen Miss Hayes in one part
only, though it is a part of many facets, I do not know

9

whether she is a great actress or not, and I do not go beyond
the statement that this was the kind of performance a great
actress might be expected to give. In the Balmoral scene
she seemed to rely very little upon make-up, but rather upon
an inward metamorphosis. Grief had left behind it a reful-
gent calm like sunset after storm-clouds have departed.
Miss Stanley, in the same scene, is still grief-crumpled.
Helen Hayes looked exactly fifty-eight; the lines painted on
the English actress's face make her look a hundred. Those
who knew Queen Victoria have always spoken of her power
to terrify. I have always felt that she must have frightened
even Mrs Kendal; and my first and last word about Helen
Hayes is that she would have frightened Queen Victoria !

Anybody who has not seen the American performance
may find the foregoing grudging to the English one.
Montague once said that it was an authentic mark of futility
in critics that they should argue whether Bernhardt or Duse
stood higher : " You cannot measure infinities against one
another." Quite ! But all who saw Hilda Trevelyan's
Wendy and then that of any other actress never talked
about pitting infinities for the good reason that there was
only one infinity to be pitted. Miss Stanley does many
things beautifully, and I think that she has at least two
moments of real emotion which, being genuinely her own,
genuinely move her audience. These are her contrition in
the quarrel scene, and her murmured " Oh, Albert !
Albert ! " after Beaconsfield has gone. But I am afraid I
find the performance as a whole a little toy-like, something
smacking of the doll's house in the pre-Ibsen sense of that
phrase, and rather like what one would have expected if the
authors of *Marigold* had been allowed to bring on the Queen.
All around me on the first night the air hummed with pretty
comments, and blasts of " Isn't she sweet ? " blew down my
neck. No one in the American audience would have thought
of this, or, if they had so thought, so dared.

The Prince Consort was capitally played in America and

is capitally played here, and perhaps comparison, being between two finites, might be odious. An eighteenth-century critic, invited to compare two public favourites, got out of his difficulty by saying that whereas Mr X had the more money, Mr Y was the taller man. I shall permit myself to say that whereas Mr Carl Esmond in this country is more like his original, Mr Vincent Price in America showed himself the better actor, and by far the better singer. That the pain of the Queen's quarrel with her Consort should be matched by our pain in listening to Mr Esmond's vocal efforts seems to me to be stretching the Pathetic Fallacy farther than it will go. Alas for the English venture, I have no doubt whatever about the advantage of Mr Abraham Sofaer's Beaconsfield over Mr Ernest Milton's ! The former had a generosity which the latter entirely lacks. Despite his exaggerated courtesies the old master of make-believe still retained a heart : his protestations had some ring of sincerity about them. Mr Milton gives us the super-charlatan and nothing more. But let Beaconsfield orate as he would, his Queen still held the stage. A nicer discretion would enjoin upon Mr Milton the necessity for not playing Miss Stanley off it !

Two superb little performances come from Mr Allan Aynesworth as Lord Conyngham and Miss Mabel Terry-Lewis as the Duchess of Sutherland, and I should have said that the English John Brown was better than the American but for a canny glance at both programmes which tells me that Mr James Woodburn is the actor in both cases. It is to be hoped that Mr Housman will make us another play out of his palace scenes ; the present mine is so rich that it is as yet hardly touched. Among the nuggets still to be brought to the surface are Lord Melbourne, Lord Palmerston, the Carlyles, Macaulay, John Stuart Mill, Martin Tupper, the Gladstones, Tennyson, Morley, Parnell, Chamberlain and Jesse Collings, the Shah of Persia, Lord Rosebery, and Kitchener explaining why he had made the Mahdi's head

into an ink-pot. " I don't quite like that, Lord Kitchener ! "
says the Queen, and Kitchener replies : " You would,
ma'am, if you saw it. It looks very handsome mounted in
silver." Perhaps I may conclude an inadequate survey of
this delightful piece, or series of little pieces, by saying that
it or they look very handsome mounted in Mr Rex Whistler's
gold.

The entertainment called *Floodlight* is largely its own
enemy. On the first night it began at ten minutes past eight
and lasted, with one short interval, until twenty-five
minutes past eleven. It should begin at a quarter to nine
and end sharp at eleven. If my calculations are correct this
means cutting one hour. The show would be all the better
for this, since at least an hour of it is quite unworthy of its
author's considerable talent. The items to go would be a
scene in a newspaper office which is desperately unfunny,
the songs about the lift-girl, the boot-black, the cinema-
organist, and the dog-owners, and all the comparisons with
the Victorian age. With the removal of this heavy and
undecorative lumber, a revue would be left which has been
put together with brains, fancy, wit, and taste. Among the
scenes delightful to the eye are the Waterloo Ball, which the
author might like one to describe as an ecstasy in scarlet.
There is a charming scene about daffodils that take the
April winds with beauty for a reason which, though strange
indeed, is the only feasible one ; this is that Mr Nichols's
Muse, arch enough elsewhere, here declines to find a rhyme
for March ! And then there is the little kitchen-ballet, an
invention of great delicacy.

Among the things nice to hear one would put first the
music to this same ballet, brilliantly scored by Mr Benjamin
Frankel, who has consciously or subconsciously found his
inspiration in the mood and manner of Wolf-Ferrari. The
music of some of the other ballets and dances proves that
Mr Nichols is no stranger to the modern style, and this being
so it is rather a pity that in the Waterloo episode he gives us

12

the waltz at its Oscar Straus or " Waltz Dream " stage of development. Possibly this is hypercritical; since Waterloo is pre-Johann Strauss and pre-Waldteufel the earliest waltzes are lost, and we should not call upon Mr Nichols to disentangle a musical mystery which even Ravel did not unravel. Among the wit we are given a first-class demolition of the ultra-modern fashionable photographer, a savage attack on the institution of the paid hostess, and an amusing skit upon modern manners at which Vanbrugh would have turned pale and even Wycherley boggled.

Miss Frances Day scorns versatility, and except in the matter of words and music all her songs are the same. Violets cannot be sweeter than the lids of this Juno's eyes, Cytherea cannot have had sweeter breath, or Proserpina letting the flowers fall from Dis's waggon have shown a more delicious affrightment. This is an exquisite piece of fragility in emotion and art, always providing that one can stand so much pulchritude quite so unrelieved. And might not Miss Day vary her gestures a little? There is a certain sameness about an evening of pink-tipped palmistry. Miss Hermione Baddeley gets about a lot more. Her work in this revue is extremely clever, and I think that she should be given more scope while it is happening and greater recognition when it has happened. Mr John Mills is a very capable young actor with charm, vivacity, and resource, and Mr Lyle Evans has one admirable turn. These three, without Miss Day, would still constitute an excellent revue.

Mr Priestley's Experiment with Time

TIME AND THE CONWAYS. A play. By J. B. Priestley. Duchess Theatre, Thursday, August 26, 1937.

WANTED FOR MURDER. A play. By Percy Robinson and Terence de Marney. Lyceum Theatre, Wednesday, August 25, 1937.

[*August* 29, 1937]

> All the beautiful time is yours for always, for it is life that takes away, changes, and spoils so often—not death, which is really the warden and not the thief of our treasures.
>
> LADY JEKYLL, *in a letter to the Earl of Lytton*

SOMEWHERE in Walkley's essays there is a passage which runs more or less like this :

> Ideas are a godsend to the critic. Give him a thesis, and you have given him his article. He can not only examine the playwright's solution, but suggest another one of his own, and in fact pass in review all the possible permutations and combinations of the problem presented. The result is apt to be a little deceptive about the play itself, because it suits the critic to travel farther afield in the region of ideas than the playwright. Nor is it merely a question of intellectual area covered ; the need for logical symmetry, for strict form, in analysis will often have tempted the critic to assume these qualities in the play when they are not, in fact, there. His picture of what the playwright has constructed will be, in Joe Gargery's phrase, a little too " architectooralooral." Hence the playgoer is often disappointed when he goes to see the play for himself. Half the ideas he has read about are not there, and those that are there are not so shipshape.

Only half of this applies to Mr Priestley's new play, which is perfectly shipshape, but the other half hits the mark exactly. Half the ideas you are now to read about, dear playgoer, are not in this piece, which I most urgently and insistently beg you to see. I will go further and say that not

14

one-tenth of what this play is really about is contained in the play, and that it would be wrong if it were. Mr Priestley works the reverse way from Mr Shaw. That metaphysical old cook will take a kettleful of ideas, and so heat them on the fire of his wit that they boil over, leaving hardly any play behind. Our younger *cordon bleu* proceeds the other way about ; the idea behind Mr Priestley's play is no more than the pinch of salt essential to every good dish.

That idea is nothing less than the new conception of Time. The old conception of Time was that of a piece of string in which the knots were years, and infinite Time merely meant more and more string. About twenty years ago it occurred to Somebody that Time might be something in the fourth dimension. Knowing what a mess a three-dimensional world makes of two-dimensional ideas, it dawned upon this Somebody that a fourth dimension must make a similar mess of three-dimensional ideas about everything, including Time and Space. The notion was even conceived that Time, being something four-dimensional, might be a part of four-dimensional Space. Ten knots ago it occurred to Somebody Else to make a mental picture of this new Time similar to that which we can make of the old Space.

Conceive a tourist leaving London and proceeding to Manchester via Birmingham, and imagine him at Birmingham. Now the traveller does not suppose that because he has left London behind, London does not exist, or that because he has not yet got to Manchester, Manchester is not in being. In fact he knows that if he could mount sufficiently high in an aeroplane and were provided with a sufficiently powerful telescope he would be able to see London, Birmingham, and Manchester all existing at the same time. This being true of the things we know as places, why, argued Somebody Else, might not the same thing hold good of the things we call dates ? If Time is a part of Space and Space of Time then even Mr Curdle would see that dovetailedness cannot end here. If one can get above, and so obtain a bird's-eye view of places, why should not this be feasible with regard to dates? It needs no more than the simplest metaphysical aeroplane to enable one to get a bird's-eye view of, say, 1066, 1588, and 1815, showing the Norman Conquest, the Defeat of the Armada, and the Battle of Waterloo all happening together and to be still going on.

Recently has come Yet Another—calling himself Mr Dunne—who conceived the notion of moving about in Time. But just as in a railway train " cows flash past the window " because it is the traveller who is flashing past the cows, so perhaps, argues this metaphysician, it is not we who move about in Time, but Time which moves about in us. Now when would Time choose to do this? Obviously when we are asleep, with the result that Time's escapades appear to us in the form of dreams. From which it follows that if you, being a lady, dream of meeting a tall, dark, handsome stranger you are probably going to, because in this new dimension of Time you have always met him, are always going to meet him, are always meeting him. Well, there is nothing new under the sun. Coming events cast their shadows before, and every servant lass with a dream-book knows all about the tall, dark, handsome stranger. It is easy to make jokes on this subject. Some little time ago I heard a man at a supper party say : " Why be afraid of Death? Since Time is not absolute, but merely something invented by Man for his convenience, we are already dead. Equally, when we are dead we shall be alive. We are both now. Past, Present, and Future are one." He then turned to the man sitting next to him and said : " Will you lunch with me to-morrow? " The man replied : " Sorry. I've got to attend the execution of Charles the First."

It is, as I say, easy to make a good joke about Mr Dunne's Experiment. But it is not so easy to make a good play out of it. This is the place and time, and both together and one as much as the other, to say that Mr Priestley has made a play which is magnificent if you grasp what it is essentially about, and first-class entertainment if you don't. The Conways are a middle-class family living in a suburb of a prosperous manufacturing town. The family consists of the mother, two sons, and four daughters. The War is just over, and it is Kay Conway's twenty-first birthday, which is being marked by a party. The first act is pure exposition, showing what each character is like now and hopes to become. Of the children the elder son is the least adventurous-minded ; he is a clerk with a dull job, and doesn't resent his job being dull. Dull jobs must have their dull doers, and why not he ? The younger and flashier son is going to make a fortune, probably out of selling motor-cars. One girl is like that daughter of Mr Bennet's who could be happy in any town provided a regiment of good-looking officers was quartered in it. (Has any critic of Jane Austen observed that her regiments consist entirely of officers ?) Another, more serious-minded, is going to reform the world, and incidentally become head of Girton : another is a little bundle of sixteen-year-old life, quivering for the fulfilment of the promises life holds out at sixteen. If these three sisters were Tchehov's how we should praise the skill with which they are drawn ! Some shred of justification for the comparison is the figure of the mother, a comfortable English Madame Ranevsky, who cannot conceive that the value of her house will decrease or her shares go down.

Remains the fourth daughter, Kay, who acts as liaison officer between Mr Priestley and Mr Dunne. Kay doesn't experiment with Time ; it is Time which tries its experiments on Kay. She is visited by waking dreams in which she has foreknowledge of the wreckage made of human hopes by Time—and, of course, by those human foibles which are Time's allies. The second act happens nineteen years later, and has a clear-cut quality worthy of Mr Granville-Barker at his best. We see what all but one of the

17

members of this family have become, the little bundle of urgent life having died. We see what has happened to the flighty daughter's marriage, and what the younger boy's love affair has turned into. We see that happiness, though of a subdued kind, comes to that member of the family who made least claim to happiness. We see a great deal which cannot be explained here, though I cannot forbear mention of that changelessness which Mr Priestley has so adroitly allotted to Mrs Conway. A little older, a little fatter, a little sillier, a little sharper-tempered, and no more.

In the third act we go back to the party, where we see the burgeoning of those hopes which the second act has so cruelly shattered. This last act is emotionally satisfying and, indeed, compulsional, since the poignancy springs directly out of Mr Priestley's thesis. I have heard a complaint that this act lacks surprise, since it shows us nothing that we have not anticipated. I regard this as the most foolish objection I have heard in the whole of my playgoing life, since novelty in this third act would be the one thing to destroy the thesis which is this play's backbone. One supercilious eyebrow raised itself to say that it couldn't for the life of it see why the play's events were not performed in their proper order. Whereby I suggest to Mr Priestley that he should adopt this suggestion on alternate nights—the present order of the acts being maintained on Mondays, Wednesdays, and Fridays for ordinarily intelligent people, but reversed as to second and third acts on Tuesdays, Thursdays, and Saturdays for the benefit of highbrows and cretins. Before the matinées the stage-manager would, of course, toss up !

Now Mr Priestley, as an experienced man of the theatre, knows that whereas a Russian piece may close in complete gloom to the plaudits of crowded houses, an English piece which did the same thing would play to empty benches. Where was the mitigating ray of sunshine to come from ? (Mr Priestley is too much of an artist to look for the ray which cannot logically exist, and if his piece had been dark with the darkness of the tomb I think he would not have written it.) His characters, he tells us, are to find their consolation in the very nature of this new Time. If the disappointment endures, so, too, does the hope ; woe does not extinguish joy. All the beautiful time in life as well as its ugly quarters of an hour is ours for always. This remains true though the quarters lengthen into hours. Not even sunset can do away with sunrise. Night cannot abolish day.

The acting of this piece is so good that it takes away the breath with surprise and gives it back with pleasure. The artists concerned are Mesdames Jean Forbes-Robertson, Barbara Everest, Rosemary Scott, Eileen Erskine, Molly Rankin, Helen Horsey, and Messrs Raymond Huntley, Wilfred Babbage, Mervyn Johns, and Alexander Archdale. Space permits me merely to say of their performances that individually and collectively they make up a concatenation of intention and display of achievement which have no parallel on the London stage at the moment. Miss Irene Hentschel has produced very brilliantly. Indeed, I see no reason why, London taste being what it is, this lovely piece should not play to scantier and scantier houses. It is only because Mr Priestley's pockets are not empty that his play sees the stage at all. For the piece is what your commercial manager insists upon calling uncommercial. By which, of course, he means that it is ten times more enthralling than the rubbish upon which he relies to fill his coffers.

I do not see why I should not say that after the production at the " Q " Theatre of *Wanted for Murder* the management consulted me about which West End theatre it would best suit. I replied that the first half should be sent to the St Martin's and the second half to Drury Lane. Full of the British genius for compromise, the management has now taken it to the Lyceum, where exactly that happens which one could have foreseen. This is that Mrs Colebrooke's drawing-room looks the size of Hyde Park, while Hyde Park shrinks to the dimensions of Mrs Colebrooke's drawing-room. The audience enjoyed it very much and with good reason. For this play is a good joke about a sexual maniac. And, of course, there may be a dimension in which sexual mania is a good joke. We must ask Mr Dunne.

Our National Theatre

CREST OF THE WAVE. A musical play. By Ivor Novello.
Drury Lane Theatre, Wednesday, September 1, 1937.
LONDON RHAPSODY. Palladium, Thursday, September 2,
1937.

[*September 5, 1937*]

> DOWAGER DUCHESS OF CHEVIOT: This doesn't mean a thing.
> DUKE OF CHEVIOT: Not a thing.

OUTSIDE our National Theatre cordons of police held back
hundreds of autograph-seekers. Inside, hundreds of auto-
graph-givers had congregated. The audience largely consisted of Privy Councillors, Elder Brethren, Hereditary
Legislators, Film Stars, Mannequins, and Lovelies. As the
conductor advanced to his rostrum a Parsifalian hush
reigned, broken only by the crackle of a too-stout shirt-
front and the rustle of an ill-mannered ruby. A Mongolian
would have realised that this was the drama nearest to the
British heart, the white elephant for which stables of por-
phyry and rose-pink marble are presently to be erected.

Crusaders chorused. These were the ancestors of the
House of Cheviot, or perhaps I mean Gantry, since heraldic
minutiæ always elude me. Anyway, Gantry Castle was the
seat of the Dukes of Cheviot, on one or other side of Tweed.
The present owner of the title was broke, and the family
apparently subsisted on the sixpences paid by visitors
desirous of viewing this malachite table or that onyx mantelpiece, presented by the Sultan of Turkey to the sixth Duke.
One by one we were introduced to the family : first the
butler ; next a pyjama'd figure causing maidens to cling
rapturously together and whisper audibly : " He's thinner."
The maidens were wrong, just as they were wrong in the
early years of this century when they applauded the actor
who played Meynard in *The Corsican Brothers*, in the belief

21

that he was Mr Martin Harvey, and just as they had been
wrong in 1880 when they acclaimed Mr A. W. Pinero playing
the same part, and under the impression that he was Irving.
This slim young man was not the Duke of Cheviot, but the
negligible Lord William Gantry (Mr Peter Graves). Next
came Virginia, widow of the former Duke (Miss Marie
Löhr) and a lady of some wit. At least she speared a breakfast kidney, and, holding it to her bosom, said : " If you
don't want to eat it you can use it as a brooch.'' Which
flashing sally was held for wit by the assembled Privy Councillors, Elder Brothers, Hereditary Legislators, Film Stars,
Mannequins, and Lovelies.

But anticipation was not long in fulfilment, for now a
figure in riding-breeches haughtily descended the stairs, and
by the breeches and the haughtiness one realised that this
must be His Grace himself. It was. It was also more than
a mere theatrical Duke. It was Mr Ivor Novello, and, as
they say at film receptions, in person. Very little older, not
a whit more rotund, with chin aloof as of yore and the aristo-
cratic gaze of Mr Beerbohm's Lord Byron about to spurn
honest English dust in favour of some greasy foreign soil.

To this family in distress entered a lady snake (Miss Ena
Burrill) poised on her tail and garbed with that sheathlike
simplicity which betokens the villainess ready to strike.
At the moment her intention was the comparatively in-
nocuous one of buying Gantry Castle on behalf of English
Quota films. His Grace indignantly refused to sell, and
would have continued in his indignation if he had not con-
fused the snake's principal—for in the film world snakes
have principals—with an underbred, generous-hearted
little chorus girl of the same initials (Miss Dorothy Dick-
son). Dropping reptilian analogy, let me say that the
villainess had no principals of any kind, was acting in her
proper person, had fallen in love with His Grace, that
her name was Helen Winter, and that His Grace mistook her
for Honey Wortle. We next saw a production number

'featuring' Versailles, in which Mr Ivor Novello doubled the part of Otto Fresch, an ageing film star. The Duchess was now hired by a steamship company to give tone to a pleasure cruise, and presently Her Grace, His Grace, Miss Winter, Miss Wortle, and Miss Wortle's Mamma all embarked. Then came a magnificent scene in which the pleasure cruiser was transformed into a battleship with guns emerging from their turrets and trained to annihilate the audience of Privy Councillors, Elder Brethren, Hereditary Legislators, Film Stars, Mannequins, and Lovelies.

But Mr Novello had not yet arrived at the apex of either his spectacle or his drama. We were therefore treated to a version of the second act of *Carmen*, the décor of Lillas Pastia, and all requisite appurtenances. "*Je vais danser en votre honneur*," trilled Honey Wortle. In return for which Helen Winter emptied a revolver into the small of Honey Wortle's ducal lover's back. After which the curtain descended and the grand staircase was filled with Privy Councillors, Elder Brethren, and Hereditary Legislators giving their arms to Film Stars, Mannequins, and Lovelies fainting with emotion.

When we returned to these revels His Grace, whose perforations had healed, was now an impoverished film extra supporting Honey Wortle, who had become a film star of the first magnitude. It now appeared that all unknown to himself His Grace possessed a genius exceeding even that of Mr Robert Taylor, which so annoyed Helen Winter that she arranged with Otto Fresch to wreck the train in which Honey was travelling to attend a film première. The penultimate scene was outside Gantry Castle on Christmas night in deep snow. Outside the ducal lodge and with a full view of the ducal drive leading to the ducal mansion, His Grace, in faultless evening dress, was holding colloquy with the Dowager Duchess, for by this time the Duke and Honey had been made one. "This doesn't mean a thing," said the Dowager Duchess. "Not a thing," said

the Duke. " But, oh, how wrong," inwardly chorused the
Privy Councillors, Elder Brethren, Hereditary Legislators,
Film Stars, Mannequins, and Lovelies. " It means the
Entire British Drama ! " Last scene of all was the great hall
of Gantry Castle filled with tenantry and vassalage. " I
cannot tell you how deeply I regret that Her Grace cannot
be with you," said the Duke. " Perhaps next year. The
doctors are afraid she may never walk again." Whereupon
Her Grace walked in without crutches, and brought this
stilted drama to a conclusion. And Privy Councillors, Elder
Brethren, Hereditary Legislators, Film Stars, Mannequins,
and Lovelies, all deeply disturbed, left the theatre, resolving to support that National Theatre which is to give us
more and more waves with bigger and bigger crests. I
myself am still under too deep a stress of emotion to do more
than thank Mr Novello for his latest contribution to a drama
which has supplanted Shakespeare in the breasts of Privy
Councillors, Elder Brethren, Hereditary Legislators, Film
Stars, Mannequins, and Lovelies.

Mastering that emotion, however, I declare the music,
dancing (by Mr Walter Crisham), and all the acting to have
sparkle—altogether a very jolly show if only one could look
on at it in any old clothes, with leave to smoke, and without the silly pretence that Here We Have an Artistic Event
of National Importance. Not that Mr Novello pretends.
He knows better. *The Happy Hypocrite* taught him not to
trust the British public with anything except sheer, un-
adulterated bosh. Then who does pretend ? Why, the
Privy Councillors, Elder Brethren, Hereditary Legislators,
Film Stars, Mannequins, and Lovelies !

There was a scene in *London Rhapsody* which happened
on Epsom Downs and was called " A Gypsy Camp." One
of the actors was a wrestling bear, but whether the bear was
real or not I was unable to determine. But there was no
doubt about the Gypsy Boys' Band, which played just as
well or as badly as you would expect a band of Gypsy Boys

to play. They gave us the old, old Hungarian Rhapsody, and you could almost hear Liszt revolving in his grave.

Nor was there the slightest doubt about the three acrobats, who experimented with a girl very much in the way that Ouspensky, Dunne, and our Mr Priestley experiment with Time. With this difference, that if our metaphysicians drop their theory nothing very much happens, whereas if our acrobats were even momentarily to loose their hold of their young lady the result would be a Frightful Bump. This was perhaps the best turn, because it was obviously difficult and obviously well done. But all the turns were admirable, and perhaps another of the best was that in which Messrs Nervo and Knox, Flanagan and Allen, and Naughton and Gold pretended to be flower-sellers sitting in the shadow of Eros. There was also a very lively representation of the London Pavilion in 1878; here Mr Harry Champion in the most famous of his songs awakened us to something between melancholy and riot.

If a trifle of criticism be permitted, then I suggest that the spoof melodrama towards the end of the programme is about half an hour too long. It is absurd to delay the appearance of the Wiere Brothers until twenty minutes to twelve. One would willingly allow any amount of rope to Mr Flanagan, in the absolute certainty that he will never hang himself, but I venture to suggest, with something of sternness, that the first joke in the scene in the milk bar should at once be deleted. However, these are unimportant matters. The important thing is to recognise that this form of entertainment, which has been going on at the Palladium for some considerable time, is far nearer to an art-form than the nonsense at Drury Lane. The Palladium's impromptu, haphazard, riotous buffoonery is far closer to that of the Commedia dell' Arte than any nonsense about Glamorous Nights, Careless Raptures, and Wave Crests. It is alive; the pretentious stuff is dead.

Body and Soul

BONNET OVER THE WINDMILL. A play. By Dodie Smith.
New Theatre, Wednesday, September 8, 1937.

RICHARD II. Revival of Shakespeare's play. Queen's
Theatre, Monday, September 6, 1937.

THE PHANTOM LIGHT. A comedy thriller. By Evadne
Price. Haymarket Theatre, Tuesday, September 7,
1937.

[*September* 12, 1937]

MISS DODIE SMITH's new play tells how a young woman
tries to turn herself into a good actress and a young man
into a good playwright by spending the night with him in a
windmill. The great actress Rachel left behind her a letter
protesting her inability, after mouthing five acts of alex-
andrines about tigresses passion-starved in Byzantine
deserts, to munch lonely sandwiches in fifth-rate provincial
hotels. But does anybody suppose that it was the refusal
to eat sandwiches by herself which made Rachel a great
actress? Perhaps the matter did not greatly trouble the
ancients, who had more sense than to divide the world into
nasty body and nice mind; it is to be doubted whether the
last nineteen centuries have ever really thought about any
other question. And to think that it was settled once and
for all in a leading article by Montague on the death of Bernhardt!

When Bernhardt played before you the last act of *La
Dame aux Camélias* you were for the time strangely
ennobled and empowered; you lived for the moment on
a plane of wisdom and sympathy unattainable by you in
your ordinary hours. All the greatest art is like that; it
is a higher power of the spectator's self, the state of
immensely quickened and thrilled perception which, it
then seems, might have been always his if some incorporeal prison-house or other had not somehow cast its

26

shade around him. Do the great artists themselves live, as a regular thing, in those high places? Scarcely, or Sarah Bernhardt would not have played some of the tricks that she did, nor would so many men of genius have lived somewhat ignoble lives. Perhaps they find in the mental excitement of practising the technicalities of their art a stimulant strong enough to give them a lift, for the time, into that state of passionate insight to which they are then able to haul up even our more sluggish selves; then they may flop down, exhausted, and even do something scrubby from mere excess of reaction, just as a soul-stirring preacher might do if sorely tried when very much tired indeed with the delivery of an excellent sermon.

Will the last nineteen centuries, the first third of the twentieth, Miss Dodie Smith, and all other intending playwrights please realise that this matter is now settled? The great artist is entitled to throw as many bonnets over as many windmills as she likes, provided she feels that way and is not doing it to show off. On the other hand, no amount of ' scrubbiness ' will make any sort of artist out of a duffer. Let us have a practical illustration. The moment I finish this article I propose visiting a gilded saloon and imbibing a weak whisky and water. But it will not be the saloon or the whisky which will have written this article —or next week's article either.

Now let us go back to Miss Smith's romantic inquiries. Really there is a Ouidaesque touch about this lady's passionate guesses. To Ouida's guardsman conquest in fulldress uniform on a settee presented no impracticabilities whatever. Similarly Miss Smith chooses the unlikeliest and least accessible places for her heroines' amorous gambits, accepted or declined. The tops of Tyrolese mountains, Scotia's rocky islets where there is hardly room to sit down, East Anglian windmills three hours from town. Putting two and two together, you will see that Miss Smith hedges herself about with a frightful lot of difficulties, all the more insurmountable because she does not begin to tackle them until round about half-past ten. The heroine is Janet, a young woman plain by name and plain by nature, as servant girls say. Despite these handicaps Janet wants to go on the stage, and first an ex-music-hall performer, who appears to live permanently on a roof in a kimono, and next a fashionable actor-manager tell Janet that she will be a good actress when she has acquired Emotional Experience. Now, the actor-manager has a friend, a good-looking, unsuccessful playwright, who is about to be lured away by Hollywood. (One has always thought it was the successful ones that Hollywood lures.) Whereupon Janet begins to wonder whether the good-looking playwright cannot be redeemed from Hollywood and made to write good plays if only he, too, is allowed Emotional Experience. (Yes, this play is strangely like *The Young Visiters*.) So Janet lures Christopher to his windmill, turns him into a better playwright, and comes back a wiser and a sadder girl. She is disillusioned for a reason perfectly well known to the audience and to every housemaid who has walked out with a soldier, but withheld apparently from Janet and Miss Smith.

Of course, if Janet had any *nous*, which must surely be part of the equipment of a potentially great actress, she would know that Christopher at six in the morning, at the end of a six hours' drive including a transformation scene in a windmill, and with a boat to catch before noon, will be in a mood making for disillusionment. It is the old story of rapturous maidens demanding too much from rapture, the essence of which is intensity and not staying power. As a modern young woman Janet would prefer Kensington to any windmill. But Miss Smith is not a realist. If she were she would not seriously tell us that a fashionable actor-manager contemplates renewing an affair with an unsuccess-ful music-hall artist turned dowdy shop-assistant, whom he met fifteen years before in theatrical lodgings in, of all places, Manchester !

Miss Anne Firth is a young actress of sensitiveness and perception, in whom there are obviously the makings of a very considerable player. There is no need to say anything about Miss Ivy St Helier's quality as an actress, yet she fails here, probably because her scenes cover too much ground. The dead love affair which turns out, on one side at least, not to be so dead after all, should be full of autumn regrets. There is no end to the play-writing possibilities here. A Jean-Jacques Bernard would show us the gay past in the dim mirror of the present; a Sacha Guitry would flick the lovers with light irony; a modern realist would make the pair wonder what it was they used to see in each other. Miss Smith has not, at the moment, enough dramatic skill. She fritters her situation away, with the result that while Miss St Helier's tears are all ready, there is nothing for her to expend them on. If tears are shed it is we who shed them because this delicious little artist has not been allowed to put the whole thing into a nutshell and a song.

Of the rompers the most successful is Miss Betty Jardine, while among the grown-ups Mr Cecil Parker almost persuades us that this is a play for grown-ups. It isn't. It is like a schoolroom farce by Mr Ian Hay edited by Marie Corelli, with contributions by Ouida and Miss Daisy Ashford as aforesaid. Nevertheless the romps are a huge success, and the serious bits will gammon many people. I am not a betting man. But I will bet any reasonable sum that this play is running long after Time has forgotten all about the Conways.[1]

It was Miss Gordon Daviot's masterly *Richard of Bordeaux* which put England's second Richard on the playgoing map of London; let us hope that Shakespeare's 'prentice play on the same theme will not wipe this monarch off that map. It is a part of polite knowledge to know what

[1] The facts are striking: Mr Priestley's play ran for 225 performances, Miss Dodie Smith's for 101.

Mr Gielgud does with the artist king. It is eight years since this well-graced actor first essayed the part; his present performance lays greater stress on the artist without losing any of the kingliness. His reading has gained in depth, subtlety, insight, power. Now indeed Mr Gielgud shows himself to be an actor at once *profond et rêveur*. This is the thing which Lewes so much distrusted in French tragedians, though I think he would have trusted Mr Gielgud. The last act is not only the peak of his achievement up to date; it is probably the best piece of Shakespearean acting on the English stage to-day. Mr Gielgud is well supported by a good company, the pick of which is Mr Frederick Lloyd's Earl of Northumberland, closely followed by Mr Harcourt Williams's Bishop of Carlisle, Mr Leon Quartermaine's John of Gaunt, and Mr Michael Redgrave's Bolingbroke, in that order.

But surely the charming firm of Motley should be invited to put the brake on a little. This production is like Pinero's French governess, " over-gowned and over-hatted." Everybody looks as though he were going to a fancy-dress ball, and the stage throughout is cluttered up with scenery, all of the most distressingly realistic kind. One example must suffice. All that is needed for the Duke of York's garden is a back-cloth and a bush, the latter because of the Queen's " Let's step into the shadow of these trees." Even the " dangling apricocks " can be off-stage. But this does not satisfy Motley, who must have a scene exactly like a model of Dorothy Vernon's steps at Haddon Hall set inside a West-End florist's. Plants in pots are exhibited on Dorothy's steps looking like stages, and so that you can almost see the dangling price tickets. The queen, hieing her to shelter, hides behind something that looks like a floral cash-desk. To cap the lot the gardener, promising himself to set a bank of rue, chooses a spot at the immediate foot of the steps, so that we visualise a line of infant Dukes of York toddling down them, only to trip over that sour herb of grace, and fall on their baby noses. Also the ladies are too much made up, with foreheads that shine like billiard balls.

Perhaps Mr Guthrie and M. Saint-Denis, who are to produce *The School for Scandal* and *Three Sisters* respectively, will give Motley leave to speak a little less of their mind. This magnificent programme is to be wound up with *The Merchant of Venice*, a quite intolerable play for dramatic critics sick to death of it, but presumably still a great favourite with the public. Doubtless Mr Gielgud is looking to the Merchant to recoup his losses on the riskier experiments, very much as the punter looks forward to Windsor to get back the money he knows he will lose at Ascot.

Some little time ago at the Shaftesbury Theatre a play called *Satyr* failed. It was a thriller. People believed it, and were profoundly thrilled. Or you might say that it was a shocker, and that people were profoundly shocked. The result was that people discovered that they did not like being shocked and thrilled. At the Lyceum a piece on the same subject of homicidal mania has not failed. It is a thriller or a shocker so liberally interlarded with humour that people are neither thrilled nor shocked. Wherefore people like it immensely. This week at the Haymarket Theatre is an example of the genre called " comedy thriller." The Lyceum genre consists of alternating scenes of thrills and comedy. The Haymarket genre is not a mixture, but a compound. That is to say, every situation, every sentence, every single word, has the edge taken off its thrill by being turned into an immediate joke. A ghost knocks at a lighthouse door, a madman gibbers, and Mr Gordon Harker is heard to exclaim : " I may be concrete from the neck up, but I haven't got cloth ears." This play continually defeats itself, and an evening which begins with the promise of things dire and macabre peters out in dismal farce. One is bored long before the end of the first act, after which there is nothing to do but wait for the end and admire the fury of Mr Gordon Harker's unavailing efforts.

31

Time Gets an Encore

I HAVE BEEN HERE BEFORE. A play. By J. B. Priestley.
Royalty Theatre, Wednesday, September 22, 1937.

[*September* 26, 1937]

In his other play, at the Duchess Theatre, Mr Priestley
propounds a theory of Time in which past, present, and
future events are like a high tea, in which everything is put
on the table together. Æons later, says Mr Priestley, tea-
time comes round again, and you sit again at the table, find
all the dishes there exactly as before, and have the same
meal. The idea is that this process goes on for ever and ever,
at, of course, æonic intervals. There is no difficulty about
this theory except the difficulty of the German railway
porter with the German train service during the War.
" Why do you ask when it goes ? " he said to some unoffend-
ing passenger. " The question is not when, but whether ! "
Even that stern moralist Matthew Arnold would have
approved Mr Priestley's notion, since if in this life you
speak out of turn or steal your neighbour's helping you
go on interrupting and stealing throughout eternity, thus
making conduct more important than ever.

Now comes this second play, which completely upsets
everything laid down in the first. The implication at the
Duchess is that we are seeing the Conways sitting down to
high tea *for the first time*. The play at the Royalty tells us
that the Conways, we, and everybody else have sat down to
high tea any number of times before, that the meal has
always proceeded in the same fashion, and will do so on the
present occasion unless we make that effort which, normally,
it does not occur to us to make. But to-day we have a
Strange Guest who begins by telling Tommy that he is going
to steal Dicky's cake, Mabel that she is about to spill the

milk, and Mum and Dad that they will have a row. There is a general chorus of " How do you know ? " The Stranger Guest replies : " Like all prophets, I have the gift of looking into the past. I know what is coming to you because it has all happened before. But there is no need for it to happen again. You, Tommy, can refrain from stealing Dicky's cake. You, Mabel, have only to be more careful with the milk-jug. And you, Mum and Dad, can pull yourselves together ! " In the new play the Strange Guest is a German professor, and, being a German professor, he lightly alludes to the foregoing as the Game of Recurrence and Intervention.

Half-way through this piece I was suddenly stung by an idea. This was the notion of Mr Priestley as a sentimental mollycoddle and dyed-in-the-wool good-behaviourist, one of those people who insist on moral wish being father to scientific thought ! This kind always thinks loosely, as when the S.G. asks : " Why should this great theatre of suns and moons and starlight have been created for the first pitiful charade we can contrive ? " Why not ? Would Mr Priestley suggest that the vaults and caverns of Gruyère cheese have been created in order to give cheese-mites a second chance ? Our author likes to play at the Game of R. and I. because it gives people a second chance, and in the theatre the people who are given second chances invariably lead better lives.

But hold on a bit. The Game is only half of Mr Priestley's theme. The other half is Pattern. All the people in the new play are as closely inter-related as the threads in a piece of cloth ; you cannot alter the life of one without a corresponding change in the lives of all the others. Now let us see where this leads. I am a naughty little boy. My schoolmaster is a brutal fellow who likes using the rod. Its use makes me grow up into a good man, and I die a millionaire at the age of ninety. This happens thousands of times. Then one fine day my schoolmaster makes his extraordinary effort,

conceives a distaste for the rod, spares it, and so spoils me
that I take to drink and die in the workhouse. And that,
dear Mr Priestley, or dear Mr Ouspensky, just won't do.

Think of the unwarrantable changes that are going to be
wrought in our lives if on some future occasion Julius Cæsar
and William the Norman decide to forgo their invasions of
this country. Think of the difference it is going to make if
the women who have rejected us suddenly make up their
minds to accept. And since, according to Pattern, everybody reacts on everybody else, the number of lives I may
have to lead amounts to 1 x 2 x 3 x 4, and so on, in a progres-
sion, the last figure of which is the entire population of these
islands ! We all remember Carlyle's answer to the lady who
told him she accepted the Universe : " Dammit, ma'am,
you'd better ! " I accept the effect of other people's Pattern
on my life because I have to. But once is enough, and if there
is a new Dimension subjecting me to countless millions of
contradictory existences because of the whims of other
people, I shall do my best to remain outside that Dimension.
No, I am afraid Mr Priestley's new piece, considered metaphysically, is bosh !

This does not prevent *I Have Been Here Before* from
being a magnificent play, for it is no argument against a
sieve that it fails to hold water. Not one but fifty ideas filter
through this piece, which, under its startlingly new guise,
one yet perceives to be the very oldest play that was ever
written. Janet has fallen out of love with her husband
Walter, who suffers from all the neuroses consequent upon
too much drink ; she is now in love with Oliver, the good-
looking young schoolmaster. A German professor who
knows his Ouspensky arrives at the Yorkshire inn where
the three are staying, and tells them that they are going to
make a mess of things because they have made a mess of
them before. Walter will shoot himself, his business will col-
lapse, and ruin hundreds of people, including the innkeeper
and his daughter and the little grandson who is at the school

to which the wife's lover has been appointed by the husband who happens to be the governor of that school. (You note the Pattern ?) The young man will lose his job. The lovers will cease to be lovers and take to quarrelling in filthy lodgings in Bloomsbury. "Now, children," says Dr Görtler, "why not make it a pleasant tea-table instead of an unpleasant one ? " In other words, Walter is to behave like a civilised man and hand Janet over to Oliver, after which Walter will not shoot himself, but devote his attention to turning teetotaller and repairing the business, thus keeping everybody prosperous. Oliver will continue in his job at the school, and in the holidays he and Janet will be on the friendliest terms with the nicest intellectuals in the tidiest parts of Bloomsbury.

Now what, may one ask, is this except the very oldest theatre ? At the Royalty on Wednesday evening I seemed to be present once again at the first night of *The Liars* at the old Criterion and to hear the voice of Wyndham's Sir Christopher Deering booming away at Faulkner and Lady Jessica. Booming with a difference it is true, but still booming. The reader will detect the variations without my help :

"I've nothing to say in the abstract against refusing to run away with another man's wife. There may be planets in which the refusal is not only the highest ideal morality, but where it has the further advantage of being a practical way of carrying on society. But it has this one fatal defect in our country—it won't work ! You know what we English are, Ned. Take my word for it, my dear Lady Jessica, my dear Ned, it won't work. You know it's not an original experiment you're making. This trick of refusing to run away has been tried before. Have you ever known it to be successful ? Lady Jessica, think of the brave pioneers who have gone before you in this act of renunciation. They've all perished, and their bones whiten the matrimonial shore ! "

I am not the first to say that there is nothing new under the sun. But perhaps Ecclesiastes was wrong, and Mr Priestley is right, in which case the whirligig of Time brings not revenges but satisfaction. In this new Dimension races are to the swift, battles to the strong, riches to men of understanding, and full houses to playwrights of skill. For Chance droppeth out, and Time and a Firm Intention to do Better happeneth to them all. But what about the firm intention to do worse? Mr Priestley's reply to this is that if the bad man persists in his badness he sinks to the lowest circle in the aspiring spiral and dies. Which seems to me like arguing that cannons go off only when they are fired in a just cause. Will Mr Priestley never realise that metaphysical thought should be free from moral bias?

The point about this play as a play is that it holds you with or without the metaphysics. Superficially it is the fashionable drama of the 'nineties all over again; actually it explores hell and glimpses heaven. It is a play of wuthering heights and depths, whose acting alone might serve for a whole column. Limitations of space permit me to say only that Mr Lewis Casson as the German professor gives the best performance, excepting Mr Bax's Socrates, of his career; that Miss Eileen Beldon as the inn's housekeeper exhibits an understanding and a restraint beyond all praise—she deliberately refuses laughs throughout—and that Miss Patricia Hilliard and Mr William Fox acquit themselves admirably. Mr Wilfrid Lawson makes of the husband a middle-aged Hamlet who has married Ophelia and bitterly regrets it. Is this a great actor? Let me shelve the difficulty by boldly stating that he is a grand one, whose present performance is something to dream about.

I advise every reader to see this play, provided that it is still running when this inadequate account of it appears. It is so interesting in thematic material, whether the argument is sound or false, so novel in treatment, so loyally produced, and so flamboyantly and dimly acted according to the integrity of part and moment, so gloriously independent of playgoing fashion—it is, in short, such big stuff that I cannot understand, playgoing taste being what it is, how the bats in this metaphysical belfry have survived to flit across the London sky for a second, third, and even fourth evening!

Robsonsholm : A Feast of Acting

AUTUMN. A play. By Margaret Kennedy and Gregory
Ratoff. From the Russian of Ilya Surguchev. St
Martin's Theatre, Friday, October 15, 1937.

MEASURE FOR MEASURE. Revival of Shakespeare's comedy.
Old Vic Theatre, Tuesday, October 12, 1937.

HIDE AND SEEK. A musical comedy. By Guy Bolton, Fred
Thompson, and Douglas Furber. Music by Vivian Ellis
and Lerner, Goodhart and Hoffman. Hippodrome,
Thursday, October 14, 1937.   [October 17, 1937]

CLEMENT SCOTT would have known *Autumn* for a smashing
good play. The youngest of present-day critics ought to
recognise it as a smashing good play. If he fails to do so he
has not theatre in his bones. Or put it that whatever is in his
bones is not theatre. This does not mean that the play has
no faults. There is in the relationship of stepmother and
stepdaughter the first of two hints that the play has been
watered down to suit English taste. At least, I strongly
suspect that in the original Russian the pair were mother
and daughter. For even in the less barbaric French drama
this is a situation which was known as long ago as 1865
when, in the Goncourts' *Henriette Maréchal*, the daughter
pretended that her mother's young man was her own. All
Russian play-writing breathes this air, and I feel that when
Ibsen died this pleasantry was among the themes left up
that unemptyable sleeve.

The piece, as Scott would have pointed out, starts with
three implausibilities. One, Lady Catherine Brooke is
deceiving her husband, Sir Brian Brooke, with his junior,
Mark Seeley. One does not believe that Mark would be such
an ass. Two, one does not believe that Lady Catherine,
who must have been on the continual *qui vive*, would have

read to her temporarily blinded husband that anonymous letter giving her away. There are at least thirty-five ways in which a clever woman like Lady Catherine would have got out of the difficulty. *A fortiori*, she would never have got into it, since even a stupid woman who is deceiving her husband will not read letters in strange handwriting aloud without having a preliminary squint at them. Three, Lady Catherine's pretence to her husband that Mark is his daughter's young man is too thin. Such thinness prepares the way for the lightest of light comedies and cannot stand up to the heaviest of heavy ones. Accepting these implausibilities —and acceptance is the first law of good playgoing—the rest of the piece is a magnificent bouquet of pure theatre in which the lover of emotional acting may shove his emotional nose and wallow.

There comes a point at which something happens to all three authors. This is the point when, in defiance of their theatrical selves, they decide to embark upon a scene of real and profound emotion. This takes up the second half of the second act, and it is all the more surprising because the first half has been extremely clumsy. In this first half the husband forces the wife to disclose her guilt before guests at a party celebrating the betrothal of his daughter to her lover, and it is immediately on top of this nonsense that our authors take their surprising dive into sincerity. For now the wife tries to make her husband see that the passion to which she and her lover have yielded has not been low. Leaving out Mr Priestley, this is as good emotional playwriting as has been seen in our theatre for a very long time. And it is emotional in the way in which your French *drame* is emotional.

The three implausibilities have been dealt with, but the second hint, *i.e.*, that the play has been watered down, is still to be disposed of. This concerns the daughter, who, after one peep into the nasty sty, runs away and takes shelter with an East-End Communist on whom she has at one time

39

been, as they say, sweet. The scene with her father when she returns is extraordinarily like that which used to move us so in the old Lyceum days when Dr Primrose had Olivia in his arms. But even Wills and Goldsmith put together could not be so simple as Miss Kennedy and Mr Ratoff pretend to be. Or perhaps they had more trust in their public. If our adapters had had greater courage they would have made an even better play, and a more moral one. At least the present piece suggests no reason why young Don Juans, tiring of ripe fruit, should not enliven autumn with the unplucked. No, nothing of what I believe to be the original should have been left out, and it could so easily have been made moral by setting it in Norway. The middle-aged husband who can never again trust his wife, the middle-aged wife who goes on hankering, the young wife who keeps one eye on her husband and another on her mother, the young husband who has another man's child to support, the child's real father whose name is Inkstand or something of the sort, a town with a rotting pier, a ring of mountains to prevent anybody getting away from anybody else—here, I stoutly maintain, would be as pretty and as moral a kettle of fish as ever came out of an Ibsenite fjord !

But the present kettleful will do, and it is superbly acted. Miss Flora Robson puts up a heartrending performance as the wife, and would be as good as Réjane was in exactly this kind of play and part if the authors would only let her, once and once only, dry her eyes, dab her nose, and round on her husband, saying : " You were always an ass, Brian. Is there any need to be such a solemn ass ? " Miss Victoria Hopper plays the daughter with extraordinary sensitivity, though in the scene with the father she should take care to be more audible. Elsewhere her playing is good enough to make the battle of sympathy between the two women sway now this way and now that. What a good actor Mr Wyndham Goldie is ! In fact, he is four times a better actor than most one knows, since with half his face he acts twice as well as anybody except **Mr Wilfrid Lawson**! And with either half! First with nose, mouth, and chin, when his eyes are bandaged, and second with his eyes alone, when the lower half is concealed by his daughter's tousled mop. **Mr Jack Hawkins** as Mark has to spend the entire evening feeling his position acutely, which he very cutely does. There is a lovely little sketch by **Mr Aubrey Dexter**. The authors may think that they have drawn a solicitor; we *know* that he is a retired manufacturer of disinfectants.

That **Mr Basil Dean** has been so long away with the films must be his excuse for a thoroughly old-fashioned production. We don't want nowadays to hear sixpences which are thrown out of windows drop into the street. We don't want tags to bring down curtains; the modern way to end a scene is just to stop. Good producing means helping to re-write, or at least cutting your authors. Therefore all that ridiculous nonsense about the wedding present in the last act should have been cut. Comedy is not wanted here, and it is a notion of the 'eighties that after a magnificently taut second act a third act must open chirpily. But when all complaints are made there still remains a smashing good play, with at least half an act of beautiful quality and four good acting parts grandly filled. Here it strikes me that I have done **Mr Dean** an injustice. He does at least make his actors concentrate on the business in hand instead of distracting us with cigarette-cases and soda-siphons. He has seen that there is something to play, and he has let them play it.

Shakespeare's great comedy is acted with a strange perversity. **Miss Marie Ney** makes Isabella a scold, and fills the mind with the odd combination of nun and ducking-stool. **Mr Emlyn Williams**, unbelievably cast as Angelo, extricates himself from a false position with diabolical ingenuity, playing throughout with the fervour of a man possessed. This is a feat of sheer acting, and promises well for the future. If **Mr Williams** can impress like this when he is unsuited,

41

what will he do when he is suited? In addition, he speaks the verse beautifully, in which he is nobly joined by Mr Stephen Murray as the Duke. Mr Jay Laurier is a superb Pompey, obviously doing for to-day's audience what his Elizabethan forbears did for the Elizabethans. That is to say, filling the part out with the by-play that goes home. This performance admirably reinforces the theory that Shakespeare's clowns should be played by contemporary clowns, always provided that the distinction between Shakespeare's clowns and unclowns is preserved. In other words, while Mr Laurier is right for Pompey and would be excellent as Bottom, neither he nor any other music-hall comedian should attempt Falstaff and Sir Toby, who are no more clowns than they are cardinals.

There is a scene in *Hide and Seek* which is very like the American ballet called *Barn Dance*. Miss Cicely Courtneidge enters and interrupts this, saying: " What is a-going on 'ere, if you please? " This inimitable artist—inimitable when she is doing that for which she has the befitting equipment—raises me to a height of ecstasy in which I think that she should interrupt any and every ballet. What Presage could be more awful than that blonde headgear? Why, oh, why, does she not come on in the Berlioz " Scène aux Champs," point to the stag, and demand to be told: " And what is this 'ere, may I h'ask? " When Miss Courtneidge is imitable she is less good, because lots of little ladies who can sing, dance, and look like the lid of a chocolate-box can imitate this sort of thing better. But Miss Courtneidge's Harringay mood is a primal creation, and in it she fills the mind with astonishing images—Henley's Barmaid, Greta Garbo, and even that divine name which I have so often vowed never again to mention.

The new partnership is an extraordinary success. Mr Bobby Howes has never been better and seldom so good, and the pair work harder than Trojans ever worked horses. Nevertheless, it should be firmly said that Miss Courtneidge is at her highest when she is at her lowest as a comedian, whilst of Mr Howes the reverse is true. There is a Priestley-ish plot in which everybody is his father or her mother. There is a clever and energetic chorus. There are any number of delightful tunes by Mr Vivian Ellis. But there is, alas, one grievous shortcoming ! This is that we see far too little of Mr David Burns, who may pretend to be a gangster, but remains a man for a' that.

Saturday-night Shakespeare and Drawing-room Ibsen

RICHARD III. Revival of Shakespeare's tragedy. Old Vic
  Theatre, Tuesday, November 2, 1937.

GOOD-BYE TO YESTERDAY. A play. By James Parish.
  Phœnix Theatre, Wednesday, November 3, 1937.

[*November 7, 1937*]

IF there is one thing about dramatic critics which is more
surprising than their omniscience it is their nescience. Only
the other day a most distinguished colleague astoundingly
admitted ignorance of what the backstairs of Paris gossiped
about in 1897! Let me in turn confess that I do not know
the correct architectural term for a triptych of five windows
one of which is a door. What I do know is that this contraption now in use at the Old Vic is extraordinarily effective. This door, which is a double door, being thrown open,
we are at once inside the Tower of London, a cell in Pomfret
Castle, and even that Limbo which ghosts inhabit.

The device succeeds everywhere except in the battle
scenes; here all that we see is a lot of highly intellectual
supers throwing themselves into attitudes reminiscent of
the forty-seventh proposition of the First Book of Euclid—
which, of course, is nonsense. One has no objection to nonsense *per se*; one objects to it only when it gets in the way of
the actor or deprives him of his means. A producer is entitled in, say, the last scene of *Hamlet* to turn fencers and
onlookers into isosceles triangles as static as jam-jars at the
grocer's. And there can be no happier instance of what I
should like to call Producer's Liberty, for the reason that
until Hamlet is pinked there is not a line worth hearing for
its own sake.

The battle scenes in *Richard III* are not nearly so ' dumb,'

44

as our American friends would say. Properly considered, they begin with the two orations to the two armies, both of which are omitted in the present production. Omitted also are those two tiny scenes, in the second of which Catesby describes how Richard's horse has been slain, and the king on foot " enacts more wonders than a man." This second scene should be retained, since it shows that Richard is only a metaphysical coward, which any man may well be who has spent half the night being gibbered at by half a dozen ghosts. In the present production Richard, in the space of two minutes, pooh-poohs the " Jockey of Norfolk " message, offers his kingdom for a horse, and is declared a bloody dog and dead into the bargain. This is all too rapid, and it deprives the actor who plays Richard of one of Richard's grandest effects.

Everybody is agreed that the worst part of being hanged for murder is the three weeks which precede the hanging. Bosworth Field is Richard's three weeks; he has long suspected what is coming to him and now knows that it has come. Nevertheless, he puts up a magnificent fight as becomes the character of whom Hazlitt uses the adjectives towering, lofty, commanding, haughty, violent, and bold. Nowhere, except when the lights burn blue, is there any suggestion that Richard is craven, and the actor ought to be given the chance to show this. Those who write of this great and grandly poetic play as though it were another version of *The Ticket-of-Leave Man* should be reminded of what Hazlitt tells us Kean did with this last scene :

> He fights at last like one drunk with wounds : and the attitude in which he stands with his hands stretched out, after his sword is wrested from him, has a preternatural and terrific grandeur, as if his will could not be disarmed, and the very phantoms of his despair had power to kill. . . .

I want even more. I want Richard to be still breathing, and therefore able to hear Richmond say : " The bloody dog is dead." I want not only the fight to stave off doom, but to see doom written in the tyrant's eyes. No actor, how grand soever, can give any of this if he is stretched under and covered by a tarpaulin.

The play stands or falls by Richard, and I shall say succinctly that when there is a Richard as good as Mr Emlyn Williams the rest of the company can afford to be as poor as it is at the Old Vic. I have never seen so false and fleeting a performance of Clarence, so dull a Buckingham, or so unvocal a trio of Queens, any one of whom in the big terzetto should be able to screech down the other two. I except from this general censure the First Murderer of Mr David King-Wood, who also speaks Richmond very well, the Tyrrel of Mr Alec Clunes, and the charming little Princes of Masters Peter Scott and Gordon Miller. This brings us back to Mr Williams, about whose performance I must not flinch from saying that it has one blazing defect. It would be vastly unfair to maintain that this Richard snoops after the kingdom of England as though it were something to be carried off in a hat-box. As in Angelo, so now in Richard, I am convinced that this actor has entirely put *Night Must Fall* behind him and out of mind. But his Richard remains plebeian. We do not believe him when he says:

> I was born so high,
> Our aery buildeth in the cedar's top.

What Mr Williams shows us is the Plantagenet upstart who has not forgotten his early grubbing at the cedar's roots. Given this, the performance is one of remarkable power and, since it is founded in imagination, of cumulative horror. It is, quite rightly, Saturday-nightish, since a lot of the part is obviously written to be ranted. But the ranting is beautifully done, and throughout we hear every syllable of every word. This coming-on actor speaks the verse admirably, his gesture and by-play are informative and entertaining, and his miming is always expressive. In other words, what we are privileged to see is a fine player in the process of turning himself into a fine Shakespearean player. One has already admitted that he is not kingly. And so what? The answer is that since Mr Williams grandly shakes all of the cedar's boughs except one, we should not grumble overmuch if the twig at the top escapes him.

Good-bye to Yesterday is no more a play about a little boy losing his reason through being shut up in a cupboard than *Little Eyolf* was a play about a little boy losing his life through falling off a pier. " Ah ! " say the clever ones. " But neither was *Little Eyolf* a play about the remorse of Eyolf's parents. It was a play about selflessness, and, since all Ibsen's plays were written to prove Mr Shaw's theories, about ' the way to Communism through resolute and un-compromising Individualism.' " I agree that Ibsen wrote plays not about fashionable wives and husbands, but round unfashionable theories using unfashionable persons as spokesmen.

Similarly, Mr Parish's play is not, let us hope, about how long it is going to take Mrs Lorimer to suspect her husband of having shut their boy up in a cupboard, how soon after this discovery she is going to find out that she can no longer love her husband, to what extent the bickerings will be prolonged, and how late in the evening it will be before proof is forthcoming that the whole thing was an accident. Let us hope Mr Parish's play is not about this, since if it were it would be false. A woman who adores her husband to the extent of preferring his stale tobacco smoke to all the perfumes of the Rue Royale is not going to cease to love him merely because she discovers a kink in him, however much she may hate that kink. Human nature is not made that way, and I shall pay the author the compliment of suggest-ing that his piece was intended to be something more than fuss in a drawing-room.

The crucial point in the drama occurs when the wife's ' advanced ' sister tears to pieces the notion that happy marriage is possible only when one partner to it believes the other to be perfect. " You have discovered that Brian has a spot of sadism. Well, I'm a scientist and I realise that all of us have got a spot of something. We have just got to accept it ! " says the sister. This is where the play's real interest lies, and it is a pity that it is not quite the play which Mr Parish has written. It is a pity that rationalising the play's emotions is not the author's reason for introducing the sister, but only the mechanical device for bringing about the suspicion that the husband can be at odd moments the monster which he is not. In other words, a play which begins by being Ibsenite ends in being Henry-Arthur-Jonesish.

It is played with all conceivable polish by Miss Gladys Cooper, Mr Philip Merivale, and Miss Marda Vanne in the three principal parts, with some deplorable comedy brilliantly done by Mr Walter Hudd, and the usual slick production by Mr Basil Dean. What it really wants is the rugged playing of Miss Flora Robson and Mr Wilfrid Lawson, and production by somebody who would firmly rewrite the play. Lastly, let me advise Mr Parish either to shilly with Jones or shally with Ibsen. A piece which dilly-dallies between the two makes the worst of both worlds.

Wuthering Depths

MOURNING BECOMES ELECTRA. A tragedy. By Eugene
O'Neill. Westminster Theatre, Friday, November 19,
1937.

CYMBELINE. By William Shakespeare and Bernard Shaw.
Embassy Theatre, Tuesday, November 16, 1937.

THE SILENT KNIGHT. A romantic comedy. By Humbert
Wolfe. From the Hungarian of Eugene Heltai. Pro-
duced by Gilbert Miller. St James's Theatre, Tuesday,
November 16, 1937.

[*November* 21, 1937]

A POLICEMAN in one of Mr Maugham's stories says : " I
don't believe remorse for a crime ever sits very heavily on a
man when he's absolutely sure he will never be found out ! "
The essence of Greek tragedy, and this play is Greek
tragedy, is that you can never be sure of not being found
out, if it's only by your sin. The Ancients couldn't call it
conscience, since Man, being the plaything of the gods, was
not responsible as we moderns know responsibility. But
even so there was something inside a man which was policeman, judge, jury, and conscience all rolled into one.

Professor Gilbert Murray pretends that Sophocles, that
determined classicist, made Electra the pivot of a drama of
matricide and high spirits. Euripides took a soberer view,
and there is no doubt in my mind that Shakespeare would
have taken the soberest of all if he had pursued the Gertrude-
Clytemnestra issue instead of losing himself in the maze of
Hamlet's mind. By the way, would Mr Shaw like to write
us a sixth act of *Hamlet* in which the poison on the rapiers
has lost its efficacy, and Hamlet is left alive to examine his
conscience in the matter of his stepfather's murder and his
mother-complex ? Like his predecessors, Mr O'Neill is
absolute for remorse, and, to conclude this part of the

49

argument, if Mr Maugham is in step a fair number of august people have been out of it !

Mourning Becomes Electra is about souls in hell. Black and spotted souls sporting on Hamlet's " couch for luxury and damn'd incest." No glimmer of hope pierces the blanket of this dark, which is thickened by pessimism and has all possible holes metaphysically stopped. Death has ceased to be the gateway to life ; we are in a limbo in which all life opens the door to universal death. In the meantime there is existence here, and by the same token we are to bethink ourselves that this is an evening at the theatre, with readers expecting to be told whether they will enjoy the play or not ! Let us inform them in our grandest style that we rate the evening among the six highest of our life, but that if they are searchers after pure diversion we recommend them to stay at home, draw up their chairs to an empty grate, and by some farthing dip discover in the pages of Emily Brontë entertainment less shiversome.

We warn such, however, that they would be missing tremendous theatre. Also that they would—and if I know anything about London playgoers they will !—miss some of the finest acting seen in our theatre since the War. Miss Beatrix Lehmann has for some time been knocking at the door marked " Great Acting Only," and with this performance she gets in one foot and one shoulder—an awkward image, but one which, I venture to think, suits the strained intensity of this performance. Whole scenes of it demand that Electra shall be as silent as the Hungarian gentleman at another theatre ; it is the actress who takes care that her silence shall shout the house down. Or you might write of this performance in terms of banked-up fires, crust over lava. The author has enjoined immobility upon his character ; it is the actress who expresses that immobility in terms of a jaw slewed round. Miss Lehmann in her magnificent playing brings to mind two images. One of these, which is not too happy, will disappear when she is more practised in a part the mere apprehension of which would have struck most actresses stone dead. In the earlier acts she is, be it confessed, a little too poker-stiff, a little too much like Judy Smallweed as " Phiz " saw that redoubtable young woman. But in the later scenes she replaces Smallweed by the great flower of French acting, Rachel, to whom she bears a remarkable physical resemblance. And on this is superimposed something else, something which is not Rachel acting, but Charlotte Brontë, who watched Rachel and realised with every fibre of her brain and body that Vashti was in hell.

Has Miss Laura Cowie quite enough guns for Clytemnestra ? The point is that Clytemnestra carries enough guns to sink a whole battleship, or any actress unprovided with extraordinary genius. What this part demands is Mrs Campbell at her greatest. Miss Cowie gives the very best of her very considerable means. There is no suggestion of failure, and perhaps the result might be described as a brilliant draw. Mr Mark Dignam's Agamemnon in its stiff obstinacy and Mr Robert Harris's Orestes in its slow awakening to lively horror are very fine performances. Mr Reginald Tate's Ægisthus is a good study in the breezy-ominous, and the whole tragedy is knit together by the superb Chorus of Mr John Abbott. Mr Michael MacOwan has produced most admirably. I congratulate him on giving Mr Brian Easdale his head with the music, and Mr Easdale on using it. But what stroke of luck or imagination was it which suggested to Mr MacOwan to make the houses of both Agamemnon and Ezra Mannon exactly like Ken Wood ? Are we to gather that the tragic spirit is the same yesterday, to-day, and for ever ?

Apology has never been Mr Shaw's forte, and I shall not be so impertinent as to apologise for him. In a collaborator's note in the Embassy programme he writes : " I stand in the same relation to Shakespeare as Mozart to Handel, or Wagner to Beethoven." But is not Mr Shaw deceiving himself? Is not the correct parallel to the Shakespeare-Shaw relationship that, say, of Gershwin to Mozart? Mozart, gingering up the *Messiah* score, took care that his pep should be reasonably Handelian. Mr Shaw's emendation of Shakespeare's score is the purest Shavian jazz.

Or you might put it that with the fifth act the texture of the play changes from brocade to calico. Good, hard-wearing, post-Ibsenite calico, but still calico. The point is not whether stout calico is or is not better than worn-out brocade; the point is that replacing outworn material by new stuff of a totally different kind is not what Mozart did to Handel. Imogen, dewy, loyal, and unquestioning, and, according to Ibsenite notions, an unawakened doll, is one character; Mr Shaw's modern young lady, realising that her husband, in making bets about her honour, has behaved like a donkey, is another. What, of course, is really wrong with Mr Shaw's last act is that he should have also re-written the previous one and shown us the steps by which Imogen the doll awakens to Imogen the emancipated woman. This last act has the air of being not a serious ending but a lark, and it has never occurred to me that Mozart looked upon his tinkering at Handel as a spree. In short, Mr Shaw has been led away by that fatal thing, an analogy. Modern orchestration is supposed to be richer than the old; I did not at Swiss Cottage hear any colour like that of:

> Hang there like fruit, my soul,
> Till the tree die!

In view of limited space, a few words must suffice for the acting. Mr George Hayes as Iachimo admirably suggested the " slight thing of Italy," Mr William Devlin gave Pisanio his full tenderness, Miss Olga Lindo, since she comes of player's stock, had no difficulty in giving flesh and blood to the shadowy Queen, and in the difficult part of Cloten Mr Skelton Knaggs made a genuine and mainly successful effort to escape from his own idiosyncrasies. Miss Joyce Bland began with a composite portrait of Imogen, half by Mary

Anderson and half by Sybil Thorndike, the whole being like
some Staffordshire potter's notion of a French actress in
Racine, all drapery, frontal stare, and tragic nose. The last
act, of course, was the difficulty. Should Imogen be mala-
pert in the Shakespearean manner or pert in the Shavian?
Miss Bland, with unerring tact, solved the difficulty in a
way Walkley would have mightily approved. She abounded
in her own sense, and even in her common sense. She was
blandly pert.

Unlike Mr Wegg I do not often drop into poetry. But
since Mr Wolfe's play is in verse, and the punishment should
always fit the crime, here goes :

> " Give me my principal and let me go! "
> Muttered old Shylock to Antonio.
> " Give us some interest, and we shall stay! "
> Murmur all those who mean to like a play.
> Such the fond hope of gentles and their dames,
> Making their way to King Street in St James,
> Putting full trust in comedy Hungarian,
> Prepared to laugh with Aryan or Non-Aryan,
> Telling the story of a lover bold
> Condemned to hold his tongue to please a scold.
> Or, if you like, 'tis coquetry's fair daughter,
> Reeking of fifteenth-century Bayswater.
> The play, they knew, had passed the acid test—
> Two years in Buda, nearly three in Pesth.
> To let them down was not the way of Miller,
> Who gave his orders thus : " Withhold no siller!
> Settings designed by Otto Niedermoser,
> Costumes by G. K. Benda. Sure the show's a
> Wow—if you'll excuse my strong Amurrican—
> To lift the playhouse roof off in a hurricane.
> Nothing to omit to make assurance sure,
> Take up the scent and follow up the spoor
> Of poet Wolfe, whose artless-artful tinkle
> Evokes delight as pin elicits winkle! "
> Thus Gilbert spake; the stage-hands roared applause.
> Not so first-nighters, whose well-mannered jaws
> Yawned to distraction, all bewailing that
> They had not stayed at home by hearth and cat,
> With pipe and book or even highbrow wireless
> To prove the tired business-man is tireless.
> Let me be fair. The show was mighty pretty,
> The verse but wanted wit to make it witty.
> Deprived of this medicament or nostrum,

THE AMAZING THEATRE

We thought of speech day and the high-school rostrum—
Guessed, though the playing could not well be properer,
The thing had been much better as an opera.
Judged that the Wynyard, languorous Diana,
Though acting grandly, lacked a grand pianner.
That Richardson, at home with king or hobo,
Needed an obligato by the oboe.
That flower-like Scott, the ox-eyed Margaretta,
Should have bel-canto'd *à la* Violetta.
Doth simile break down 'neath brave Lyn Harding?
We and our halting Muse must then beg parding.
Dressed, mounted, acted, everything to please
Th' expectant tiers, why should the thing just tease?
Why should romance modelled on old Cyrano
Not prove what Curzon called a grand be-ano?
Why sate the audience something bored and glum?
Plain stared the reason—the whole play was dumb!
Nor Grimm nor Andersen wrote story sillier
Than this of tongue-tied Peter and his Zilia.

Two Moderns and a Classic

ROBERT'S WIFE. A play. By St John Ervine. Globe
Theatre, Tuesday, November 23, 1937.

PEOPLE AT SEA. A play. By J. B. Priestley. Apollo Theatre,
Wednesday, November 24, 1937.

THE SCHOOL FOR SCANDAL. Revival of Sheridan's comedy.
Queen's Theatre, Thursday, November 25, 1937.

[*November* 28, 1937]

EDMOND DE GONCOURT has said: "*Le vrai bon théâtre,
c'est une émotion ou une gaîté procurée n'importe comment.*" Judged by this standard Mr Ervine's play is very
nearly a complete success, since except for an apparently
directionless twenty minutes in the second act the audience
is consistently interested and amused. Mention of one
Frenchman paves the way for another one. It is recorded
of Balzac that, walking in Paris, he met a friend who began
to pour out his domestic woes. Balzac cut him short: " Let
us talk of real things—who do you think is going to marry
Eugénie Grandet ? " Mr Ervine's characters have the
supreme gift of becoming alive. Novelists, we know, talk of
their characters acting out of their own volition. Thackeray
could not prevent Rawdon Crawley from striking Lord
Steyne, and Dickens was powerless to stop Mr Micawber
from dropping the ruler across Uriah's knuckles. Similarly
I feel that Mr Ervine could not have prevented his Miss
Orley from coming forward with that gift of £5000 which
secures this good play's happy ending.

Yet I am to show how a good play might have been made
better. In Russia there is a contraption called a troika. This
is a sledge drawn by three horses whose harness includes a
large hoop binding the animals together in a rainbow-like
unity. Mr Ervine's play is harnessed to three major themes

having to do with self-sacrifice. Now, the point about jumping into a canal to rescue somebody is not so much the keeping of another's head above water as the fact that if you don't jump you will never again be able to hold up your own head. In other words, the essence of self-sacrifice is not material efficacy, but the spiritual effect on the doer of the sacrifice.

Now for our three themes. Robert, a vicar and the apple of his bishop's eye, insists upon a young man jumping into marriage with a shiftless gadabout for the sake of their un-born child. The baby dies. The vicar's son jumps into the pacifist breach by writing seditious letters to a soldier. The soldier remains constant, not one penny less will appear in the Army estimates, and the vicar's son goes to gaol. Robert will be dean if his wife Sanchia renounces her post in that clinic whose speciality is birth-control. It may be argued that Mr Ervine burkes the general issue by concentrating on an extreme example, and I agree that there is a play to be written on the intense annoyance Torvald Helmer would have felt if Nora had developed into a successful novelist, or Morell if Candida had blossomed out into a St James's Hall pianist. But this is not Mr Ervine's play. The case he presents is that of a wife whose work runs acutely counter to her husband's; at least the parish does not want to hear the vicar preach from Sanchia's text. In the play as we now have it, Sanchia's sacrifice of her career is made easier be-cause Miss Orley, the parish worker with " Prossy's com-plaint," insists on coming forward with the £5000 enabling the clinic to carry on. Whereupon Robert gets his deanery and the pattern goes to pieces.

The play as it stands is like two perfectly matched carriage-horses with a third animal of a different colour running alongside them. It could be made into a troika if Sanchia, having irrevocably resigned from the clinic, reads in the evening paper that the deanery has gone elsewhere. Our artistic consciences would then be satisfied, and we could leave the theatre debating whether people should indulge in the luxury of self-sacrifice or discipline themselves into more looking and less leaping. I agree that the play's failure in pattern is more than compensated by the fight it puts up for not looking so long and so blindly that leaping ceases to be a function of mankind. There is a noble cogency in the sustained argument that throughout history the result of shackled minds has been tethered limbs.

Alas that no sooner are Mr Owen Nares and Miss Edith Evans on the point of being extremely good than some lesser character comes along and snatches the play from them! First it is Mr David Horne, trailing episcopal clouds of sheer Trollope. Next it is Miss Margaret Moffat, consolidating all working-class motherhood into one bitter etching. Then it is Mr David Markham in a fine temper and pulling young Oxford down about old ears. Then, just when our leading pair seem like getting a look in, Miss Margaret Scudamore floods the stage with the blessed gossip of a rich old silly, after which we must concentrate on that reservoir of beautifully pent-up emotion which is Miss Edith Sharpe's parish-worker. This exquisite tank removed, you would say the stage was now clear for our star pair, when lo and behold Mr Robert Holmes comes in as a forbidding rival priest and sweeps his betters into corners! I shall not be surprised if one of these nights Mr Nares and Miss Evans forget to go down to the theatre!

The genre of philosophic thriller, which Mr Priestley now attempts, is one which must always fail. When a schooner is derelict in no matter what ocean, putting aside fire and fever, only two things can break out. These are mutiny and argument. Your play, then, either consists of, say, Mr Lyn Harding crawling about the rigging pursued by, say, Mr Edmund Willard with a knife in his mouth like Mr Hands going after Jim Hawkins, or it just calls itself *Heartbreak Houseboat*. But you cannot have Hands and Hawkins crawling about Captain Shotover's rigging. Why? Because the spectator is not going to be thrilled by murders which are mere pegs for further argument, neither will he be dumbfounded by your argufier spacing out his thuggeries with intellectual small change.

Twelve people are adrift on a steamer whose other pas-sengers are either drowned or have taken to the boats. Yet the day after this frightful happening, and with the danger of the ship breaking up at any minute, even the rational members of the party still dress for dinner ! In the case of the film star varnishing her nails for the Day of Judgment this would have been a pretty touch ; its general application destroys actuality. Later on the senior wrangler empties his pistol into the stomach of the chief mutineer ; after which he goes on with his theorising, whereas in real life even a philosopher would put aside philosophy to put himself right with the captain of the approaching rescue-steamer. Mr Priestley's answer here is that since he has not posed his piece on the strictly factual plane, one must not be factually critical. Whereupon one comes back with the knock-out blow that if the argument is about how to reconstitute society on derelict steamers the late Sir James Barrie argued more picturesquely. That if it is about the remaking of the soul the late Jerome K. Jerome argued more effectively. That if it concerns the rights of stokers Mr Eugene O'Neill argued more forcefully. That if it is all summed up in the two failures who take a header into eternity *via* the Carib-bean Sea Mr Sutton Vane argued with more splash.

This, then, is a play of reminiscent action and unremem-berable talk, and in the theatre coma never settles quicker than when listening to small talk on big matters. Still, there are bits of nice acting to look at. There is Mr Torin Thatcher's stoker, a Hairy Ape who would fit into a better play. There is Miss Vivienne Bennett's lady's-maid, first cousin to Lady Dedlock's Hortense, and also going about " like a very neat She-Wolf imperfectly tamed." There is Miss Jean Muir giving a witty impersonation of the bit of nonsense which the cinema calls a great actress. There is Mr Edward Chapman booming away about nothing in particular. There is Mr Martin Walker staging his familiar easy drunkard. And there is Mr Carl Jaffé, who for the second time in my experience, and by no discernible means, plays everybody else off the stage.

But it is a dull evening all the same, and the pity is that it could so easily have been avoided. Mr Priestley is a major dramatist, and one appreciates that even one of these may have a playlet in his system and want to get rid of it. Very well, then; let such a playlet be voided in, say, the Outer Hebrides. But let it not be brought to London, where the author is in full tide of success with two first-magnitude plays. In allowing *People at Sea* to be staged Mr Priestley is like an orchestral conductor who should connive at a programme of Elgar's two symphonies with the same composer's " Salut d'Amour " coming after.

I am in something of a quandary about the Queen's revival of Sheridan's masterpiece. Mauling is too rough a word, fantastication too smooth, and treatment too colourless for the way in which this revival has been mishandled. A good principle is that the direct and, if you like, unimaginative approach to this play is always better than the ' amusingness ' of Bloomsbury. The one way to stab this masterpiece in the back is for the producer to express himself through it. It is all so simple. You find out when the play was written, build one room each in the houses of Lady Sneerwell, Sir Peter Teazle, Charles Surface, and his brother Joseph, as they were at that date, fill them with the real furniture, real curtains, and real chandeliers of the period, and do the rest with drop-scenes. You stick to elegant costumes and period acting, and if any of your players starts to dance you tell him sternly that the note of the production is the Old Vic and not Sadler's Wells. At the Queen's Theatre these rules are broken. The scenery is billowy and impressionistic, so that the spectator is made to look at the year 1777 through the patronising, self-conscious eyes of 1937. Curtains and candelabra are painted, and where the setting is realistic it has the colour of dust on a skeleton. Finally, the majority of the costumes are of an unexampled hideousness.

This brings us to the acting. This is so generally out of tune that Sir Oliver Surface, whom Mr Frederick Lloyd manages to keep grandly in key, becomes the play's central figure—so much so that a young colleague has written of Sir Peter and Lady Teazle as " the by-play." I wonder what any of the great Sir Peters would have thought at being relegated to a sub-plot, a thing which could not happen if the character were authentically played. Charles Lamb praised King, the original Sir Peter, for giving him an old, hard, withered face " like a john-apple puckered up into a thousand wrinkles." Mr Quartermaine makes him too young, too smooth, and too gentle, less like an apple than a pensive autumnal tree shedding melliflous fruit. One who is not a Lamb might put it that Sir Peter is a testy old fool ; Mr Quartermaine is without an atom of testiness or folly. The result is that the screen scene is ruined an hour before we come to it. As Lady Teazle Miss Ashcroft is breathless with innocence when she should be panting under a smother of acquired elegance. Apart from this her performance is charming.

Can it be thought that those brilliant actresses, Miss Dorothy Green and Miss Athene Seyler, left to themselves, would have hung such clouts on Lady Sneerwell and Mrs Candour ? What is the point of a Charles Surface who is without glitter, wears worsted, and talks with the home-spun accents better befitting Goldsmith than Sheridan ? Surely to ruin oneself with extravagance and wear an air of parsimony is to make the worst of both worlds ? Again it is a case of a good actor, Mr Michael Redgrave, being miscast. Why is Trip a boor who would not have dreamed of emulating his master's elegance ? Why must Mr Alec Guinness put

an inch of putty on to Snake's nose? And why is Mr George
Howe, as Crabtree, forced to roll and grimace like a plebeian
Rowlandson? Why are the pictures in Charles's gallery such
modernistic daubs? And why does Charles look to find his
ancestors in the audience? Even first-nighters are not so
ancient as that! In the slang of to-day a predominant actor
is said to be " out by himself." On Thursday evening Mr
Gielgud, who played Joseph Surface, was within these old
doors by himself, always with the exception of Mr Lloyd.
And at the end of the play nobody was indoors, for the
reason that all the company had gone to join the Russian
Ballet.

Macbeth Yesterday and To-day

MACBETH. Revival of Shakespeare's Tragedy. Old Vic
Theatre, Friday, November 26, and Wednesday after-
noon, December 1, 1937.
[*December* 5, 1937]

> We have each our private ideal of Macbeth, Hamlet,
> Othello, Lear; we have all of us read of, if we have not seen,
> great performances of these parts; so that every actor who
> undertakes them has to pass through a triple ordeal, en-
> countering, first, our imagination, kindled by Shakespeare;
> second, our idealised memory of performances which used to
> please our, perhaps unripe, judgment; third, our conceptions
> of the great actors of the past, gathered from the often ex-
> travagant panegyrics of contemporaries.
>
> WILLIAM ARCHER

PERHAPS this is the place to say—and if it isn't I shall still
say it !—that I have been more ' got at ' over Mr Olivier's
performance than by any other in my recollection. Chelsea
semaphored, "Unable conceive Macbeth as gigolo."
Bloomsbury signalled, "No use for Macbeth as mountebank." A young gentleman in corduroy trousers and a
velvet smoking-jacket opined to my face that Macbeth
should not be like a retired Army colonel. Reflecting that
what the young gentleman stood in need of was an active
drill-sergeant, I proceeded to turn a deaf, but not altogether
deaf, ear to another of the mincing brigade, who suggested
that the new Macbeth shouted too loudly.

I say " not altogether deaf " because even the austerest
critic is none the worse for knowing what is being said by
the mob ! I am persuaded that those monuments to incor-
ruptibility, our judges, take a good keek at anonymous
letters before they consign them to the wastepaper-basket.
Now my mentors, though self-appointed, were not anonymous, and it so happens that I have the greatest respect for
their opinions in the domains of art and music as well as

drama. Nor did I get the impression that the plushy young gentleman was altogether a fool. Why, then, should a performance which interested me throughout and at times excited me greatly fail so completely with these others? Can it be that they were judging Mr Olivier's performance by some preconceived standard to which this actor's physical means, even if he were Garrick and Kean rolled into one, would still not let him conform? Can it be that they were like a man going to the circus expecting to see lions and who, confronted with a cage of tigers, says: " These lions are poor ! " Or can it be that I was wrong?

Anyhow, I was sufficiently intrigued, as they say, to pay a second visit and sit the play out a second time. And sufficiently conscientious to consider whether one's rules for measuring performances in classic parts stand in need of revision. I look at it in this way. Every critic has his ideal Macbeth, Hamlet, Othello, Lear. But the attitude he must adopt is not that of a schoolmaster correcting schoolboy answers. A critic has not finished with Mr Jones's Hamlet by allotting it, say, 65 marks out of a possible 100. If I am not being too nice in this matter, let me suggest that this arithmetical judgment may be the only practicable method of assessing a newcomer about whom the critic knows nothing more than the immediate impersonation. Hazlitt, writing about Kean on his first appearance as Shylock, was in a very different position from Hazlitt years later considering Kean's Lear, when the actor's virtues and limitations, mental as well as physical, had become well known to him. This is why when it comes to allotting marks for a performance the critic must take into account not only how much that performance falls short of the ideal, but by how much it exceeds, or fails to exceed, that which the critic could reasonably expect from previous performances by the same actor.

Of course Mr Olivier's Macbeth, now presented for the

first time, is inadequate, ideally considered. And perhaps
we may first glance at what has been said of the adequacy
or inadequacy on the part of actors greater than Mr Olivier
pretends to be. First there is Garrick, about whom Francis
Gentleman winds up a fulsome panegyric with the request
to know " who has heard Macbeth's speech, after receiving
his death wound, uttered with the utmost agony of body
and mind, but almost pities the expiring wretch though
stained with crimes of the deepest dye ? " One reflects that
this speech, not to be found in Shakespeare, must have been
uttered not only with the utmost of Garrick's bodily and
mental pain, but at considerable cost of the great actor's
invention as well ! Quin " could not be expected to exhibit
the acute sensations of the character." Barry " made a
lukewarm affair of Macbeth." Powell " dwindled into boy-
ish whimpering." So much for Francis Gentleman.

According to Hazlitt, Kean, being deficient in the poetry
of the character, " did not look like a man who had encountered the Weird Sisters." This critic greatly preferred
Kemble's Macbeth, although " his tones had occasionally a
learned quaintness, like the colouring of Poussin." Of
Macready, Lewes said that " though unsurpassable in some
aspects, he wanted the heroic thew and sinew to represent
the character as a whole," and that his Macbeth " stole into
the sleeping chamber of Duncan like a man going to purloin
a purse, not like a warrior going to snatch a crown." Henry
Morley was so greatly overcome by, and wrote at such length
of, Helen Faucit's Lady Macbeth that he dismissed Phelps's
performance of her great partner as a " rude, impulsive
soldier," while a lesser critic of the 'forties complained that
in the banquet scene " dignity and kingly courtesy were
wanting." Irving, according to Ellen Terry, thought that
his Macbeth, though universally discredited, was his finest
performance, and of his last act she writes : " He looked
like a great famished wolf." Of Bourchier's over-acting in
the part Allan Monkhouse once said, if he did not write,

that one left the theatre wondering whether murder was as serious as all that came to !

Since from the foregoing it would seem that a great Macbeth has never been in the calendar, it is reasonable to expect that the new one should be lacking in perfect adequacy. It is a part demanding great natural and physical gifts, to which Mr Olivier at present can only oppose natural and physical shortcomings. He does not, for example, look like coping with Russian bears, Hyrcan tigers, and rhinoceroses, whether armed or unarmed. His voice, which in the " To-morrow and to-morrow " and the " Sere and yellow leaf " speeches should vibrate like a 'cello, is of a pitch rather higher than the average. In other words, he is not a natural bass and has some difficulty in getting down to baritone. All the same, he brings off some magnificent vocal effects, and his verse-speaking has improved throughout. Ideally, Macbeth might be likened to some oak, magnificent in outer shell but lacking roots, and presently to be riven by the lightning of conscience. But Nature has not so endowed Mr Olivier, who is forced to play the whole part nervously among the high-tossed branches.

The whole performance, then, is a study in nerves, and, so far as I am concerned, this actor, largely by force of highly expressive play of feature, makes a notable conquest over what might so easily be monotony. He begins in a low key. We realise that Macbeth is rapt, as Banquo says, in something more than contemplation of the Witches' pro-mises ; his mind harks back to the earlier occasion when to his wife he tentatively broke the murderous enterprise. He hesitated then, and is not ready now, and this reading gives a chance upon which any great Lady Macbeth would eagerly seize. But, alas, Miss Judith Anderson throws it away by suggesting that " He that's coming must be provided for " is no more than an allusion to clean sheets ! As the murder draws near this Macbeth's passion increases. Many actors play the " dagger " speech with the aplomb of a concert-

singer reeling off " Hybreas the Cretan " ; the speech as it is
now rendered is shot with apprehension. The ascent and
descent of the staircase are done superbly, the voice falling
at the duetted " Amen " and rising to a magnificent resonance with the " Sleep no more " speech, which has a Nordic,
barbaric, and what I may call a Sibelius-like ring of doom.
I pass over the nicely calculated scene with the murderers
to welcome the beautiful and intensely Shakespearean
delivery of

> Light thickens; and the crow
> Makes wing to the rooky wood.

The banquet scene a little disappoints in the same way
that Phelps disappointed. Macbeth, who has put on king-
ship, should be more royal, and I am inclined to think that
jumping on to the table is too much in Hamlet's vein after
the play scene. This brings us to the last act, which is the
best of any of the Macbeths that I have seen. It is played
at white heat of both imagination and energy, so that it
becomes a molten whole. Here the actor gathers up all his
forces and all his knowledge of what ought to be done. It is
the reverse of " all over bar the shouting." Mr Olivier, who
has made enough noise, and some people think too much,
now gives the part the finest edge of his brain. " Liar and
slave ! " is uttered with a cold, Irvingesque malignity. If
the voice, expressing Macbeth's melancholy, still cannot
accomplish the 'cello, it achieves a noble viola. The fight
at the end is grandly done, and when sword and dagger are
gone Macbeth's final gesture, in which he would fight Macduff with his bare shield, shows that not even the poetry in
which he has been enwrapped, nor all the metaphysical stuff
which has embroidered his wife's death, has robbed this
soldier of his first valour.

To sum up, this may not be the whole of Macbeth. Ideally
considered, the performance lacks grandeur, and the actor
should look to his gait, which smacks too much of the
modern prize-ring. But the mental grasp is here, and so

too is enough of the character to take one spectator out of the Waterloo Road and set him down on that dubious heath. Further, is it not a point that whereas a stripling can fly at Hamlet, Macbeth is a weighty business which requires the momentum of age? Mr Olivier will probably play this part twice as well when he has twice his present years. Meanwhile he registers another step in a career of considerable achievement and increasing promise. Alas that he is insufficiently helped by his Lady Macbeth, about whom I shall echo what an earlier critic said about an earlier actress : " Miss Laura Addison has a good conception of the part, draws a just outline of it, but is incapable of filling it up. She is a clever actress, with a very laudable intelligence of the character, but with natural powers inadequate to its just exhibition." Where Mr Olivier is admirably aided is by the production of M. Michel Saint-Denis, by Motley's scenery, of dried-blood hue and consistency, and by the incidental music of M. Darius Milhaud. The perkiness of M. Milhaud's themes and the irrelevance of their toylike colouring suggest by audacity of contrast the time's form and pressure.

Two Great Plays and a Witty Revue

VOLPONE. Revival of Ben Jonson's comedy. Westminster Theatre, Tuesday, January 25, 1938.

THREE SISTERS. Revival of Tchehov's play. Queen's Theatre, Friday, January 28, 1938.

NINE SHARP. A revue. By Herbert Farjeon. Music by Walter Leigh. Little Theatre, Wednesday, January 26, 1938.

THE INNOCENT PARTY. A comedy. By H. M. Harwood and Laurence Kirk. St James's Theatre, Thursday, January 27, 1938.

[*January* 30, 1938]

DE GUSTIBUS and so on. Speaking for myself, I had as lief see a comedy by Ben Jonson as any by Shakespeare. Perhaps liefer, though the unfamiliarity of the one and the over-familiarity of the other may have something to do with it. But then I would sooner live surrounded by Hogarths than by Watteaus, since to me the English painter, despite the ugliness of his subject, is warm and alive, while the Frenchman, despite the elegance of his, is cold and not so alive. And there the analogy must end, since, if we take Hazlitt as our mentor, Shakespeare's humour " bubbles, sparkles, and finds its way in all directions, like a natural spring," whereas Jonson's " is, as it were, confined in a leaden cistern, where it stagnates and corrupts."

Still holding each to his own taste, I submit that it is possible to prove Hazlitt all wrong about this play. Consider Volpone's speech, which begins : " Why droops my Celia ? " and goes on :

> See, behold
> What thou art queen of ; not in expectation,
> As I feed others, but possess'd and crown'd.
> See here a rope of pearl, and each more orient
> Than that the brave Ægyptian Queen carous'd ;

68

> Dissolve, and drink them. See, a carbuncle,
> May put out both the eyes of our St Mark;
> A diamond would have bought Lollia Paulina,
> When she came in like star-light, hid with jewels
> That were the spoils of provinces; take these,
> And wear, and lose 'em. Yet remains an ear-ring
> To purchase them again, and this whole state.

Look over the exquisite passage beginning:

> Thy baths shall be the juice of July flowers,
> Spirits of roses, and of violets,
> The milk of unicorns, and panthers' breath,
> Gather'd in bags, and mix'd with Cretan wines;
> Our drink shall be prepared gold and amber,
> Which we will take until my roof whirl round
> With the vertigo. . . .

It seems to me that Faustus himself would not have disdained

> When she came in like star-light, hid with jewels,

and that Perdita would have been at home with

> The milk of unicorns, and panthers' breath.

Yet Hazlitt's adjectives for Jonson's verse are " dry," " literal," and " meagre." The point is that the great essayist, like every other playgoer who ever lived except me, is a sentimentalist and will take no pleasure in a play unless he can find in it some nice person with whom to identify himself :

> There is almost a total want of variety, fancy, relief, and of those delightful transitions which abound, for instance, in Shakespeare's tragi-comedy. In Ben Jonson, we find ourselves generally in low company, and we see no hope of getting out of it. He is like a person who fastens upon a disagreeable subject and cannot be persuaded to leave it.

But, in heaven's name, who wants anybody to leave a disagreeable subject if he can make it more interesting than an agreeable one ?

Hazlitt thinks that the trouble with Jonson's comedy is

69

that it is mean. This is palpably absurd, since one of the concomitants of meanness is littleness. I would rather call Jonson's comedy riotous and his humanity of the cartoonist's size. Volpone bestrides his world as Valmont bestrides that of Choderlos de Laclos and Vautrin Balzac's; the lesser rogues have still something Michael-Angelesque about them. Hazlitt denies Jonson gusto because he does not like the things the gusto is about, and because, like any other sentimental playgoer, he wants to warm himself at the spectacle of good men routing bad ones, and sees no fun in villains destroying one another. It dismays him that Volpone should be undone by Mosca, and that both should be punished by a bench of zanies. He dislikes the caperings of Volpone's minions because he would not have them behaving so in his own drawing-room.

To sum up, Hazlitt desires that comedy should make him think better of mankind, whereas I demand of comedy only that it shall make me think. So long as the comic dramatist is writing well and not ill I am indifferent whether his characters behave well or ill. " Jonson had a keen sense of what was true and false, but not of the difference between the agreeable and disagreeable." This proves my case against any playgoer demanding more that the things shown him in the theatre shall be agreeable than that they shall be true. Judged by the West-End standard of popularity, *Volpone* is " cross-grained," " prolix," " improbable," " repulsive," and even " revolting." Yet in a critic as good as Hazlitt the critical habit dies hard, and he cannot help saying that " this best play " of Jonson " is written *con amore.*" This sentence clinches my argument. It is all very well for its author to recover by saying that the play " is made up of cheats and dupes, and the author is at home among them." The gibe comes too late; the *piece is written con amore*! So saying, Hazlitt puts himself in the position of a batsman who should at one and the same time hit the ball twice, obstruct the field, and tread on his wicket. The

70

play is written *con amore,* and not merely to supply a demand, please a manager, or create a part for Miss Prompt-worthy !

In the revival at the Westminster the same boundless spirit is at large. Mr Michael MacOwan has given their heads to Mr Peter Goffin and Mr Edmund Rubbra, and, thus encouraged, Mr Goffin responds with a gold-encrusted Jacobean tableau which Mr Sickert ought to paint, and Mr Rubbra, meeting his producer more than half-way, conjures from the throats of clarinet, oboe, and bassoon a concourse of sounds even more obnoxious, in a Hazlittean sense, than the scenes they accompany. This spirit extends to the players. Mr Donald Wolfit makes a splendid mouthful of the Fox; he is right in presence, and he speaks the verse as the actor of Jonson's day must have spoken it. There must be many ways of playing Mosca, and Mr Alan Wheatley has chosen to be a silk thread among the hempen villainy. Mr Mark Dignam is the vulture-lawyer of all time, and Mr Stanley Lathbury is a most pointed, witless crow. As I wish this revival immensely well, and as at this point the praise of the acting must get thinner, I stop.

Though one has still to justify Ben Jonson to dunder-heads, with Tchehov that necessity is past. I think it may have been this recognition which was behind Mr Giel-gud's obvious emotion when making his little speech of thanks—recognition that a public which screams itself silly over French without tears can be got to listen in deepest silence to Russian with tears. Mr Gielgud would be the first to recognise his debt to his predecessors, to Mr Philip Ridge-way, who first entrusted the masterpiece to Komisarjevsky, and to the Old Vic management, who gave it to Mr Henry Cass's charge.

The henchman on the present occasion has been M. Michel Saint-Denis, and one would briefly say that his read-ing is as good as theirs. There is no copyright in these things. Furtwängler does not steal Toscanini's thunder, nor Beecham crib from either. Therefore it is right that nobody should have stolen Komisarjevsky's shadows on the bedroom ceiling. Nor does M. Saint-Denis attempt Mr Cass's pyramidal grouping, perhaps because Miss Ffrang-con-Davies is not tall enough. But our producer has his own bent and follows it. There is a moment in the first act when all the characters retire into the inner room and leave the front stage to the five armchairs. Here one has an odd thought of Wordsworth, and says to oneself : " Dear God, the very furniture seems to breathe ! " But one's mind throughout the evening is a jumble of all sorts of right things. On the arm of one of the chairs Miss Carol Goodner, posed for a quarter of an hour in a black dress, has looked like some exquisite Manet. Mr George Devine's imaginative lighting has given another part of the stage the indeterminate look of a Vuillard, while the right-hand window of the house in the last act is like a bit of unusually gay Utrillo.

" Conductors, poets, painters—what a muddle the man's mind is ! " somebody may say. But it is part of this drama's genius to make you think in terms of other media —of lilts and cadences, of brushwork, of wind and strings. Play-writing of this order calls for a corresponding fluidity of acting for which every spectator must find his own simile. He may liken each little performance—for in this great play all performances are little—to a wavelet merging into the general sea. Whatever terms appreciation uses it will not dwell too much upon excellences and shortcomings.

Yet something must be attempted. Vershinin will never be among Mr Gielgud's great parts. His reading is too light, and he misses the melancholy of the man who has nothing to expect from life but whose mind will not lie down. The trouble, of course, was the necessity for subduing the Gielgud graces to this play. Well, they just won't be subdued ! If you subdue them there is nothing left but compromise, since if there are two things which the Terry blood for ever forbids, they are the warped and the sombre. But Mr Gielgud's triumph is not in his acting-share in a piece in which there is no part for him. I shall say that the intensity of longing and will-power which has included this play in his programme ranks with his finest performances as an actor.

Nor does Mr Redgrave approach Mr William Devlin as Tusenbach, though it is a much better Redgrave than we have previously seen, and always very good. But all this is the very ecstasy of ingratitude. Let us rather be grateful for Mr Byam Shaw's Solyony, rightly mad as a man should be who pours eau-de-Cologne over hands smelling of blood; for Mr Lloyd's Tchebutykin, not rivalling Mr Cecil Trouncer's, but shining with its own smoky flame; for Mr Devine's very adequate Prozorov; for Mr Quartermaine's Kuligin, who once again makes us think that the putting on of the false beard is the highest point in the whole tragic farce; and collectively to the ladies—Mesdames Ffrangcon-Davies, Carol Goodner, Peggy Ashcroft, Angela Baddeley, and Marie Wright—for the limpidity and translucence of their acting. You have seen a landscape mirrored in water; the wind ruffles the surface, and the scene is gone for ever— yet remains. So with this play and this acting.

My apologies to Mr Farjeon for having left myself in- sufficient space to discuss his revue. Enough, perhaps, to say that it takes rank with the one or two masterpieces in the genre of intimate revue which flourished soon after the War and one thought had now been lost. With the excep- tion of three numbers which have now been removed, the piece—for it has enough unity to make it so—is brilliantly and consistently entertaining, and as one little jewel of wit glides from the stage another slides on. It has all been beautifully pared and polished. The show is a worthy pendant to this week's two great plays, and for making it so Mr Farjeon has to thank Mr Walter Leigh for his music, Mr Hedley Briggs for his scenery, Miss Hermione Baddeley, Mr Cyril Ritchard, and a very clever company.

The convention persists that plays put on by fashionable

playwrights at fashionable theatres must be noticed, whether they are good or bad, because they are news. Space must therefore be found for *The Innocent Party*, in which there are no people that interest, nothing happens, and it is all a question of whether A is going to Divorce B, and whom C and D are going to run off with. Is it witty ? In my view playwrights of the pre-Waugh period should not try to write light comedies of the post-Rattigan order. Mr Harwood, who is an admirable master of the older-fashioned play with a plot, should stick to this last. For no man can successfully cobble on to his own work the wit of a generation which has outdistanced him, or receded from him—anyhow, a generation to which he does not belong. The piece has, however, a lot of something that might pass for wit.

Miss Mary Ellis impersonates a sulky Romney refusing to have any truck with that variety which is the spice of femininity. Mr Basil Radford imitates an American so inadequately that I rage to take the next boat to New York to lay my apologies at the feet of that continent. Fortunately Miss Elizabeth Allan, by individuality and newness of approach, and Mr Cecil Parker, by immensity of polish, do something to retrieve the evening. And I frankly admit that for people who find Jonson nasty and Tchehov not nice this play about modern amativeness is the very ticket !

Irving's Centenary

[*February* 6, 1938]

Hume having told Boswell that he was no more uneasy to think he should *not be* after this life, than that he *had not been* before he began to exist, Johnson thundered : " Sir, if he really thinks so his perceptions are disturbed ; he is mad. If he does not think so, he lies." If anybody thinks Irving was the greatest English actor of modern times and does not say so, he lies. If he does not think so, he is mad. That Irving would be laughed at to-day is the parrot-cry of hop-o'-my-thumbs. In 1893 he put on *Becket*, and it would be easy to say that in 1935 he would have put on *Murder in the Cathedral*. But I do not think this is true. Irving was undoubtedly influenced by Tennyson's prestige, and to encourage a rising dramatist was never any part of his business.· I think in 1935 he would have revived the old play and snubbed young playwright and young actor. And I know which side of the street the laugh would have been on.

Mr Gordon Craig has said that since it may be supposed some day that Irving was either a bravura or a quietist actor, he had better put it on record that he was neither, for the unshakable reason that Irving was a genius, and " a genius is both a quietist and a bravurista." " I will speak daggers to her, but use none," says Hamlet. Lots of middling actors can speak daggers ; I have never seen Irving's equal at looking them. To-day your player comes on the stage with one look and keeps it, always with the exception of Charles Laughton, who can pull his face about in the way the street-merchant manipulates an indiarubber doll. But Irving *made* faces, and when he made one it was in granite. I have never forgotten, and to my dying day shall not forget, his expression when as Dante he saw Ugolino starving in his tower. He made faces for every part he played—macabre, jaunty, diabolical faces. He had a pathetic face, a saintly face, and a regal one : " The splendour falls on castle walls." He had faces for everybody, for Mathias, Jingle, Louis XI, Dr Primrose, Corporal Brewster, Shylock, Robespierre.

Yet people would tell you that he was " always Irving." And so he was, if they meant that in every part Irving played there was a hint of Mephistopheles. They said he never ' acted.' Nor did he if by ' acting ' they meant pretending to be somebody else. Hear Max :

> Irving could not impersonate. His voice, face, figure, port, were not transformable. But so fine was the personality to which they belonged that none cried shame when this or that part had to submit or be crushed by it. Intransformable, he was—multi-radiant, though. He had, in acting, a keen sense of humour—of sardonic, grotesque, fantastic humour. He had an incomparable power for eeriness, for stirring a dim sense of mystery ; and not less masterly was he in evoking a sharp sense of horror. His dignity was magnificent in purely philosophic or priestly gentleness, or in the gaunt aloofness of philosopher or king. He could be benign with a tinge of malevolence, and arrogant with an undercurrent of sweetness. As philosopher or king, poet or prelate, he was matchless. One felt that if Charles the Martyr, Dante, Wolsey, were not precisely as he was, so much the worse for Wolsey, Dante, Charles the Martyr. . . .

Irving had more pathos than any player I have ever seen, and whether this was an emanation of the soul or a trick of the larynx does not seem to me to matter. Much has been written of the waves of magnetism, or whatever you like to call it, which in *The Bells* Irving sent over the footlights even before he had shaken the snow off his coat. I would prefer to dwell upon the extraordinary pathos with which Mathias suggested the man tormented and conscience-stricken. For years nothing in the theatre haunted me so much as that first act's unhappiness. It filled the theatre so that there was nothing else left in the universe.

How would Irving have fared to-day? Could he *at any time* have tackled Ibsen's Borkman, Strindberg's Adolph, Tchehov's Vershinin? I think not. Put him in the dingy Russian uniform of this last, and those three sisters, their visitors, and everybody in the little town and even Moscow itself would have disappeared and left the world to darkness and Henry Irving. No; Irving is not thinkable in the great plays of to-day. I even venture to hold that he was a Shakespearean actor only on condition that it was Irving's Shakespeare rather than Shakespeare's that was being performed. His notion of Shakespearean acting was himself and two hundred and fifty supers. Comparing the piano concertos of Brahms with those of Beethoven, the staunch classicists of fifty years ago said that they were not concertos, but symphonies with pianoforte obbligato. Irving knew nothing about providing an obbligato to Shakespeare or anybody; he insisted on being the entire bag of tricks.

Ellen Terry, who was a more radiant actress than Fanny Kemble and a wittier diarist than Fanny Burney, has left what are easily the best descriptions of the outer man and the inner artist:

> I have never seen in living man, or picture, such distinction of bearing. A splendid figure, and his face very noble. A superb brow; rather small dark eyes which can at moments become immense, and hang like a bowl of dark liquid with light shining through; a most refined curving Roman nose, strong and delicate in line, and *cut clean* (as all his features); a smallish mouth, and full of the most wonderful teeth, even at 55; lips most delicate and refined—firm, firm, firm—and with a rare smile of the most exquisite beauty and quite-not-to-be-described kind. His hair is superb; beautiful in 1867, when I first met him, when it was blue-black like a raven's wing, it is even more splendid now (1895) when it is liberally streaked with white.

Yet Irving could never have said of Ellen: "Look how our partner's rapt!" For she was not rapt. There was no moment when her critical percipience about him was not busy. She was not blinded by his genius as an actor to his defects as a thinker : " He never admires the right thing." " Oddly enough, Henry was always attracted by fustian." And here are some bits found in a notebook after Ellen's death :

> His work, his work ! He has always held his life, and his death, second to his work. When he dies, it will be because he is tired out. Now, double performances (Saturday mornings and evenings) oblige him to stimulate himself with wine, and at about midnight he looks like a corpse. . . .
>
> He is a very *gentle* man, though not in the least a *tender* man. . . .
>
> His illness has made him look queer. He is stouter, very grey, sly-looking, and more cautious than ever. Bother ! . . .
>
> A quite common young fellow in the company plays all the good parts, which might befit Laurence, but H.I., thinking only of H.I., fancies L. an inch or so too tall to act with, so down goes L., and up goes himself ! . . .
>
> He has terrified me once or twice by his exhaustion and feebleness. Then he appears grateful to us all, for we *all* give him *all*. But when he gets a little better, anything so icy, indifferent, and almost contemptuous, I never saw.

And all the time she is noting the extreme beauty of his hands, and how he always makes them up a gipsy brown.

My father, who was a great theatre-goer, would not allow that Irving was a tragedian at all. In his view, Macready, Phelps, Fechter, Barry Sullivan, Salvini were all better tragedians. On the other hand, he held that as Jingle, and in purely melodramatic rôles like Mathias and Dubosc, he was unapproachable. What, in my view, was the matter with Irving's Shylock was that it was neither Jewish nor foreign. Indeed, I used to have the impression that he never really studied Shylock, and that the trial scene was just Becket and Wolsey stuck together. But I now know that I was wrong. I realise now that Irving's Shylock was a Sephardic Jew—that is, a Jew of Spanish-Portuguese descent—in contradistinction to the Ashkenasic Jew of Eastern origin. It was this which accounted for Shylock's nobility and stiffness. I admit Irving's weakness as to legs and diction. Nor was the voice good, and Wilde wrote the purest bosh when he ended his sonnet to Irving:

Thou trumpet set for Shakespeare's lips to blow.

Truth to tell, that trumpet was much nearer the wrynecked fife. Yet I say that Irving's natural deficiencies and wilful faults became him better than their virtues and graces have become any other actor of my time. He was unescapably and without qualification the greatest player, male or female, that I ever saw. He possessed not more talent than any other player, but talent of another order. When I first saw him he had turned fifty, and I like to think I had enough schoolboy wit to go about proclaiming:

He above the rest,
In shape and gesture proudly eminent,
Stood like a tower; his form had not yet lost
All her original brightness, nor appeared
Less than archangel ruined, and th' excess
Of glory obscured.

The years passed and

deep on his front engraven
Deliberation sat and public care;
And princely counsel in his face yet shone
Majestic though in ruin; sage he stood,
With Atlantean shoulders fit to bear
The weight of mightiest monarchies; his look
Drew audience and attention still as night. . . .

And would again to-day. That is all Milton and I have to say about Henry Irving.

Those Dodsworths

DODSWORTH. A play. Adapted by Sidney Howard from
the novel by Sinclair Lewis. Palace Theatre, Tuesday,
February 22, 1938.

LAND'S END. A play. By F. L. Lucas. Westminster
Theatre, Wednesday, February 23, 1938.

HEAVEN AND CHARING CROSS. A play. By Aubrey Danvers-
Walker. Players' Theatre, Thursday, February 24,
1938.

[*February* 27, 1938]

WHAT an occasion is going to be missed here! What a
chance to compare Mr Sidney Howard's play with Mr
Sinclair Lewis's novel, and the impersonations of Mr Philip
Merivale and Miss Gladys Cooper with those of Mr Walter
Huston and Miss Ruth Chatterton in the film! Only, of
course, to be able to do this one must have read the novel and
have seen the film, and, alas, I have not done either! This
is the place to come forth boldly and say that that " Alas ! "
is the purest hypocrisy, since not to have read the book
from which a play is adapted is this world's nearest approach
to your counsel of perfection! Indeed, the good critic sitting at your novel-turned-play spends half the time in which
he should be regarding the adaptation in trying to disregard
the original. And, of course, it can't be done! I have no
doubt that Meredith wrote

> Tell the grassy hollow that holds the bubbling well-spring,
>   Tell it to forget the source that keeps it fill'd . . .

after the first night of *East Lynne*.

Mr Merivale had not been on the stage five minutes before
one guessed that his agglomeration of charm, looks, and
knightly bearing had no resemblance whatever to Mr Lewis's
Middle-West magnate, soul-destroyed by the insides of
motor-cars. In the mind's eye one saw the original Dods-

80

worth as a tired, paunchy, middle-aged, unattractive automaton discarding the shell of twenty years' huckstering and trying to resume that spiritual self which twenty years of the motor business had obliterated. One sensed that the original Dodsworth was an unattractive ' dear ' whose virtues, after twenty years, his over-attractive wife, Fran, would both recognise and resent. What, therefore, seemed to be wrong with the stage Dodsworth was that Mr Merivale made him too fascinating a ' dear.' And, of course, one realised that he was far, far too little American. Inasmuch as Miss Cooper's Fran was far, far too English, it followed that as a representation of the adventures of two Middle-West hicks in search of European elegances the piece was a hundred per cent. betrayal of the novel.

How about Fran Dodsworth ? Conceding that one started, so to speak, from scratch, a quarter of an hour seems a reasonable time in which to have deduced that Miss Cooper's portrayal was the best part of a hundred per cent. unfaithful. Certainty was attained half-way through the fourth scene of the first act, the scene in which Clive Lockert, having kissed Fran, suddenly came up against a blast of wifely indignation. Now, if there is one thing for which Miss Cooper's acting stands it is steeliness of purpose. Alter the pronoun, and the couplet about Jim Bludso—

> He seen his duty, a dead-sure thing,
> And wend for it thar and then—

might have been written about this actress, the secret of whose art is bull's-eye concentration. She is an actress who never fluffs. How then does she manage when called upon to impersonate the fluffy ? The answer was provided in that moment of *volte-face*. In the early part of the scene we saw Fran deploying for the seduction of Lockert virtuosities of sophistication as much exceeding Madame Potiphar's simple guile as the gowns worn in this piece exceed the devisings of primitive *couturières*. What next happened was as though poor Joseph, tending his lips, should have both cheeks soundly smacked. *C'était magnifique, mais ce n'était pas Potiphar!*

Since neither Mr Howard nor Mr Lewis is a duffer, how could this meaningless scene have come about? Obviously only if the actress had deprived it of its meaning, which, one concluded, had been brought about by Miss Cooper having put too much meaning into the first part of it. Remember, reader, that your critic had not read the book. He deduced from the complete ruination of this scene that Fran in the original must be one of those *étourdies* who live in a world entirely of their own making—one of those women whose heads are half feather and half chuckle; a woman who, while indifferent to flowers, insists upon being loaded with orchids; a woman who, unlike the flower, decks herself out for pure vanity and then gets huffy with the mistaking bee. In other words, a vapid woman. And if there is one quality which Miss Cooper cannot express it is vapidity, unless express trains and bullets seeking billets are vapid. Whence Fran was betrayed, unless she was so complete a vixen, to use the Victorian phrase, as to *simulate* annoyance. And Miss Cooper did not appear to simulate.

This is not to say that the performance was not a glittering one. On the contrary, it glittered like the Matterhorn at daybreak. I have never seen the Matterhorn, and rarely the daybreak. But the conjunction is irresistible. And then the wonderful clothes this accomplished piece of acting had on its back, including a dinner gown for whose colour I coin *soupir de lilas fané*. Over this was presently drawn a cloak for which I suggest the tint *rose blessée par son épine.*

And last the backgrounds, that mazy succession of royal suites giving on to Piccadilly, Paris, Vienna, Swiss mountains, Italian lakes—all that *mise-en-scène* dear to Baedeker and Pinero! Yes, I thought it was a lovely evening, and a sumptuous play quite perfect except perhaps as a transcription of Mr Lewis's novel. Surely as far as Fran is concerned the book must be a tragedy ? The only possible tragedy in connection with the show at the Palace would have been to fail to turn up in a white tie and a waistcoat dazzling, as Maupassant says of other beauty, *dans tout l'éclat de sa blanche nudité!*

Sometimes at country shows the horse-judge is presented with a mixed class containing, say, three hunters, two hacks, a shire, three Hackneys, a child's riding pony, and four nondescripts. The only possible way of placing these is to proceed on the principle that a good van-horse is better than a bad show-horse. I propose this week to regard London's current plays as such a class with myself as judge. Note, reader, that I am not concerned with the reputation of the authors, length of run, subject-matter, or the fact that you may prefer anecdotes about Queen Victoria to speculations as to the nature of Time. I am not concerned with anything at all except the value of the pieces as contributions to the drama, always remembering that a good farce is better than a bad tragedy. Here, then, is my list, leaving out Shakespeare and the musicals :

1. *Three Sisters.*
2. *Mourning Becomes Electra.*
3. *Time and the Conways.*
4. *I Have Been Here Before.*
5. *Land's End.*
6. *Victoria Regina.*
7. *Room Service.*
8. *Autumn.*
9. *Robert's Wife.*
10. *The Island.*
11. *Whiteoaks.*
12. *George and Margaret.*
13. *Dodsworth.*
14. *I Killed the Count.*
15. *Black Limelight.*
16. *Welcome Stranger.*
17. *Housemaster.*
18. *Mary Goes to See.*

The reader may wonder at the high place occupied by **Mr F. L. Lucas's** new play. This is a very bad play. Its major fault screams to heaven with a voice so loud that even our youngest critics have heard it. What is this fault? Simply the flagrant breaking of Walkley's rule that a work of art must be consistent with itself. The first act is talk. The second act is over-violent action. The third act would, if this were a novel, be turned down by a publisher vowed to the production of twenty detective stories a week. What right, then, has this very bad piece to fifth place in my list?

The point is that **Mr Lucas**, while writing this very bad play, has achieved two things which are missing from all the plays below it. He has created characters which are entirely alive. They may do violent things—and one feels that the violence is that of a scholar writing for what he believes to be a coarser medium—but life flows quietly in them. They are something more than the polished, smooth-working, efficient automata of more practised playwrights. I except from this reality the figure of the explorer who wants to drag his faithless wife by the hair of the head to live with cannibals in that Central Africa which he holds to be so much more civilised than Central London. But this figure is no more intended to be real than **Mr Shaw's** Captain Shotover was intended to be real; he is not a person but an explosive. It is the wife growing old in Cornwall, the essayist who makes bookish love to her, the callow **Left Wing** son, the hard, virginal daughter who thinks her mother should renounce happiness because it is " not nice " —it is these who are real. In comparison with reality of this order **Mr Ervine's** bishop and **Miss de la Roche's** grandmother in *Whiteoaks* are as figures on a mantelpiece. And what Disraeli said to Mr Pepys ceases to be evidence!

The second remarkable feature in the play is the quality of its talk. The dialogue does not scintillate. Two or more characters together do not coruscate. There is no attempt at sparkle. Instead we are given the conversation of the members of a decently bred and decently educated family discharging their full minds about things that matter. This talk is only possible because Mr Lucas has a mind. Forsaking our horse-show metaphor, I shall say that the plays standing below this one in my list are like so many well-made cabinets with perfectly fitting drawers containing little or nothing. Whereas the drawers of Mr Lucas's rough-hewn chest are full to bursting.

Miss Cathleen Nesbitt and Miss Mary MacOwan, Mr Alan Napier and Mr George Astley, play together with extra-ordinary understanding and sensitiveness, and Miss Deirdre Doyle is quite shuddersomely good as a Cornish crone. And then, just when the play needs lifting up, in comes Mr Cecil Trouncer to blow the lid off family introspection as though he were Captain Shotover, Mr Boythorn, and the Giant Blunderbore all in one. One enjoys this performance as one would enjoy a trombonist who should play fortissimo throughout a concert, provided fortissimo was right.

Neither Mr Danvers-Walker nor anybody else must ask for criticism of a play in which a working-class youth strangles a working-class sweetheart with her cheap beads and comes home to tell his mother all about it. Such a play, if good enough to be put on at all, is bound to wring the critical sensibilities. What musical critic has ever had anything to say about " Home, Sweet Home "?

And, of course, Mr Danvers-Walker must not expect commercial success for a piece which commits the funda-mental mistake of being about the working classes. Does he not know that the story of how he languidly throttled some jade with a rope of Bond Street's best must be told by a jaded young man in faultless dinner-wear leaning gracefully against a jade mantelpiece somewhere near the Green Park ? Mr Danvers-Walker has obviously a talent for brilliant humour about the working classes. Does he not realise that what the public wants is smart patter about the leisured classes ? As a matter of fact, this is a very good little drama, which I place round about eighth in my list.

Two Exasperating Pieces

THE KING OF NOWHERE. A play. By James Bridie. Old Vic
Theatre, Tuesday, March 15, 1938.

OPERETTE. By Noel Coward. Music by Noel Coward. His
Majesty's Theatre, Wednesday, March 16, 1938.

[*March* 20, 1938]

As I sat listening to Mr Bridie's farrago and raking my
mind for any reasonable image for it, I thought first of how
Mrs Amanda Ros's Delina Delaney, having partaken of
some slight breakfast, entered Madam-de-Maine's study,
where " a pile of wit, humour, and interminable talent lay
on the table before her." How she sat " with fingers buried
deeply in the tufts of hair that adorned her forehead, but
with her mind too irritated by the disturbed force of the
bare-faced pages that lay exposing their grim surface to
glean much knowledge from their instructive talent." Next
I thought of that colloquy for which I have ransacked
Boswell in vain :

> BOSWELL. Did not Dr Goldsmith argue beside the
> point ?
> JOHNSON. Sir, he argued beside *my* point !

Then a lot of other images, concluding with that of the
irritable customer who snarled : " Waiter ! Is this beef or
is it mutton ? " Now the waiter was old, and the day had
been hot, and he was tired. So he snarled back : " Can't
you tell by the taste, sir, which it is ? " The customer said
he couldn't. " Then what the devil does it matter ? "
barked the waiter.

At first sight the waiter was justified in his retort. So long
as food is palatable or inobnoxious it is unnecessary refine-
ment to ask what it is. But let a nicer logic be employed,

and we shall see that the waiter was wrong. The discontent of a customer ordering beef and getting mutton comes through not getting what he asked for, this not being the day on which he prefers mutton. Thus your playgoer, expecting a melodrama, is disappointed by the best of comedies, while he who has gone to see a farce will not be fobbed off by a tragedy, though it be *King Lear* itself. Let us apply this to Mr Bridie's new play, whose wit, humour, and interminable talent were huzza'd to the echo by the first-night audience, and next morning were so coldly received by the critics. The reason is summed up in the single word ' discrepancy.' Discrepancy not in the matter of what the audience wantonly, as Mrs Ros would say, expected, but in the matter of the author's implied promise.

The King of Nowhere is Mr Bridie's title. Now who are Kings of Nowhere? Obviously dictators. Therefore this play must be about a dictator. But there is no ' must ' about Mr Bridie or any of the plays which he has invented " by his lane." This author is, indeed, a law unto his lane ! No man can begin a play better, or end it worse. All of this author's plays begin with some Terrific Thesis, and then go on to prove something else. Or with some story that winds up with the ending to some other story. They are turnings without any road. The present play shows how a leading actor, suffering from megalomania to a degree considered excessive even for one of his profession, is sent to a mental home. He escapes, and a parched, elderly virgin, with queer notions about uplift and who sees in him the saviour of her country, puts him into dictatorial leggings, and the silly fellow imagines that he is the Panjandrum of Panjandrums. Like all of Mr Bridie's starts, this one is magnificent. But once again he finds himself better at starts than at fits, for his ending, in which his dictator executes, imprisons, and sends to concentration camps the other inmates of the asylum, is no ending at all.

It was incredible that we should be asked to encumber our minds with a play about dictatorship only in the sense in which, according to the madman's hallucination, it might equally well have been about anything from pitch-and-toss to manslaughter. Does not Mr Bridie see that his hero *must* develop into a real dictator? Given a real dictator, the full range of satire was open to the author. He could then have shown that dictatorship can have as its seed the teeniest-weeniest smack of self-complacency, the passion of aggrandisement, madness itself. It were satire's crown of satire to show a lunatic swelling to become a country's master-mind. Normally it is a capital mistake to criticise a play for not being what the critic wants it to be. But that is a different thing from criticising a play on the score that it has not fulfilled its initial promise. Suppose a piece called *While Rome Burns*. Must not such a title promise inquiry into the callousness of emperors? Is its promise fulfilled if the play merely exhibits the abstraction of fiddlers? Or even the exsufflation of actors?

Mr Bridie's title promised an inquiry into the vagaries of dictators; it was not fulfilled by a play dealing with the ramifications of lunacy. It promised all of a dictator's facets and gave us one facet of dementia. In other words, Mr Bridie has made exactly the same mistake that he made in the case of his play about Dr Knox. There the last act should have shown us what happens to a great scientist when he is disgraced and thrown upon a hard and unsympathetic world. All that Mr Bridie showed us was how a middle-aged man, who might equally well have been a distinguished judge or a general full of honours, felt when the lady he was courting turned out to be hard and unsympathetic. I have been trying for seven years to instil into Mr Bridie that after announcing his intention to get from A to B he must not tell us that he has completed his journey because he finds himself at C. Mr Bridie, as his plays show, is fond of biblical illustration. Has he not once more put himself into the position of a Jacob who, having worked seven years for Rachel, volunteers to Laban that he prefers Leah ?

There is a kind of play which, the better it is acted, becomes thereby the more annoying. I therefore withdrew my attention from Mr Laurence Olivier and thought of what he will presently do with *Coriolanus,* a play which has a point and sticks to it.

Better known should be that rebuke administered by a clever woman to a young highbrow offering some more than usually blatant puerility. The rebuke consisted of the two words "Hush, darling!" So some Egeria, when Mr Coward smote his brow and said : "Hanged if I don't do another *Bitter Sweet*!" ought to have smoothed that temple and murmured : "No, darling!" Does not Mr Coward know—and it really is astonishing of how many playwrights I am impelled to ask this question !—that the better is the enemy of the good ? I see nothing in *Operette* that was not brought better off either in *Bitter Sweet,* or *Cavalcade,* or *Words and Music,* or *Conversation Piece,* or *To-night at 8.30.* The story of the new piece is all about a musical-comedy actress who refused to marry the heir to a peerage because he would have to resign his commission. This is trite. But for Miss Peggy Wood it would have seemed still triter. Mr Coward probably realised that it was no good asking an actress of Miss Wood's resilience and buoyancy to impersonate a chorus-girl going into a galloping consumption because she can't marry a galloping major. But I have written "trite," and the word sticks.

The *milieu* is the lighter stage in 1906, and Mr Coward should know without my telling him that the musical comedies of that period were nothing like so dull as *The Model Maid* pretends to be. He should know this if only because he wrote the "Mirabelle" scene in *Cavalcade.* Does Mr Coward really think that his present back-stage quarrelling is a patch on the same thing in *Red Peppers* ? But it would be tedious to go through the whole piece item by item and show where the same author has already done them better. I doubt even whether Mr Coward's tunes are as good as they used to be, though I waver not in my allegiance to Miss Elsie April and Mr Charles Prentice, who, with cor anglais, triangle, contra-fagotto, and harp—are the *glissandos* of this last paralleled save on the Cresta Run?—once more sweeten the air with patchouli'd sound.

Mrs Calthrop's décor? What other designer could so have caught the exact Edwardian note:

> The windows were draped with deep gold-coloured plush curtains, lined with pale-green silk, and edged with a fringe bathed in both these hues. . . . A Wilton carpet, blending in these colours, covered the highly-polished floor, as could be seen by its glittering sides. . . . Two pianos, differing much in material and design, stood in opposite corners of the room; while two low-lying lounges graced the others. All sorts of easy chairs, some of them odd specimens of handicraft, stools, settees, ottomans, etc., etc., rested here and there throughout the room. . . . Great bronze pots of choice flowers bloomed on marble tables, naïvely and neatly arranged. Spreading ferns peeped high in abundance above their decorative rests, throwing a fanciful shade over their marble pedestals. Statues claimed a fair share of space, too, as they stood in martyrdom, sneering at the varying criticisms that passed from the lips of their many shocked admirers. . . . " Good Queen Bess " sat in regal dignity, dressed in a full, flowing robe, apparently horrified at Nature's naked form; while Milton smiled with satisfaction because he was robbed of the pleasure or displeasure of expressing his opinion. . . . A fine old drapery hung over the lofty door, completing the meagre description of this room.

Yes, one glimpse of Liesl Haren's drawing-room in *Operette* convinced me that Mrs Calthrop had been reading Mrs Ros on Clapham Hall! It strikes me that that same masterpiece contains a brilliant description of Liesl herself:

Moving to one of the sweetly-toned instruments, Madam-de-Maine struck its keys, sending from them strains, at one time loud and long; at another, grave, low, and pathetic. Then she would send from its ivory octaves notes of ringing bitterness, as an introduction to magically-mastered, sweet angelic sounds. . . .

But enough of Amanda! Mme Fritzi Massary is a bravurista of the highest order; any one of her gestures reduces the English notion of acting to the likeness of a milk pudding with a grating of nutmeg. Does the reader consider this rude to Miss Wood? The reader is wrong. Miss Wood is an American actress, and the English parallel for her is not a pudding, milk or otherwise, but an honest, domesticated rose. Nobody else matters very much except Miss Irene Vanbrugh, whom I nearly forgot. To look at acting like this is like wearing a suit that fits so perfectly that you forget you have it on. Such suits have not been made yesterday; nor is acting like Miss Vanbrugh's.

Sermon in Slapstick

IDIOT'S DELIGHT. A play. By Robert E. Sherwood. Apollo
Theatre, Tuesday, March 22, 1938.

FLOOD TIDE. A play. By William Boehnel. Adapted from
the novel *The House by the River* by A. P. Herbert.
Phœnix Theatre, Wednesday, March 23, 1938.

ROAD TO GANDAHAR. A play. By Boris Trainin. Garrick
Theatre, Thursday, March 24, 1938.

[*March* 27, 1938]

> Ils virent Barnabé qui, devant l'autel de la sainte Vierge, la
> tête en bas, les pieds en l'air, jonglait avec six boules de cuivre
> et douze couteaux. Il faisait, en l'honneur de la sainte Mère de
> Dieu, les tours qui lui avaient valu le plus de louanges.
>
> ANATOLE FRANCE, *Le Jongleur de Notre-Dame*

THIS is not the occasion or the place for an essay on the
difference between the average Englishman, who probably
exists, and the average American, who certainly doesn't.
But any such essay would fail if it did not stress the
Englishman's view of art and artists. In England no man
is considered a serious artist who does not take himself
seriously. Not his art, mark you, but himself! Consider
the esteem in which, since he composed oratorios, Michael
Costa was held, and the regard lavished upon Edwin Long,
whose 'religious' pictures, framed in black velvet, drew
a congregation rivalling Spurgeon's.

Another odd thing about your Englishman is that the
more serious the matter, the more he likes to be bored.
Murder is a serious matter. The most successful serious
play of the last year or two is undoubtedly Mr T. S. Eliot's
Murder in the Cathedral. Since I have only read this play
but not seen it, I am not competent to pronounce upon its
entertainment value as an acted thing, though I suspect
it of not being wholly gay. I base my suspicion on a sentence

98

by my ever-trustworthy colleague Mr Ivor Brown, who in his notice of the play's production at the Duchess Theatre, suggested that the piece wanted the actual fane : " Exposed to the holy chanting, the smell of incense, and the sermonising of Becket, one soon, a trifle wearily, decides that no play in London more thoroughly deserves to be let off entertainment duty."

Now, modern warfare is mass murder, and your serious Englishman desires that mass murder should be treated *ex cathedra*. Therefore, he argues, a play about war should be in verse, chanted by a chorus of flat young ladies singing slightly sharp. Is such a piece of work a feeble echo of that great war play which Euripides called *The Trojan Women*? Never mind. War is a serious subject and must receive serious treatment. And the audience, having yawned its fill of edification, goes home to uninterrupted sleep.

But since bombs fall upon serious and non-serious alike, what about the frivolous-minded and their right to expression? Shall they not be permitted juggler's licence? Mr Eliot does not write in the Sherwood manner. Why should we expect Mr Sherwood to write in the Eliot manner? If one wanted a serious American war play, Mr Maxwell Anderson is, as Bunthorne would say, the shop for it. Mr Sherwood is a horse of a very different colour. He writes pungent, satirical comedies to please the hard-bitten, hard-boiled audiences of New York. His vein is lighter than Anderson's, though less light than Kaufman's. *Idiot's Delight* is true to this vein. It is that new thing—a tragic farce. In a postscript to this play Mr Sherwood has written : " I believe that a sufficient number of people are aware of the persistent validity of the Sermon on the Mount." And here is his offering in support of that belief.

No ! The weakness of this play is not the form in which it is cast, or its plot, which is a harum-scarum affair about the guests at an hotel in Central Europe demolished by enemy aeroplanes. (Perhaps I am not quite satisfied about the mechanics of the imbroglio, and perhaps I find the character-drawing a shade wobbly.) But the real weakness is in the polemics which are this play's kernel. Among the characters is one of those rich international thugs who, as financiers, armament-makers, or what not, pull the strings releasing the bombs. His mistress rounds on him in a tremendous tirade prophesying the end of an English boy and girl honeymooning in the hotel. She foretells that he will die as a soldier, and here is the rest of the speech as given in New York, though stupidly weakened here:

> Before the moment of death he consoles himself by thinking: "Thank God *she* is safe! She is bearing the child I gave her, and he will live to see a better world!" But I know where she is. She is lying in a cellar that has been wrecked by an air raid, and her firm young breasts are all mixed up with the bowels of a dismembered policeman. . . .

Mr Sherwood has seen that for his piece to rise above melodrama he must provide his thug with an answer. He does his best, but it is not good enough.

Readers will not have forgotten the magnificent case which Mr Shaw made for the burning of that innocent and pious maid Joan. Some dazzling polemic would doubtless make a case for the burning of the innocent and the pious in a world war. Did not Henley write:

> In a golden fog,
> A large, full-stomached faith in kindliness
> All over the world, the nation, in a dream
> Of money and love and sport, hangs at the paps
> Of well-being, and so
> Goes fattening, mellowing, dozing, rotting down
> Into a rich deliquium of decay.

And did he not go on to argue that "if the Gods be good, if the Gods be other than mischievous," then comes the swoop of war?

> And in wild hours
> A people, roaring ripe
> With victory, rises, menaces, stands renewed,

Sheds its old piddling aims,
Approves its virtue, puts behind itself
The comfortable dream, and goes,
Armoured and militant,
New-pithed, new-souled, new-visioned, up the steeps
To those great altitudes, whereat the weak
Live not. But only the strong
Have leave to strive, and suffer, and achieve.

Henley's poem is dated 1901, and it may be that he would sing another tune to-day. But his case, weak though it is, is better than that of Mr Sherwood's armament-maker :

Apply your intelligence, my dear. Ask yourself : why shouldn't these young people die ? And who are the greater criminals—those who sell the instruments of death, or those who buy them, and use them ? You know there is no logical reply to that. But all these little people —like your new friends—all of them consider me an arch-villain because I furnish them with what they want, which is the illusion of power. That is what they vote for in their frightened Governments—what they cheer for on their national holidays—what they glorify in their anthems, and their monuments, and their waving flags ! Yes—they shout bravely about something they call " national honour." And what does it amount to ? Mistrust of the motives of everyone else ! Dog-in-the-manger defence of what they've got, and greed for the other fellow's possessions ! Honour among thieves ! I assure you, Irene—for such little people the deadliest weapons are the most merciful.

Of the play's theatrical effectiveness there can be no question ; my only doubts are as to its cogency. It is not a masterpiece of argument. It is very nearly a masterpiece of light theatre with a core of thought, and, as such, a play which nobody else could have written. There is one brilliant performance. This is Mr Raymond Massey's impersonation of a third-rate cabaret-artist travelling with six blonde dancers. This is a death's-head spouting braggadocio, chap-fallen and boasting. It catches perfectly the American note —the inferiority complex hiding behind a shield of strut

and bombast. There is a fine piece of hysteria by Mr Carl
Jaffé as a professional agitator, and the honeymooners are
played with beautiful simplicity by Mr Valentine Dyall and
Miss Janet Johnson. Mr Franklin Dyall accomplishes the
feat of submerging his very strong personality in that of a
German scientist, but I must be forgiven if I do not think
that world-thugs have the sensitiveness which Mr Hugh
Miller inescapably suggests.

And now I come to the delicate question of Miss Tamara
Geva. Delicate because the part of the armament-maker's
mistress was written for Miss Lynn Fontanne, who is a
superb comedienne, and because, though Miss Geva is a
very intelligent young lady, she obviously lacks experience
and authority, and Irene must be crammed to the teeth
with both. To put it kindly, I think her art wants another
ten years.

Mr A. P. Herbert may well have asked himself, as the
play at the Phœnix proceeded, what further violence was
to be done to his original story. There was some justification for the initial divergence, that of making the murdered girl Stephen Byrne's ex-mistress instead of his
housemaid. For a play needs a lot of plot, and a discarded
mistress is always good for a complicated first act. Then
it looked as though the play was going to have too much
plot, for Stephen, before he murdered his mistress, had
unloaded her on his friend John Egerton, another painter.
However, it was not the complication but the alteration
of Stephen's status from author to painter which turned
out to be the snag. Mr Boehnel conceived the notion of un-
masking his murderer by making him betray his murderous soul in a mural he was doing for a church. Stephen,
painting Judas, had given him his own face.

This seems to me to be rank nonsense, unless we are to
find traces of dissipation in Morland's cart-horses, and
detect Van Gogh's ear lying on his Chair. When I got
home I turned up Mr Herbert's novel to find that page in

which he deduced Stevenson's phthisis from *Treasure Island* and Maeterlinck's boxing prowess from the nebulosities of *Aglavaine and Selysette*. But even if there is anything in the theory that as a man is so shall he write or paint, I do not think Stephen would have been such an ass as to consciously give away his villainy in his painting. Split my infinitives if I think he would! However, it is a poor stomach that cannot warm a cold potato, and he is a poor playgoer who cannot warm up to a fantastic bit of psychology. And, after all, when you have a cast thick with emotional actresses you have to give them something to be emotional about.

But not necessarily audible! Or so it would appear by this first night's mumbling, in which the important lines were confided to sofa-cushions, lampshades, and anybody except the audience. I am not concerned with possible reasons for such inaudibility. But I do know that Mr Ernest Thesiger, acting extremely well, contrived to give every syllable its weight and to be perfectly heard. I am inclined to think that Mr Basil Sydney, who can be very frightening when he wants, a little over-rationalised both play and part. At least, he seemed to me to discard the substance of a thriller for the shadow of a psychological study which wasn't there.

Mr Trainin's rich drama is part-produced by Mr Franklin Dyall, thus justifying the wit's overheard " You know the sort of thing. At the end of the second act Franklin Dyalls the police! " But there are no police in the desert to be dialled; cargo is white and tongues are black, and mammy-palaver leads to the slakings of vengeance, and there is no slaking like that of Mr Martin Walker's thirst. To alcohol add heroin, flavour with a more feminine sort snatched from something worse than something in a Cairo bazaar, serve with a dash of honesty in the shape of an English doctor who has done eight years for murder in a criminal lunatic asylum—and you get what I regard as a thoroughly satisfying drink; the sort of play in which one man will say to another : " Carruthers, old boy, before we shake hands on our friendship there is something *the audience* ought to know ! "

Road to Gandahar will presently be filmed. While Mr Charles Boyer wallows, Miss Dietrich wilts, and Mr Colman woos, Mr Robeson will lead to the defence of Persian womanhood impis of Zulus chanting hot jazz. To behold this millions will queue up. Why not see it while Mr Walker, with consummate art, tact, and *vraisemblance*, nails to the counter of reality some odd fragments of the flying nonsense ? Mr Malcolm Keen, as the stiff-lipped British medico, is equally good whether full-faced or in profile; Miss Lilli Palmer is a much better little actress than anybody quite so young, pretty, and blonde need be ; and last, one Mr Orest Orlov presents a handyman from Persia with a smile ingratiating as an eel's, and more slippery.

The Stratford Festival

MACBETH. Revival of Shakespeare's tragedy. Stratford-upon-Avon, Wednesday, April 13, 1938.

WILD OATS. A musical comedy. By Douglas Furber and Firth Shephard. Music by Noel Gay. Prince's Theatre, Thursday, April 14, 1938.

[*April* 17, 1938]

WRITING on the death of Chaliapin and comparing his acting with that of Edmund Kean, a leader-writer in *The Times* has said that " the emotional or nervous strain of the great ' moments,' the ' flashes of lightning,' is so great that, unless the actor has the simplicity of a Chaliapin, it knocks him to pieces, and as likely as not drives him to the dissipation which was the ruin of Kean, as man and as actor." This starts a train of thought which may be worth pursuing. I pursue it all the more eagerly because within the last few weeks I have received from the daughter of Clement Scott a magnificent present, nothing less than a gigantic newspaper-cutting book belonging to her father—it is not known where he got it from—containing some six thousand dramatic criticisms written between 1811 and 1833. Among these is a defence of Kean, which appeared on the last day of March, 1816, the great actor having failed to turn up at the theatre and excusing himself *next day* because " having dined a few miles in the country, and returning at a very quick pace to keep his engagements at the Theatre, he was thrown out of his gig, and had his arm dislocated, besides being stunned and very much bruised with the fall."

The old writer undertaking Kean's defence had this passage :

With respect to the extravagance of actors, it is not to be wondered at : they live from hand to mouth, and they plunge from want into luxury. Chilled with poverty, steeped in contempt, they sometimes pass into the sunshine of fortune, and are lifted to the very pinnacle of public favour, but even there cannot calculate on the continuance of success. . . . With respect to the habit of convivial indulgence, an actor to be a good one must have a great spirit of enjoyment in himself, strong impulses, strong passions, and a strong sense of pleasure, for it is his business to imitate the passions and to communicate pleasure to others. A man of genius is not a machine. The neglected actor may be excused if he drinks oblivion of his disappointments; the successful one, if he quaffs the applause of the world in draughts of nectar. The intellectual excitement inseparable from those professions which call forth all our sensibility to pleasure and pain requires some corresponding physical excitement.

Now for some later corroboration. Compare Montague on the death of a great French actress:

All the greatest art is a higher power of the spectator's self, the state of immensely quickened and thrilled perception which, it then seems, might have been always his if some incorporeal prison-house or other had not somehow cast its shade around him. Do the great artists themselves live, as a regular thing, in those high places? Scarcely, or Sarah Bernhardt would not have played some of the tricks that she did, nor would so many men of genius have lived somewhat ignoble lives. Perhaps they find in the mental excitement of practising the technicalities of their art a stimulant strong enough to give them a lift, for the time, into that state of passionate insight to which they are then able to haul up even our more sluggish selves; then they may flop down, exhausted, and even do something scrubby from mere excess of reaction, just as a soul-stirring preacher might do if sorely tried when very much tired indeed with the delivery of an excellent sermon.

But our modern leader-writer has another passage, in which instead of contrasting the men he compares the artists : " Both had the mysterious, unanalysable actor-power, which does not bother about the rules, does as little as possible by thinking, and as much as possible by the actor's uncanny power of merely being." This is only another way of saying that great actors are born and not made. From which one might deduce that the most any academy or conservatoire can hope to do is to make a bad player less bad, and a good player better. We need not bother about what makes a bad actor; we know him at sight. What makes a good actor is that he is magnificent in his successes; what makes a great actor is that he is magnificent even in his failures. Few actors have succeeded in Macbeth, and Irving's was deemed a failure, though he would not have it that it was, and Ellen Terry has written :

> He told me that by intuition [in the days of the Bateman management] he had got the right idea of the character, and had since come to know from fresh study that it was *right*. His confidence in the rightness of his conception was not in the least shaken by criticisms of it, and he always maintained that as Macbeth he did his finest work.

In the last act he " looked like a great famished wolf," which is a very different thing from your good hungry actor looking forward to his supper !

An old playgoer with whom I was talking the other day remarked that when the Third Witch said to Irving : " All hail, Macbeth, that shalt be king hereafter ! " there came into his face a look of malignant covetousness that was dreadful to see. Two things connote the great actor ; these are the looks that come into the face, and the tones that come into the voice. Recently we saw a Macbeth which was good enough to win considerable praise. This young actor used his voice as soldiers unfurl a flag—quite rightly he hung out his accents on the outward walls—but throughout the part he used an unvarying mask like the grin of a Chinese dog on a mantelpiece. No look came into his face, and equally no look departed from it. This made it, strictly speaking, only half a good performance.

At Stratford Mr James Dale does not even compose a mask, and while his performance is vocally semi-satisfying, visually it is not satisfying at all. One hardly expects a Macbeth dogged by the thought of murder to wobble like a jelly. But one does not at all expect him to intone the words " shakes so my single state of man " with the rock-like unemotionalism of a toast-master. One might sum up this performance, then, by saying that it is " smother'd in surmise, and nothing is but what is not." But acting's the oddest thing : Mr Dale played the whole of one scene far better than I have ever known it played. This was the little scene with Macduff before the discovery of the murder. Here for a moment Macbeth became real. One was afraid for him, afraid lest his demeanour would in the light of later discovery give him away.

Now how about Lady Macbeth ? The first thing to be said is that Miss Neilson-Terry appears to have broken all the rules. At least she gives one the impression of having prepared for the great rôle by taking the unprecedented step of reading the play ! Most actresses begin their first scene like some celebrity-pianist sitting down to the C minor Concerto with every appearance of wondering why on earth Beethoven must waste three pages on orchestral preliminaries. In other words, they rush Macbeth's letter as though they knew it by heart, their real concern being the solo part which starts at " Glamis, thou art." Miss Neilson-Terry actually reads the letter as though she did not know any of its contents until she comes to them. But throughout there were evidences that she brought her own mind to the play, though I do not agree with all of her readings. I do not think, for example, that as Macbeth goes up the stairs to commit the murder Lady Macbeth should descend them so that they meet half-way. This suggests the complicity of a smash-and-grab raid. On the other hand, it is extremely effective that Lady Macbeth, in the sleep-walking scene, should descend from her bedroom, cross the stage, ascend to Duncan's chamber, keep the stage waiting, and then descend again.

One or two little things did not quite come off, as when the lady on hearing of Duncan's proposed visit said " Leave all the rest to me ! " as if it were merely a question of fruit-knives and finger-bowls. Here, and in one or two other places, Miss Neilson-Terry was handicapped by excess of physical beauty. Too many Lady Macbeths look like the serpent, but speak out of a buttercup-and-daisy intelligence ; Miss Neilson-Terry has to convey total guile while looking like a Gloire de Dijon. Only the other day Miss Julia Neilson was telling us she had failed in some rôles because she was not a Terry ; some of Lady Macbeth will always escape her daughter because she is !

Wild Oats is a go-as-you-please, happy-go-lucky, steady, and stolidly jolly Bank Holiday piece of nonsense, and I defy any critic, however cultured, to distinguish the gems from the paste. Events begin at Little Giggleswick, which I know better than Mr Douglas Furber, go on to Paris, which Mr Furber doubtless knows better than I do, and proceed ultimately to Bibbi Abbouba, of which I doubt if either of us knows anything at all. Much of the piece is couched in that vein of easy French so popular at the moment on the alleged legitimate stage. " These trousers," says Mr Sydney Howard, in the course of a conversation with a Frenchman, " are too loose and too long ! " And the Frenchman is delighted to hear that Mr Howard has been to both places. I first heard this joke when I was a little Giggleswickian, which, of course, doesn't make it any worse. There are also Mr Arthur Riscoe and Mr Jack Donohue and Miss Josephine Houston. But the evening's real tower of strength is Miss Vera Pearce. And what a tower !

Poetry Takes a Holiday

CORIOLANUS. Revival of Shakespeare's tragedy. Old Vic
Theatre, Monday, April 18, 1938.

THE MERCHANT OF VENICE. Revival of Shakespeare's play.
Queen's Theatre, Thursday, April 21, 1938.

THE MASQUE OF KINGS. A play. By Maxwell Anderson.
Gate Theatre, Friday, April 22, 1938.

[*April* 24, 1938]

W HAT is all this about *Coriolanus* having no poetry?
Well, there was once a man who was prosecuted because
his dog had bitten a tramp. His defence was that the dog
had not bitten the tramp. Alternatively, that it wasn't
his dog. If I were defending this play for its alleged lack
of poetry I should plead that it is full of poetry, and,
alternatively, that it doesn't need any. I think I should be
defeated on the first head; I know I should win on the
second. But why this absolute solicitude for poetry whatever the subject, this Musset-like demand—" *Poète,
prends ton luth* "—to stand and deliver blank verse? Ask
some Trojan, tromboning it in Berlioz, why he doesn't
make his instrument sigh. This drama is a concerto for
the trombone; those who can hear nothing but the flute
must seek another play.

The best defence is Hazlitt's : " The cause of the people
is indeed but little calculated as a subject for poetry; it
admits of rhetoric, which goes into argument and explanation, but it presents no immediate or distinct images to
the mind, ' no jutting frieze, buttress, or coign of vantage '
for poetry ' to make its pendent bed and procreant cradle
in.' " In other words, Shakespeare's play of *Coriolanus* is
full of such magnificent rhetoric that you can almost plead
that the tramp enjoyed being bitten ! Anyhow, the title-
rôle is something for an actor to get his teeth into.

105

Then how about the suggestion that the whole thing is a perfunctory job done by Shakespeare to order? We are always being told how Haydn was commanded to produce a quartet because the Elector of Umlaut was coming to dinner, and how Mozart was ordered to prepare a serenade to please the Landgrave of Dankeschön. To the musically uninstructed quartet and serenade now sound like pure genius, as against the superior view that they are merely the common form of the time, with certain idiosyncratic pribbles and prabbles which are the composers' finger-prints. Similarly, I will maintain that *Coriolanus* is full of Shakespeare's finger-prints, provided you have the ear to hear them.

Vocally Mr Olivier's performance is magnificent; his voice is gaining depth and resonance, and his range of tone is now extraordinary. Physically the performance is admirable, containing one startling leap and a superb fall at the end. If one has any reservations at all it is to suggest that this steadily improving actor should abandon that make-up like a Javanese mask and trust more to his own features. At present his face is not so much made-up as buried beneath loam and plaster. I think, too, that he must resolve to discard that clowning which he probably adjudges to be mordancy. There is not much of it in the present performance, but what there is is wholly bad. For where it is used it turns into a naughty boy a figure whose dignity should be pauseless. It is not right that Coriolanus, whose whole point is his refusal to tickle the mob, should play even to the Old Vic's gallery. These things being said, I regard this performance as Mr Olivier's best to date, for it has a pathos we have not yet observed. The playing in the great scene with mother, wife, and son has great tenderness. The famous speech, " I banish you !", is delivered not in the Kean manner of " ungovernable passions " but with Phelps's " cold sublimity of disdain." The end is the full organ of acting, with all the stops out. It brings the house to its feet cheering, and yet those pajocks the high-brow critics must hurl at the playwright Horatio's " You might have rhymed ! "

Dame Sybil Thorndike discovers in Volumnia's early scenes a genial humour which would have made Geneviève Ward relegate this acting to something less than the top drawer. But mark this actress's face when her son comes back from the wars, and note how all the rest of her playing has the full authentic sweep. I doubt whether the Old Vic has ever had a more valuable secondary actor than **Mr Cecil Trouncer**, whose Menenius is a beautiful piece of oddity, warm and shrewd, testy and true to life. His baiting of the Tribunes is wholly delicious. **Mr Casson's** production strictly denies that Rome at any time looked like the pictures of Alma-Tadema. The first act is even grubby. But there is fine lighting throughout, and when necessary a fine darkness, as that in which the red cloak of Coriolanus glows like sullen fire. Yes, this is good Shakespearean producing, even if it does suggest that Rome was built in a day !

Reader, have you ever, passing Queen's Hall, been caught up in a stampede and wondered what it was all about? I will tell you. It was the outrush of musical critics who just cannot bear to hear again Beethoven's Fifth Symphony or *the* Tschaikowsky Piano Concerto. The reason dramatic critics do not stampede from *The Merchant of Venice* is that they may not. Your musical critic can say that this symphony or that concerto was performed, and leave it at that. But you cannot so dismiss a play, because of the essential difference between music and drama. *Pace* Mr Newman, there is no more to be done with a piece of music than play the notes of it ! It does not matter how the performers look or are dressed, and they do not move about. But you do not begin to perform a play if you only recite its words.

How much more reason for stampeding would that critic

have who even in his schooldays loathed this play, clearly perceiving that it is nothing but a glorification of the meanness of the Gentile when put to it! Who, twenty years ago, desired no further instruction about the sleeping propensities of the moon, the carrying power of candles, the quality of mercy, the deception of gold, the fraud of silver, and the honesty of lead. But just as there are people who are hearing symphony and concerto for the first time, so there are people coming new to this play. Indeed, judging from the laughter provoked the other night, nobody in the audience had seen it before! These innocents, then, are entitled to be told what can reasonably be thought of the way the play was produced and acted.

In the matter of production let me say that I can understand a boxing-ring or some disused stable being called Venice or Elsinore or the Forest of Arden. But that I neither understand nor sympathise with a Venice which looks like a boudoir by Boucher. I don't mind a setting so blank that it may be anywhere. But when it is so detailed —for the boudoir contains a bridge and a canal and a house—that it is obviously somewhere, why not let it be the place the play says it is? I do not want to see fortunes spent on clothes or on seventy-five candlesticks—I know there were seventy-five because I counted them! I would rather spend the money on scene-shifters who have something to shift; Shakespeare says nothing at all about moonlight sleeping on a staircase. And when the scene was not looking like a boudoir it resembled a circus-tent before the side-curtains are put up. A play is not a ship, and I do not think that Shakespeare intended this one to scud under bare poles.

The acting was better, at least in regard to the minor characters. As Bassanio Mr Richard Ainley had so much personal glitter that one could not see that personage at all, which is the best thing that can be done with a thoroughly bad egg. Mr Alec Guinness made of Lorenzo a dark flame of great intensity. Mr Howe amusingly suggested that in not becoming Princess of Arragon Portia escaped more than she wotted. As Old Gobbo Mr Morland Graham gave a display of tittery-tottery rubicundity to which every heart warmed. Miss Baddeley made of Nerissa a stocky handmaiden obviously flabbergasted by the handsomeness of Gratiano's calves. Over Mr Lloyd's performance I shall draw a veil, assuring him that his admirers know the difference between his Tchebutykin and his Prince of Morocco. About Miss Ashcroft's Portia I find it difficult to pronounce. Portia, to my way of thinking, is arch, sophisticated, tiresome, ready for a bout of wit with anybody, a complete mistress of herself, and something of a *prétentieuse*—in short, the ideal part for a leading lady who is young enough to look it. This may be a legacy from Ellen Terry ; it is an inalienable one. Now, Miss Ashcroft's talent lies in conveying innocence, and her chief difficulty is to look old enough to play anything. Whence it follows that I did not believe a word of her Portia throughout the entire evening. If, however, Portia is rightly represented as a child, then Miss Ashcroft's performance was perfect.

But I shall make no concessions about the Shylock. The Jew is the stuff of the play, which is over when he leaves the court-room. The suggestion that Shylock must be subdued to make the play, fifth act and all, a complete frolic is, in my view, untenable. But perhaps Mr Gielgud's careful underplaying was rendered necessary by the setting ; you could not have contained Irving in the bandbox at the Queen's, and, coming to current times, one breath of Mr Oscar Homolka's terrific verisimilitude would blow it away. One could find many things to say in favour of this performance. One could praise its measure, restraint, intellectuality, if one thought that those qualities ought to be in Shylock. But suppose one holds that what the part calls for is hatred and dæmonic fury? Suppose one sees Shylock as a storm-centre, malignant and terrible, ready to shatter the inconsiderable world about him? What, then, holding this view, is one to say of a Shylock who is merely a wet blanket at a party?

I shall hold my fire about Mr Anderson's piece, which must obviously come to Shaftesbury Avenue. It has everything the commercial theatre wants—swift-moving action, excitement, love scenes. Its only handicap is that it has aspects which the commercial theatre doesn't want. It is a serious discussion of autocracy and rebellion. It is magnificently written, every line demanding and repaying attention. There are fine performances by Mr Eric Portman and Mr Milton Rosmer, and Miss Jill Furse does not get in the way. In other words, the evening is a grown-up one. Nevertheless, I am persuaded that the piece will come to Shaftesbury Avenue, always providing that room can be found for it among the horde of titter-traps about twittermice.

The Lunts Have a Word For It

AMPHITRYON 38. A play. By Jean Giraudoux. Adapted
by S. N. Behrman. Lyric Theatre, Tuesday, May 17,
1938.

HAPPY RETURNS. A revue. Devised by Charles B. Cochran. Adelphi Theatre, Thursday, May 19, 1938.

[*May* 22, 1938]

RICHARD STRAUSS begins his *Elektra* with a bang which
says to the spectator: " Sit up and listen ! " This play's
start is the visual equivalent. The curtains part to disclose
an inverted Jupiter and Mercury, who obviously know
their Blake, with their chins supported on a cloud. The
heads and arms are those of Messrs Alfred Lunt and
Richard Whorf, the bare rest of them is papier mâché.

Is the old fable dull or isn't it ? It is true that Dryden
also starts off with a bang:

> MERCURY. There has been a devilish quarrel, I can
> tell you, betwixt Jupiter and Juno. She threatened to
> sue him in the spiritual court for some matrimonial
> omissions; and he stood upon his prerogative. Then
> she hit him on the teeth of all his bastards; and your
> name and mine were used with less reverence than
> became our godships. They were both in their cups;
> and at the last the matter grew so high, that they were
> ready to have thrown stars at one another's heads.
> PHŒBUS. 'Twas happy for me that I was at my voca-
> tion, driving daylight about the world; but I had rather
> stand my father's thunderbolts than my stepmother's
> railing.
> MERCURY. When the tongue-battle was over, and the
> championness had harnessed her peacocks, to go for
> Samos, and hear the prayers that were made to her. . . .
> PHŒBUS. By the way, her worshippers had a bad
> time on't; she was in a damnable humour for receiving
> petitions !

But almost at once the farce degenerates into another Comedy of Errors.

How about the Molière, relieved though it is by crystalliastion of Gallic common sense? In all the plays and novels about marriage that have been written since 1668 has anybody—and you can throw in Meredith—added to Mercury's last word on the subject:

> Diantre! où veux-tu que mon esprit
> T'aille chercher des fariboles?
> Quinze ans de mariage épuisent les paroles;
> Et, depuis un long temps, nous nous sommes tout dit.

But all of Mercury's part in the Molière is admirable, and twice at least the author seems to be speaking in his own person. For example, when he makes Mercury say:

> Et je prendrois pour ma devise:
> "Moins d'honneur, et plus de repos."

And again:

> J'aime mieux un vice commode
> Qu'une fatigante vertu!

But has any modern playgoer enjoyed Molière's play as a whole? Could anybody to-day sit it through without a yawn? This is the place to say that while some hovering of the hand might be permitted during the first act of this latest Franco-American version, any member so offending during the second and third acts should be instantly cut off. One must suppose that every country's handling of the story has appealed best to the audiences of that country. If Plautus is for your Roman, Molière for your Frenchman, and Dryden for your seventeenth-century Englishman, it would seem natural that Mr Behrman's American version—one suspects that M. Giraudoux's text has been freely handled—is best suited to American audiences. If in this country some of us judge a play's poetry to be the better part of it, it is probably because, whereas wit may be local, poetry must be universal. Is Mr Behrman astonished to find himself dubbed a poet? Perhaps the answer is that one can be a poet without knowing it. Poetry does not, as certain American dramatists seem to think, consist in cutting a line of prose into halves and printing it so that it reads:

> Good morning, Mr Smith,
> I hope I see you well!

The poetry of *Amphitryon 38* is the poetry of idea, not of phraseology. Its subject is the old contradiction—immortals who have so much time on their hands that nothing in particular is worth their enjoying, and mortals whose intensity of pleasure depends on the meagreness of the span during which that pleasure may be tasted. Jupiter would make Alkmena a goddess, or at least a star. She refuses, as Stephen Phillips's Marpessa refused before her. She believes that her own fibres have their self-sufficient persistence, that they will come up again in the form of grass or flowers, that she, Alkmena, will endure as long as the earth bears on its face a single vegetable. What is this except Marpessa's decision to

> Accept the perfect stillness of the ground,
> Where, though I lie still, and stir not at all,
> Yet shall I irresistibly be kind,
> Helplessly sweet, a wandering garden bliss.

This play being a comedy, it is right that Alkmena should see immortality in the shape of the garden pea as distinct from the field!

When all is said and done, wit has always been the essence of this farce, and it would be as imbecile to pretend not to know what the wit is about as to deny that the gross impropriety of theme finds its condonation precisely in that wit. " *C'est un peu leste, le mariage!* " exclaimed Balzac's de Marsay. Listening to that breakfast-table discussion as to whether the precedent hours should be described as divine, perfect, charming, pleasant, or connubial, one feels that the dandy might have summed up this farce in the phrase: "*C'est un peu leste, l'adultère mythologique!*"

The piece is beautifully acted, though there could be no worse description of Miss Fontanne's Alkmena than Phillips's "helplessly sweet." Helpfully sour would be nearer the mark, the evening owing its flavour to the sharp, quince-like property of this Hellenic fruit. I cannot think of any actress since Réjane who would have put up quite such a performance in the part—infinite in resource and variety, wonderfully witty and extravagant, yet informed with all that common sense with which it pleased Arnold Bennett to endow femininity. Mr Lunt's Jupiter is a hyacinthine joy; the least of his jovial utterances has spring in it like the curls of his beard if you were to pull them. And there is nothing in the whole production better than Mr Whorf's Mercury, too much of the earth to be Ariel and too little of it to be Puck. Like a dragonfly in dart and poise, he keeps the play quivering between two media.

That which brings it too solidly to earth is the music. This ought to be witty and even perky in the way in which M. Milhaud or M. Poulenc or our own Mr Walton understands wit and perkiness; instead we are offered a lacerating study in transatlantic *morbidezza*. As music Mr S. L. M. Barlow's score may be good; it is not good for the occasion. "It occurs to me," says Jupiter, echoing Beaumarchais, "that a first-rate god may make a second-rate man!" Alas, that the music does not catch the witty echo! These Amphitryon Blues are too solemn. What this farce demands is an unpretentious little score, one that doesn't mind rattling away nineteen to the dozen.

If Mr Cochran's revue had failed—which it didn't and isn't going to!—I can imagine him throwing up his hands and saying: "What in heaven's name *do* they want?" In his new revue he gives us certainly three, and possibly

five, scenas about which I will only say this: I do not
believe there is any other revue-producer in this country
who could have contemplated them, and I do believe that
there are few revue-producers who, if they had been given
a glimpse of them, would not have turned them down at
sight. For their concern is not fun or fashion or *réclame*
or oddity or any kind of vulgarity. Their concern is sheer
visual beauty! Worse than that, it is not the sort of
beauty which it attained by plastering stucco balustrades
with gold foil. It is beauty in the painter's sense, and
yet worse again, the sense of your French Impressionist
painter. I am not enough of a connoisseur to label all the
scenes, but I know that the last one, entitled " Sunday in
the Park," is a perfect Bonnard. The best of these five
pictures, the one entitled " Piccadilly," also by Professor
Stern, is good enough to be a painting in its own right.
The same compliment should be paid to Miss Doris Zinkeisen for her " Highland Swing."

Now the trouble with an English audience is that it
likes beauty only provided the strain of beauty is plen-
teously relieved. Students of Henry Morley will remember
his remarks about the necessity for humour in any entertainment your Englishman is to approve: " The phrase
with thousands even among our educated men for not
finding a thing acceptable is ' seeing no fun ' in it." Therefore our revues must alternate between absolute beauty
and applied humour. To whom, then, has Mr Cochran
applied?

First of all to Miss Beatrice Lillie, who is pronounced
on all hands to run away with this show. All I have to
say about this is that if Grock himself came into my room,
and if my room were hung with Matisses and Cézannes,
Dufys and Duncan Grants, I do not believe that the great
clown would run away with them! No; a fair view of
this production might be that you never want to turn the
pictures to the wall, and yet cannot bear it when Miss

Lillie leaves the stage. It is difficult to imagine what her present studies must seem like to those who are viewing them for the first time. I can only remember the impact of delight with which I first saw in New York these impertinent little cameos. "Impenetrability!" said Humpty-Dumpty; and I think if he had seen this performance he would have changed the word to "Imperturbability!"

In her infinite self-sufficiency this great little artist is immune from all the natural and unnatural shocks that flesh is heir to. If Vesuvius erupted under her delicious nose she would first arrange some errant hair, or flick from her lap some unnecessary, offending crumb, before greeting the lava with her flat, dazzling smile. She places herself in positions in which she must woo discomfiture, and, being discomfited, emerges the winner. If she were to meet a mad bull in a field it would be the animal which would retreat in disorder. She is a Mrs Cryptic Sparkler whose epigrams are looks. She has a new face for every social catastrophe, appalling or merely untoward, and a shrug of the shoulders connoting what a metaphysical friend has called "the philosophy of misunderstatement." And all of this is conveyed in precise, economic, wonderfully-timed skits at the expense of a torch-singer, a bad-mannered first-nighter, a foreign diva, a bad actress, and a Queen of Night. Also a feminine version of St Simeon Stylites, or, in case people have forgotten who that was, of Shipwreck Kelly, the world's champion flagpole-sitter, who, ten days before I left New York, perched himself on a pole on top of a music-hall and when I left had not descended.

And then some impish familiar appears to have whispered to Mr Cochran that some more substantial relief was needed. The choice fell upon Messrs Flanagan and Allen, an admirable pair in any other setting. But mixing brands of humour is rather like mixing drinks, and to add the bottled stout of this pair's self-imposed craziness to the full body of that Burgundian décor and Miss Lillie's dry champagne is not quite to solve the problem of the revue which hangs together. Yet this, one repeats, admirable pair do very well indeed in a number called " Down-and-out Blues " in which they are joined by Miss Phyllis Stanley. This is easily the best of their material, which too often is dull and boring in itself. They should at once be released from two of their sketches, and to make good the gap a librettist in their own kind should be secured and locked in a room as Sheridan was locked until he has produced the requisite material. The name of the librettist ? Why, Mr Teddy Knox of course !

Last Words on Irving

HENRY IRVING CENTENARY MATINÉE. Organised by the *Daily Telegraph and Morning Post*. Lyceum Theatre, Monday afternoon, May 23, 1938.

GLORIOUS MORNING. A play. By Norman MacOwan. Duchess Theatre, Thursday, May 26, 1938.

[*May* 29, 1938]

NEVER until this matinée have I understood how anybody could go to the stake. But then never until that moment had I come across a principle worth going to the stake for. I mean worth *my* going, not the going of some medieval loony in a nightshirt. Must I believe that black is white? Very well, then, black is white. Must I agree that two and two make five? Charmed! That the earth is flat? *Cela se peut.* That water runs uphill? *Je n'y vois pas d'inconvénient.* But the supremacy of actors is another matter. That is what stakes are for.

The matinée was in honour of the greatest actor any of us has seen or is likely to see. It was finely inspired, ingeniously designed, magnificently organised, beautifully pageantried, and executed by the players of to-day with a cheerful resignation beyond all praise. One by one they went to annihilation as determinedly as Charles I went to the scaffold. "Remember Irving!" each seemed to be saying with a look in the tail of his eye which signified: "And for heaven's sake forget about us! This isn't our job, and we know it."

"We are all mighty fine fellows," said Stevenson, "but we can none of us write like Hazlitt." The actors of to-day are mighty fine fellows, but they cannot act like Irving. It was a mistaken kindness to insist that they should try, and that is what appearing in the old rôles

118

amounted to. What about the suggestion that they were not imitating Irving, but giving their own interpretations? This is too naïve. You cannot interpret Liszt's Studies in Transcendent Execution; you can only execute them transcendently. You cannot be capricious about Paganini's Caprices; the notes are there to be played, and that is all. Similarly you cannot 'interpret' characters like Mathias and Dubosc. There is nothing to be discovered about them. They are parts which yield everything to a great actor and nothing to a middling one. Whoever plays Mathias must get as much effect out of shaking the snow from his coat as Lear does by shaking off his daughter's scolding; and Richard's wandering through slaughter to a throne must not be more effective than Dubosc's paddling in the postboy's blood. So don't let us have any nonsense!

I never saw Irving's Jingle, but my father used to tell me that it was a mixture of intellectual ascendancy and gentlemanly sad-doggishness. Mr Olivier made him an Elizabethan cut-purse who would have been happy in the company of Pistol, Bardolph, and Nym. In other words, Irving's Jingle could have sat at Mr Pickwick's table; Mr Olivier's couldn't. Yet Mr Olivier is an admirable actor.

Somebody complained that in the excerpt from *The Bells* whereas the wind outside was blowing hard, the cycloramic snow fell in flakes as vertical as the spots on a curtain. I didn't mind that; it is a mark of the present age to invent a thing and then not know how to use it. I did not mind when Mr Tearle came in without even one of the myriad flakes through which he had plodded. What I did mind was the way he took off his gaiters. He took them off like an ordinary man, whereas Irving took them off like an extraordinary man. About this simple action Mr Gordon Craig has written:

Now you might think that the act of taking off some boots could be done one way only—but the way Irving did it had never been thought of till he did it, and has never been done since. It was, in every gesture, every half move, in the play of his shoulders, legs, head, and arms, mesmeric in the highest degree. . . .

Or you might put it that the difference between Irving's fingers and those of Mesmer was this: when Mesmer came, fingers acquired a new art; when Irving went, they lost it. And why didn't one feel drawn to this strange creature? Why was one not fascinated, mesmerised if you will? Yet Mr Tearle too is an admirable actor.

Of Irving's final scene as Charles I, Ellen Terry, writing, like Hazlitt, monosyllabically, says: "It was not a man coming on to a stage to meet someone." And again: "However often I have played that last scene with him, I knew that when he first came on he was not aware of my presence nor of any *earthly* presence: he seemed to be already in heaven." On Monday Mr Nares arrived in the pink of earthly condition, as though he had not undergone any trial greater than that of sitting to Vandyck. Yet Mr Nares is an admirable actor.

No one will accuse me of underrating the talents of Mr Lawson. Yet about his Dubosc my displeasure actively gathered. Why didn't some one tell Mr Lawson how Irving threw open that window and lay on the floor on his stomach drumming with his toes and hurling imprecations and flower-pots at the crowd below? This Dubosc did not even enjoy himself, let alone gloat. And where was the extraordinary rumble which Irving managed to keep going throughout the scene, like a ground-bass? Yet Mr Lawson, again, is an admirable actor.

Mr Farquharson gave one the impression of having seen Irving's Louis XI, and this was admirable in this actor. Contrariwise, Mr Richardson gave one the impression of having seen some other Becket! What had become of all that subtlety and pride, and how did Mr Richardson hope to replace it by honesty and forthrightness? Nature has given this actor many qualities. But she has not given him the quality of a prelate, or of any kind of monk, save those who in the old comic operas trowl jolly bowls. Yet Mr Richardson too is an admirable actor.

But so are they all, all admirable actors in their own kind. The trouble is that their kind and Irving's kind don't mix. With this further difficulty—that sallies out of the two kinds meet with vastly different results. Obviously Irving would have wholly ruined a play like, say, *Eden End*. Mark, however, that Irving would have remained intact, the only thing in smithereens being somebody's play. Whereas when your team-actor attempts to transform himself into a virtuoso both play and actor perish, because without the actor there is no play. The point is dealt with by Mr Craig:

> Frédéric Lemaître took *L'Auberge des Adrets*, which was a sinister little drama, a plain-sailing trifle, such as went down with the public—went down in the strict sense of the words, as a ship sinks and is lost for ever: but Lemaître rigged it out anew, and it came sailing in as though it were a Spanish galleon. Paris was astounded.

So, if Irving were alive, would all these old plays come sailing in like Spanish galleons, and London would be once more astounded.

No! This part of the matinée was a mistake. Playgoers who had seen Irving were tempted to think too poorly of modern acting; playgoers who had not seen Irving were bound to think too poorly of the old plays. But the rest of the celebration was beautifully conceived, largely by Mr Knoblock, and perfectly carried out by Mr George Bishop, Mr Charles La Trobe, and Mr Ernest Irving. There were prologues and epilogues and middlelogues. There was a scene in Irving's dressing-room. There was the Lyceum pit queue as the eighties knew it. There was a supper-party in the Beefsteak Room at the

Lyceum. And there was a scene in the hall of the Midland Hotel, Bradford, a few days after October 13, 1905. If Irving came to life at all at this matinée it was in this last episode at the moment when Mr Edward Chapman, with extraordinary reverence, lifted the chair to show where the porter had marked it with his initials.

And Irving himself? It may give young people some true notion of what he was like if I say that his aloofness would have been untouched even by all this incense. Let me remind them of Mr Beerbohm's account of seeing Irving in a brougham on his way to catch the train to Windsor on the day he was to be knighted: " His hat was tilted at more than its usual angle, and his long cigar seemed longer than ever; and on his face was a look of such ruminant, sly fun as I have never seen equalled." He was preserving, says Max, " in the glare of fame that quality of mystery which is not essential to genius, but which is the safest insurance against oblivion." How would he have behaved if he could have been present on Monday afternoon? I imagine that he would have said to the young actors who were re-creating him what he once said to the brawling Montagues and Capulets striving to impress him: " Very good, me b'ys. But don't fidget ! "

I suggest that the three postulates of *Glorious Morning* —man's right to believe in God, the futility of materialism, and the invincibility of spirit—are like three oranges on a plate. A stage-carpenter like Wilson Barrett does nothing whatever with his three oranges except exhibit them on the plate. Then comes a dramatist of ideas like Mr Shaw who, spying the oranges, says: " What are these? " and begins to juggle with them. *Glorious Morning* seems to me to be *The Sign of the Cross* all over again, except that the oranges belong to the 1938 crop instead of the 1896.

The play's heroine, Leda, is a visionary in a totalitarian State. She believes that God has appeared to her and enjoined her to go about telling everybody that He still exists though the State has denied Him. She comes into contact with a general sent to put down sedition, and the rest may be summarised as follows:

> GENERAL. You lie when you say you have seen God.
> LEDA. I have seen God, and I speak the truth.
> GENERAL. We will force you to say you have been lying.
> LEDA. You can hurt only my body.
> GENERAL. If you persist you will be shot.
> LEDA. You cannot kill my spirit.

But Wilson Barrett said all that, and if the dramatist is not going to say more it does not matter whether his heroine is called Leda, Joan, or Mercia, or whether his mob is Red, Rouennais, or Roman. What, then, could Mr MacOwan have said? It is not up to any critic to re-write a man's play. On the other hand, the critic who complains that nothing is said must be prepared to indicate a line along which something might be said. Mr MacOwan could have closeted his general and Leda together, when the general might have addressed her as follows:

> My dear young lady, you have read *St Joan*. You know that she was burned, not for being a bad heretic, but for being a good one, and because good heretics give the lead to the bad ones who come after. You say God exists. I agree with you, though I shall deny it outside these four walls. If you were wrong about this it would still be my duty to shoot you, but as you are right about it, it becomes my duty to shoot you ten times over. Voltaire, whom you have also studied, said: "If God did not exist Man would have to invent Him." The State says to-day: "Even if God exists Man must abolish Him." The point is not whether God does or does not exist. The point is that Man's belief in God has led him to turn God's world into a hell impossible to endure, always in the hope that things may be better in the world to come. Now that is just not good enough, and the State has decided that the world may be made

better by abolishing the belief in God. It is possible that Man, having no God to believe in and no next world to rely on, may decide to make a better use of the here and now. And as you, my dear young lady, insist on putting yourself in the way, the State finds itself under the painful necessity of shooting you, though holding that under the old *régime* you are an entirely admirable young woman!

This, or something like it, would have made a play. Without it, or any other kind of thinking, *Glorious Morning* remains as empty as the stratosphere or a removal van between removals. Lastly, let me deal with the argument that countries abroad may have audiences which would not assent to this play's three propositions. Agreed! But the fact that something might be a needful sermon abroad does not make it a good play at home. I agree that *Glorious Morning* would be an admirable play for Nazi Germany and Communist Russia. But so would *The Sign of the Cross*! In London to-day it is no more than an anecdote acted by Miss Jessica Tandy as the visionary and Mr Herbert Lomas as her grandfather with a simplicity which simple people may find moving.

The Trough of the Wave

COMEDIENNE. A comedy. By Ivor Novello. Haymarket
Theatre, Thursday, June 16, 1938.

BABES IN THE WOOD. A comedy. By James Bridie.
Embassy Theatre, Tuesday, June 14, 1938.

TRUMPETER, PLAY! A play. By Vere Sullivan. Garrick
Theatre, Monday, June 13, 1938.

[*June* 19, 1938]

THERE are certain retorts, familiar as household words,
about whose provenance there is no arguing. Everybody
knows who said: " You will, Oscar, you will ! " and in
reply to what. Everybody knows who boasted of having
dined in every great house in London, and who immediately said: " Yes, Frank. *Once !* " Everybody knows
who was a better judge of mutton than any sheep. Everybody knows what great English lady, on being asked by
Napoleon III whether she thought of staying long in Paris,
countered with: " *Et vous, Sire?* " Everybody knows
the name of the great English actress who begged to inform Sir George Alexander that she never laughed at him
till she got home.

The point about these stories is that people would still
know to whom they referred if you changed Oscar and
Frank to Tom and Jack. This being so, it is idle for Mr
Novello to think that if he changes Alexander's name to
Marchmont we do not know what actress he is referring to.
Part of the evening's fun—and the evening has a great
deal of fun—consists in wondering how far Donna Lovelace's witticisms are authentic, how far they have been
doctored, and how far some of them are skilful counter-
feits. Perhaps it would be brainsickly to inquire into the
good taste of all this. The wit is cometary in both the
original and the´ reproduction, and when comets flaunt
themselves the matter of taste hardly arises. Equally, of

course, if you do not want to be scorched you should keep out of the way of a comet, and of this wit which has always been willing to wound and never afraid to strike. Its owner, said an American critic, could be best likened to a sinking ship firing upon her rescuers. And in all fairness to the gallant captain, let it be said that she has never hesitated to turn her guns about and give the vessel a taste of its own broadsides. I have before me a letter from a lady about this great actress's performance of Hedda Gabler under the ægis of some provincial reportory company : " It was miraculous ! What I most enjoyed were Hedda's asides to the scene-shifters ! "

But oh ! what a tangled web the playwright weaves when he starts to mingle fancy with fact ! Mr Novello spends his first hour in indicating in the fullest and most explicit manner possible who Donna Lovelace is intended to be, while to make assurance doubly sure Miss Braithwaite obliges with a music-hall ' impersonation ' of the famous voice. We are as certain of the lady's identity as we are that Mary Parnell, the actress who is to make a success of a play from one side of America to the other, thinly disguises Miss Katharine Cornell. Having established his leading character, Mr Novello has then to invent an imbroglio which isn't supposed to be true, and so far as our observation goes does not fit. It is all very much as though an historian, having told us the anecdote about the burned cakes, which identifies his hero, were then to set him to signing Magna Carta prior to marrying six wives. Any small boy reading this travesty would say : " But that isn't King Alfred ! " Similarly, anybody seeing this piece would, when he got to its catastrophe, say : " But this isn't the lady we are all thinking of. At least she knows her job ! " For the point of Mr Novello's play is that the great actress, Donna Lovelace, has so undermined her genius by faults of temperament and lack of self-discipline, that having given an amazing performance at the dress rehearsal she has shot her bolt, and has so far unlearned her job that on the night itself she has nothing left to give. J'ever hear such nonsense? Ju'believe it of the original?

One might be prepared to believe that a Donna Lovelace had betrayed her talent to the point of inability to conceive, learn, and execute a new rôle; the theory that a really great actress can burn herself out at a dress rehearsal and then go phut is mere playwriting nonsense. There would have been more point in Mr Novello's tale if the dress rehearsal had been a frost, and if author, backer, cast, and even the actress herself, with the theatre's insane optimism, had held that it would be " all right on the night," on the principle that the gamest of old war-horses cannot be expected to sniff the battle until the battle is joined. And if, on the night itself, Nemesis had had her unexpected way. But I am not going to re-write Mr Novello's play for him. I merely raise a mild eyebrow when Donna Lovelace says she is glad that she has failed. And why is she glad? Because she likes the play's boy-author, who happens to be her husband's illegitimate son, and her failure will enable his play to be performed right across America, not by a waning English star, but by a rising American one! At this odd concatenation of the magnanimities I confess that my other eyebrow goes up to join its fellow.

There is a brilliant cast—Miss Fabia Drake deserves special mention—which gets itself on the stage as unobtrusively as possible, and as expeditiously off again, thus leaving the coast clear for Miss Lilian Braithwaite, whose Donna is as *mobile* as the original. But why *Lovelace*? Everybody must find his own answer to this. Mine is that I could not love the copy so much, loved I not the original more! Did not Donna say to me as I was leaving New York: " I don't think I shall return to England. London doesn't want me. It seems quite satisfied with Miss

B—— ! " In the art of paying back new scores in advance we must certainly hand it to Donna !

At last Mr Bridie has finished the same play with which he began ! It may or may not be a very good play—that is a matter of opinion—but at least it is the same play throughout. The story tells how a Scotch schoolmaster sees in the evening paper that his work on the Rhythm of the Universe has sold twenty thousand copies. Normally one would expect a publisher to tell his author that he is selling pretty well. But this publisher is a queer fish who apparently spends his time floating in a pond in Sussex. Anyhow, the author decides to sell his school and come south.

In the second act the author and his wife arrive in Sussex to find themselves plunged in the middle of the naughty nineteen-twenties. Mr Bridie is a Scot and therefore possessed of sufficient courage to pursue that of which he disapproves as persistently as if he approved it. This play reads to me as though its author, having taken up Mr Waugh's *Vile Bodies* for the first time, decided to show the irresolute Sassenach what resolution could do with such a theme. For this reason the publisher, the old beldam who is his mother, the bearded artist, and his light o' love—the whole *ménage* and caboodle is of a raffish nastiness exceeding Sassenach invention.

In the third act we have echoes of *What Every Woman Knows*. Probably there ought not to be a third act at all, and I am not quite satisfied that, with the exception of ten hilarious minutes with a little boy, there ought to be a first act ! Yes, I think the piece is really a one-acter. Title ? I am ashamed to ask the question. For obviously this skit without a before and after can only be called *Shall We Join the Nineteen-twenties?* It is extremely well acted by Miss Angela Baddeley and Mr Alexander Knox.

Now for Miss Sullivan. Countess Marion von Ahlenfeld was an English girl who had married His Excellency General Count Armin von Ahlenfeld. Therefore their son,

Flight-Lieutenant Count Karl von Ahlenfeld, was half-English. When Peggy Fortescue, whom one took to be a sort of cousin, went to stay with the Ahlenfelds, the Flight-Lieutenant fell in love with her and presently married her. She was preparing to have her baby at her mother's house in England when war threatened to break out between the two countries. Whereupon the Flight-Lieutenant insisted, against the doctor's orders, on Peggy's going back to Germany to have her German baby born on German soil.

So we all trooped back to the Fatherland, and the German doctor, announcing that he could not save both mother and child, gave the Flight-Lieutenant his choice. The Flight-Lieutenant chose the baby, England was given one more chance to submit to Germany's terms, and the Leader himself, whom one might have supposed to be closeted with his Chief of Staff, had nothing better to do than to come marching down the street outside the drawing-room of His Excellency General Count von Ahlenfeld in a garrison town in a corner of Germany. The moral? That you can't make military omelettes without breaking eggs. Which perhaps some of us suspected before entering the theatre.

Mr Peter Murray Hill as the Flight-Lieutenant took that hop which in the case of this improving young actor one confidently predicts must precede many skips and jumps. Mr Malcolm Keen and Mr C. M. Hallard gave terrific studies in dignity, German and English respectively. Miss Cathleen Nesbitt as a pacifist aunt in a hot-bed of German militarism resembled a snake in the grass that hadn't bothered about any grass. Mr Leon M. Lion did very well in a game of metaphysical blind-man's buff in which there was only one player, while an actor who shall be nameless put up one performance which was far and away more embarrassing than any war.

129

Honouring Irene Vanbrugh

IRENE VANBRUGH JUBILEE MATINÉE. In aid of the Elizabeth Garrett Anderson Hospital and the Theatrical
Ladies' Guild. His Majesty's Theatre, Monday afternoon, June 20, 1938.

GOLDEN BOY. A play. By Clifford Odets. St James's
Theatre, Tuesday, June 21, 1938.
[*June* 26, 1938]

COOL and flippant like bunting, that eminent prologuist
Mr Noel Coward began the afternoon by giving us a taste
of the English language as Shakespeare did not write it,
and as Miss Irene Vanbrugh has never spoken it :

> Dead shepherd, now I find thy *sorr* of might,
> " Who ever loved that loved not at first sight? "

This brings me to an essential and perhaps unavoidable
florr in all of these stage-jubilee celebrations. The point
is the presence of the critics. Should they or should they
not attend ? If, attending, they function, they commit
the indescribable gaffe of looking a bevy of beautiful gift-
horses in the mouth ; if, still attending, they desist from
functioning, they must join in the general conspiracy of
taking the will for the deed, of excessive sweetness, of
regarding the whole affair as a ju-jubilee.

It is not suggested that critics should seize the occasion
to cry its heroine's faults to heaven. Odd, by the way,
that it is always heroine and never hero ; I cannot recollect
an actor's Jubilee since Macklin ! No, at such times the
lady abides no question. What is questionable is the effect
on the audience, who are told by implication that this was
the impact produced by such-and-such a scene in such-
and-such a play thirty or forty years ago. It isn't, and
it wasn't ! Take the other afternoon's scene from *The Gay
Lord Quex*. In 1899, Mr Evelyn Waugh being minus four,

the world could still be shocked at the notion of an elderly roué betraying his young fiancée to the extent of imprinting a farewell kiss on the Félix Poubelle-stained lips of his erstwhile—I think they then called it inamorata, the Duchess of Strood. Nowadays if a young girl batted an eyelid at such a proceeding her classmates at Snowdene would at once tell her to stop being so indecently frumpish.

But this wasn't the worst. Did Hare pronounce the champagne's *carte d'or* as though he were talking about a cart-door? And why omit all mention of those then crashingly modish cigarettes called Argyropulos, if my memory serves me? (No, I have not looked it up!) And why was Quex, the grave Bond Street roué, turned into that very different thing, the thirtyish cumberer of raffish lidos? And what a Duchess! Let me repeat that anybody who thinks that last Monday he was seeing the third act of *The Gay Lord Quex* was, except in the matter of Sophie, mistaken.

And now to a much graver matter. No critic minds shutting up; what he dislikes is being shut up. He dislikes feeling out of it at that moment when acclamation is at its height and the star must unload her fifty years of gratitude. Authors who have written their pitiful best for her, managers who have mismanaged her, fellow-players who have trespassed on her boards, call-boys whose memories she has had to jog—everybody comes in for a meed of praise except the critics whose august phrases have made her memory worth while. Here stands Rosalind showering praise on all her world, but as far as her critics are concerned without a word to throw at a dog. Had I been the master of ceremonies at His Majesty's I should have printed in the programme a golden passage written by Montague and perpetuating for ever, as all great critics do for all great players, what else had been a little day:

Miss Irene Vanbrugh is far the best of English actresses at expressing a certain kind of salt, sane, wayward honesty of ill-will and generosity, the temper that jumps in a semi-calculable way up and down the whole scale of equity and magnanimity, from uncompromisingly Mosaic doctrines of an eye for an eye to superChristian prodigies of self-sacrifice. Small shame to her that this time she does the Old Testament ethics the better of the two, for Mr Pinero does them vastly better. Indeed, the whole theory of retaliatory justice, with its set contrasts and its spirit of pat, triumphant repartee, is much more easily dramatised than the mild, blond sort of moral beauty that answereth not again. The vivacity with which Miss Vanbrugh's Nina routed the advanced guard of Hilary Jesson's heavy brigade of arguments for the wearing of haloes did good to the natural man in all of us, though there were other and less momentous moments at which her art was even finer. Like Irving and Bernhardt, she can shout through a door into a passage in a way that turns scenery real, or sit dead still in a room full of people and turn the rest into mere faint sketches, so importunate is the sense she conveys of the greater authenticity and vehemence of her own emotions.

Anybody fifty years hence picking up a programme containing this would know what Irene Vanbrugh was like; Monday's programme will tell him nothing. I charge the entire theatrical profession with remembering only the unfavourable things the critic says about them, and, when he enskies a great actor or actress in words worthy to endure on the ceiling, of trampling the picture underfoot!

Miss Vanbrugh will have less of the salt, sane common sense with which I credit her if she detects anything in the foregoing of adverse personal application. Her bearing, physical and spiritual, can never have been finer than on this most trying occasion. She did not pretend that the whole thing was a surprise. She did not claim to be unworthy of it. And why should she? Any actress for whom two great playwrights like Pinero and Barrie persistently wrote dramas over a course of years must know her own worth. If I were asked to sum up Miss Vanbrugh's quality I should say—English. A whole essay might be written here, but I shall condense it into two images of two English ladies. One shows Miss Draper her garden; the other lives in the provinces with Miss Delafield. Both are feminine abstractions of Hamlet's essential qualities in the good player—discretion, smoothness, temperance, modesty. All these were present in Miss Vanbrugh's speech, the best I ever heard on such an occasion. They gave her a gold casket containing a cheque to buy a jewel. But all afternoon the audience had been giving her something which cannot be bought—its unforced love for a good actress and a good woman.

Flop or wow, your dramatic critic sits more or less up and writes the notice he is paid for. It is a very different thing when an audience which has paid for its seats sits up and takes notice on its own account. Three plays, and only three, this season have been winners from the moment the curtain went up. These are the three New York successes, *Idiot's Delight*, *Amphitryon 38*, and now *Golden Boy*. That one American play should stir an English audience more than all the English plays of the season may be a fluke. That a second should do it may be no more than a coincidence. But when a third achieves it, it begins to look uncommonly like cause and effect.

What is there in American play-writing which turns your listless English first-nighters, each wrapped in his own concern, into an excited, spellbound, homogeneous audience? Whatever differences there may be between Messrs Sherwood, Behrman, Murray, Boretz, Kaufman, and Hart, they all have something of Mr Odets, and he has something of them. At any rate, the play under notice is his play, and he shall be whatever is the opposite of whipping-boy.

Let us look at one or two English plots. Shall a nice young woman marry a nasty butcher? Shall another nice young woman marry her father's stud-groom? Shall a wife give up medicine because her husband is in the Church? May a wife blackmail her husband into providing for her daughter? None of these, we may agree, is any great shakes. But is the plot of *Golden Boy* so very much better? It needs no dramatist come from the American Group Theatre to tell us that a young man with the soul of a violinist who abandons fiddling to make money in the prize-ring deserves to be unhappy. Ibsen may be out of date, but I, personally, should not rebuke his ghost for whispering to Mr Odets that spiritual tragedy is not achieved by accidental manslaughter and a motor smash. Mr Odets, of course, knows this, and part of his American cuteness is that while tickling the groundlings with an accidental catastrophe he gives the judicious any number of hints as to the real cause of the boy's misery.

Let us now consider Mr Odets's characters and dialogue. Each one of his characters has been freshly imagined and has an urgent life of his or her own. Space is limited, and this is not the place for an essay on dramatic creation and what it is in the dramatist which gives him the power to instil into his characters the breath of life. In the outer world it may need a scientist to tell living matter from dead. In the theatre your meanest playgoer is never in any doubt. The people in this play feel intensely, and appear to be feeling for the first time.

These characters have no background. They are unaware that anybody has had feelings like theirs before. They have no common experience to draw on. They know nothing of intellectual resource or spiritual solace. They fly to the senses to cure maladies of soul they cannot diagnose. This boxing boy is unhappy because he is not fulfilling himself. But he has never heard of frustration, and thinks to find the cure for unhappiness in high-speed motor-cars. One takes the best part of this play to be its love scenes, for here the boy's passion is, though he does not know it, a return to single-mindedness. The writing here is wilfully disjointed and inarticulate, and if we do not know quite where the play is drifting, it is because the boy and girl cannot size up what is happening to them. And we are conscious that their modern despair is strangely like an old one. Sitting on that bench in the melancholy twilight, these lovers cease to be a vulgar American boxer and a common little drab; they are creatures from the world of Turgenev.

The name brings me up sharp. Anybody might think from the foregoing that this play was the miasmatic exhalation of the Sewer Group at the Mantrap Theatre, whereas it is a sparkling cross-section of life lived in New York's most garish noonday, a world of scorching asphalt, not peat. The characters move in a light as brilliant as that of the boxing-ring. They give us life as nearly, as humorously, and as trenchantly observed as in our own Sean O'Casey. They belong to that new genre which America has invented in the last dozen years or so, the vortex with a still and bitter centre—in a word, the tragic farce. Add first-class direction, and a furious energy of acting as though that art had just been invented, totally unlike the English duplication of esteemed successes, and we may perhaps be on the track of discovering why, to put it bluntly, the American theatre is so much more alive than the English.

I cannot think of any English actress who could play the girl as Miss Lillian Emerson plays her, without fuss, yet giving the character its full value. Your English actress would either get nowhere near it or overplay the part out of all recognition. Is there any actor on this side who could convey the passionate reality of Mr Luther Adler's puzzled, sensitive, angry boy? Or the dumb rightness of Mr Morris Carnovsky's father? Or the weakness of that beflustered maelstrom which is Mr Roman Bohnen's boxing manager? Or the unsizeable and indescribable quality cf humour in Siggie, the taxi-driver? The answer is threefold. There isn't, there isn't anybody trying, and there are no plays to try in.

Countercheck Quarrelsome

GOLDEN BOY. A play. By Clifford Odets. St James's
  Theatre. [Second notice.]
THE TEMPEST. Revival of Shakespeare's play. Regent's
  Park, Tuesday, June 28, 1938.

[*July 3, 1938*]

No, I have not revisited *Golden Boy*. Nor do I intend to
re-write my notice of last week. But so much has sprung
from that article, and the play itself has aroused so much
controversy, that I gladly return to it. And then, consider
the alternatives! Does anybody want to read a column
by me on Shakespeare's *Tempest*? No! Does this worn-
out machine want to write one? No! Very well, then.

One of the most distinguished of living English dramatists has written me a letter beginning: " I must remon-
strate with you about the fuss you make over these
Americans." The letter ends: " The fact is, of course,
that it is a pleasant change for you to see American
hokum after so much English nonsense. But you must not
begin to over-estimate the hokum merchants." And the
middle of the letter informs me that *Golden Boy* is a
hokum play without integrity: " Practically every scene
is jazzed up, given more punch and excitement and noise
than it should have, without reference to reality at all."

But who has brought *Golden Boy* to the tests of integrity and reality? Who has implied that judged by
these standards *Golden Boy* is anything but a highly
meretricious piece of theatrical impudence which happens
to hold an audience pin-still? Scanning my article, I cannot find the least hint that Mr Odets's play begins at any
time to be a work of art. If it were I should immediately
have ranked it with *Juno and the Paycock*, and people
would have gone to see it for a respectful week or two and

137

then stopped. But Mr Odets has written at least two other plays which are works of art. Why, then, did not Messrs O'Bryen, Linnit, and Dunfee produce one of these instead of *Golden Boy*? Because Messrs O'Bryen, Linnit, and Dunfee are theatre-managers who rightly prefer making money out of an exciting, sentimental melodrama to losing it out of a jumble of integrity and reality that nobody cares twelve-and-sixpence about.

It has been left to me to disclose—which I do here and now—the full cunning of these astute gentlemen. They have been able, and knew that they would be able, to print on their programme the magic words: " By Arrangement with the Group Theatre, New York." Now if there is one thing an English audience likes it is to think it is being edified when it is actually being amused. In English ears the words " Group Theatre " cover a multitude of artistic sins. Nor must Mr Odets be left out of the astute catalogue. To ' think up ' a theme which might be Ibsen's, that theme being the clash of idealism and money-getting, to deck this theme with the glamour and glitter appertaining—as the film-magnates know well—to boxers, backers, bullies, and drabs, with a soppy Poppa in the background, and to soak the whole in a racy Italianate idiom—how Mr Odets must have rubbed his hands over an audience-trap as superb as this !

Of course your young violinist, being a world-genius who decides to betray his art, does not abandon that art ; he sells it to the jazz-merchants. *Of course* the penalty is not to be drawn against a boxing champion with a weak heart so that he must needs commit manslaughter. *Of course* Nemesis knows her business better than to deal in motor smashes. *Of course* Mr Odets knows all this as well as any English playwright who ever had a play of integrity and reality flop in New York. In this case Mr Odets just wasn't having those playwriting virtues at that price. But he also took care that the characters involved in his piece of rank commercialism should be people in whom we take a warm interest. *We mind what happens to them.*

Let me put it another way. Nobody disputes that Ibsen's *Ghosts* is a better play than *Golden Boy*. We all know that Ibsen did not make the mistake of sending Oswald and Regina on a joy-run and tipping the toboggan into some retributional fjord. But how does that help towards our liking or disliking Ibsen's characters? I have never had the slightest interest in Oswald except as a pathological pawn. Whereas I have an affection for Mr Odets's young couple. Oswald's talks with Regina may be real, but I do not particularly want to hear them. Joe's talks with Lorna may be " high-falutin' bosh," as my letter says. But I like listening to them, and am concerned for the talkers.

Then there is the question of entertainment. Is it not conceivable that a play of " punch and excitement and noise," when you like sitting at it, is better value for money than a play of integrity and reality which somehow fails to hold you? For even in the highest playwriting these austere qualities alone do not suffice. A dramatist of complete integrity may yet be the dullest fellow, and his characters, though real, may be the dullest people. That seamstress who can no longer sew because she is blind, and, starving, puts her head in the gas oven, is doubtless a very real person. But I suggest that a play about her must have something more than integrity if an audience is to be as irresistibly drawn to it as the poor girl is to her oven.

Here is something which your highbrow playwright always forgets—*nobody is forced to go to the theatre.* The one thing which drives people into a playhouse, particularly in the summer, is a compelling interest in what is going on in it. There are so many alternatives to playgoing. For curiosity's sake I have looked up the files to see what new plays I have visited in the last twelve months. And I have supposed that I was not a dramatic critic, and that somebody had come up to me in the middle of each new play and said: "They're just tuning up for *Elektra*!" Or, "You'll be in time for *Coq d'Or* and *Le Beau Danube*!" Or, "The last film at the Cyclops is said to be better than *Carnet de Bal*!" Or, "The Heavyweight Eliminating Bout at Harringay comes on at ten!" I made myself answer the question—on how many occasions would I have stayed in the theatre? And I had to answer—five, the plays being *Time and the Conways*, *I Have Been Here Before*, *Mourning Becomes Electra*, *Idiot's Delight*, and *Amphitryon 38*. In other words, two plays by Mr Priestley and three plays by American authors. I then asked myself—would I have left *Golden Boy* in the middle even to hear Toscanini, whom I have never heard, conduct the Sibelius No. 2, which I cannot hear too often? And I answered—no!

Now it is quite possible that when I dislike a play I may be mistaken. I may be jaded through over-much play-going. The public may be righter than I think. It may be right in liking some inanity which in my tired view would make a giraffe vomit. But when a critic in the course of his weary round finds himself glued to his seat and ranged with the public and sharing their emotion and excitement, then that critic is surely justified in holding that the play has plenty to say for itself. And as long as that critic keeps that play and his praises of it in the category to which it and they belong, it seems to me monstrous to object that he does not condemn it by standards to which it does not pretend. The public are flocking, or near-flocking, to *Golden Boy*. I do not conceive it to be my duty at a time when plays are coming off right and left, *or even at any time*, to dissuade the public from going to see something which I like as much as they do.

I do not believe that any of the dramatic critics from Hazlitt downward could, if challenged, have produced *on the spot* a coherent account of the parts played in the imbroglio by Alonso, Sebastian, Antonio, Gonzalo, Adrian, and Francisco. But that doesn't prevent *The Tempest* from being (a) a great masterpiece and (b) a pleasant way of spending the afternoon.

After which exhaustive analysis I shall say that Mr Philip Merivale played Prospero as well as most, that it was moving to hear the son of a regretted brother-critic speak Ferdinand's verse with the feeling for beauty which Mr David Tree obviously possesses—perhaps he should give more value to his consonants—that Miss Peggy Bryan as Ariel looked pretty in woad, and that Mr Robert Atkins made one of the best Calibans I have ever seen. This fine actor used his 'cello-deep voice and mastery of make-up to suggest something half ape and half Early Man, and there was extraordinary pathos in the beatings of that primitive brain against the imprisoning skull. Sullivan's music was enchanting, and the whole thing seemed to me to be as good as anything ever done at Regent's Park.

Max and Aristophanes

LYSISTRATA. Revival of Aristophanes' comedy. English
version by Benjamin Bickley Rogers. Regent's Park,
Tuesday, July 19, 1938.

DIVERSION. Revival of John van Druten's play. "Q"
Theatre, Thursday, July 21, 1938.

[*July* 24, 1938]

ONE of the most inconvenient properties of newspaper-
readers is the propensity to pin down the newspaper-
writer. They are in the position of those who would nail
a truth to the counter. Several readers have challenged
me to produce that article by Mr Beerbohm in which I
recently stated that he debunked—O monstrous vulgar-
ism!—Greek tragedy. Obsequiously I turned up Max's
two volumes. Obsequiously and after enormous labour.
For, alas, I do not possess a complete Max, and the two
volumes of dramatic criticism are not sold separately!
Blank after blank I drew, until finally a friend who is in
the country has lent me the two books without knowing it!

There, lo and behold, was the evidence I wanted in the
essay entitled *Bygones Up To Date*. The play under notice
was the *Andromache* of Euripides:

> If the Greek legends are for all time, then we can be
> moved by a contemporary version of them as deeply as
> were the original Greeks. But the fact appears that we
> cannot be moved by a contemporary version. Mr
> Murray's *Andromache* proves that we cannot. Instead
> of being purged, according to the ancient prescription,
> by pity and awe, we are utterly unaffected. We are
> even disaffected. The superstitions that were impressive
> to us in the old version become definitely absurd in the
> new. The deeds that were inevitable and pitiable
> become merely incredible phenomena of brutality. We
> feel as though we had stumbled into a cave of moon-
> struck butchers.

I also re-discovered that delicious article entitled *An Hypocrisy in Playgoing*, and it is this which I propose to take as my theme now. It is said that all things fade, change, and pass away. But I hold this not to be true of theatre-going hypocrisy, which is fadeless, changeless, and eternal.

Take that visit of a company of, I doubt not, excellent Jewish actors acting in Yiddish. Is there any critic who will admit to being flummoxed by his ignorance of the language to the point of not knowing whether some be-lauded outburst is dictated by anger, jealousy, bereavement, loss of fortune, or just toothache? No! Beard after beard is ecstatically received. To me ignorance of the language reduces such acting to just this matter of bar-bigerousness, whereby he who has the longest beard becomes the best actor. Since this must be nonsense, I have for some time forborne to criticise performances in unknown tongues. But are the voices of my colleagues similarly hushed? No! What happens is that which happened to Mr Beerbohm's colleagues when Duse came. Their voices " are uplifted in unisonant dithy-rambus."

Let us say that the play is *Hedda Gabler*. You read your English version, says Max, feverishly, like a timid candidate for an examination, and when you get inside the theatre you are utterly lost until " from the welter of unmeaning vowels and consonants ' Ejlert Lövborg ' or ' Hedda Gabler ' suddenly detaches itself, like a silver trout rising from a muddy stream." But there was a time —and I grow hot all over when I think of it—when I presumed to judge that of which I wotted nothing. In a paroxysm of nervousness I have turned up my scrapbooks to find what I wrote about, for example, Signor Ruggeri's Hamlet:

> Let it be confessed that my courage failed me on Signor Ruggeri's first night, and that I went to the

flyweight championship at the National Sporting Club, where at least the boxing was in English. My impressions of the Italian actor are culled from the Wednesday afternoon performances, and it must be definitely understood that they are only impressions.

After which I proceeded to make what I now know to have been a complete fool of myself: " The great soliloquies failed of their immemorial effect." But, by St Patrick, of course they did! Would not Wordsworth's sublimest sonnet lose its immemorial effect if read in English to a Hottentot? I have some knowledge of the soliloquies in *Hamlet*. Yet I swear that an actor delivering them in a language I do not know has but to wade three lines deep and I am utterly at sea. In plain English, I know no more of what he is talking about than any Hottentot.

The hypocrisy I have in mind at the moment concerns certain Aristophanic proceedings at Regent's Park. Here I desire to walk with the utmost nicety. I do not say that my colleagues, joined together in unisonant dithyrambus, have written hypocritically. What I do say is that I should be guilty of that sin if I added my voice to theirs. Am I to confess that I was bored? Unwillingly, yes. Lysistrata's long set-speeches, magnificently declaimed by Miss Gladys Cooper, fell as sheerly as a yard of pumpwater. But though the water was Attic and the pump Parian marble, the stillicidium remained pump-water all the same. It possessed every quality except interest. Then had I not gone to the theatre taking the thing for a witty, even impermissibly witty comedy? The belief was induced by recollection of M. Donnay's version, at which the flowers in Regent's Park must have pudically folded petals, and of certain Beardsley drawings any one of which would have made amnesias and aphasias, glubjullahs and damphobias, wish they had never blossomed. Listening with modern ears, which are all I possess, I heard nothing save the agelastic. This old entertainment did not now entertain.

Rooting about what I call my library prior to the performance, I came across an arrangement of this play by a Miss Winifred Ayres Hope which seemed to suggest that the thing might be seeable to a wider audience than that of moonstruck pedants. For two reasons. First, because it was short enough to be got through within the hour, and second because Lysistrata's " It is a ridiculous custom, this arming oneself with shield and helmet, to go into the market-place and purchase a mackerel ! " is exactly in the key of any one of Alkmena's utterances in *Amphitryon 38*, and we all know how amusing Miss Fontanne can make that sort of thing sound. As hour after hour sped—O verb ironic ! —by, the conviction grew upon me that the way to make the old Greek comedy both seeable and hearable would have been to use the Donnay as libretto and set that to appropriate music. A colleague, Mr Alan Dent, has suggested Gluck as the apt composer—but with profound respect I disagree. What we want is a modern Offenbach. And if we cannot have the intoxication of Strauss in his *Ariadne auf Naxos* vein, then I suggest the mockery of Mr Walton in the mood of *Façade*. And, of course, décor by Mr Messel, who in the theatre has Nature beaten to a frazzle !

By the oddest coincidence I find that the very week which saw the production of Mr Cochran's *Helen*, in which Meilhac and Halévy, Mr A. P. Herbert, and *feu* M. Offenbach all had a hand, saw also a performance of Ben Jonson's *Volpone* freely adapted by Stefan Zweig and re-translated by Ruth Langner, which free adaptation was freely slanged in this column. Why then, asks the logical reader, demand a modernisation of the old Greek play ? For the reason, my dear fellow, that I agree with George Meredith, who has dismissed Aristophanes with perfect laconism : " He is not to be revived." But this way

brickbats lie ! Dipping yet again into Max, I come across
this astonishing passage :

> But who, really and truly, in his heart of hearts,
> wants to see a performance of a play by Ben Jonson or
> any other Elizabethan or Jacobean, or by Congreve or
> any other Restorationist ? These plays are interesting
> curiosities, and many of them may be read with enjoy-
> ment. But as plays they are dead utterly ; and a
> theatrical production of any of them is a mere rattling
> of dry bones.

And I restore Max to my friend's shelves, happy in the
knowledge that if I have relegated Aristophanes to a mere
rattling of dry bones I err in exquisite company.

Mr Robert Atkins did everything possible to marry the
old with the new, and his production had for obvious aim
Gilbert's " gay but classic measure." Let me end with a
chorus whose model will be familiar :

> Merry were the cymbals' soundings—
> Gaily blew Pandæan pipes—
> Turning Daphnephoric boundings
> Into bread and cheese and swipes!

In a production wholly admirable for those whose taste it
meets let me particularly commend Mr Atkins's stage-
lighting. Were ever sward and brake and toy Acropolis
so bathed in luteous glow the exact hue of lemon-pudding ?

There is perhaps not very much subtlety about *Diversion*,
which is a murder story simple almost to the point of
crudity. But it has at least one advantage over the type
of murder play most popular at the moment—the murder
happens at the end instead of at the beginning ! The
revival is well done at Kew, though Miss Gina Malo does
not quite give Rayetta Muir the quality with which Miss
Cathleen Nesbitt endowed her. In the West-End performance the boy's father was, so to speak, kept guessing
about Rayetta ; though she might be a bad woman she
had the manner for good drawing-rooms. Whereas at

Kew two minutes would have told Harley Street's Sir Charles all he wanted to know. Again, while Miss Nesbitt's end was unexpected, Miss Malo made it appear that Rayetta's was only a matter of time. In other words, though the present performance is a clever one, it needs putting up a social peg or two.

Mr Peter Glenville is coming on hand over fist, and his performance in the first part of the third act is extremely good. Passivity is easy, and we are always being told by the quietists that passion is a mere affair of shouting. Since, according to that school, acting is all an affair of whispering, I submit that rising passion must be a differentiation in whispers. And that, surely, calls for some doing? Whether it does or not, Mr Glenville acts admirably. As the medico Mr Walter Hudd adroitly unties the knot of predicament with the fingers of toxicology, and in two small parts Miss Elaine Hamill is unusually promising and Miss Marjorie Clark astounding as usual.

The Malvern Festival (I)

GENEVA. A play. By Bernard Shaw. Monday, August 1, 1938.

MUSIC AT NIGHT. A play. By J. B. Priestley. Tuesday, August 2, 1938.

CORONATION TIME AT MRS BEAM'S. A comedy. By C. K. Munro. Wednesday, August 3, 1938.

[*August 7, 1938*]

AGE, Molière might well have told us, has nothing to do with the affair, and it is agreed beforehand that Mr Shaw's eighty-two years do not affect the quality of his new play *Geneva*. Does this play show its author to be in his dotage? Yes, if dotage means vigour unimpaired and vision undimmed. A young man was once rebuked by an older saying: "Goethe in his extreme age hoped that he had not grown to be such a fool that he could not change his mind." The young man replied: "My extremely youthful mind is not so foolish that it needs changing." Mr Shaw is both old and young. He is old enough, and by now has become sensible enough, to alter his way of playwriting if he saw the necessity; he has also remained young enough to think that he knows his own business best. That is why we had to put up with Miss Begonia Brown, of Camberwell, one more of those lifeless dolls which have lain about so many of the Shaw nurseries, but are still held tight against a childishly believing bosom. If Begonia, with her talk of insulting the British flag, ever existed, be sure it was in the time of the Boer War and "Good-bye, Dolly Grey," and not to-day, when the type Mr Shaw has in mind concentrates solely upon beach-wear, nail-tint, and the new one-sided veil suggesting a bandaged mump. And did femininity, Camberwell or otherwise, ever in Mr Shaw's or anybody else's time, use the word " Egad " ?

The first two acts of *Geneva* have been likened to paltry antechambers leading to some august and noble hall. To me they were like the hinterland of a Brighton or a Blackpool, the cluttered approach to the open sea. But, when you got to it, what a sea, with nothing left out that rightly appertains, a sea full yet with plenty of sound and foam, breakers of argument, rollers of philosophy, tang of salty dialogue thrown at you like spray. Irene Iddesleigh, who " paced the beach of limited freedom," was a poorer creature than we who are made free of Mr Shaw's limitless ocean. Three points stuck out, like Needles. These were the bringings to trial of Bombardone garbed like Nero, Battler displayed as Lohengrin, and General Flanco in the military uniform of to-day. To the charge that he had destroyed democracy Bombardone retorted that democracy had never existed unless he, Bombardone, as the world's greatest vote-puller, was to be reckoned the first democrat. Called to account for brutal and ruthless anti-Semitism, Battler argued that the Nordic attitude against Hittite invasion was Australia's and California's against Oriental submerging. And the upshot ? That Man, having made a mess of things, deserved to be put against a wall and shot up.

The play, Mr Shaw explains in a note, is not supposed to end ; it just stops. The only possible criticism is that it did not stop soon enough. What was wanted was not scissors, nor yet shears ; scythes only could have done the needful. Æons hence, when Mr Shaw's copyright falls in, I foretell that producers will throw away all of the piece except the last act, which they will stage by itself under the title of *Shall We Leave the League* ? Only, of course, by that time there may be no League to leave, and perhaps no nations to leave it. As Bombardone Mr Trouncer

gave his brazen, bull-necked best, a trumpet performance
with odd little grace-notes of malice and mockery. As
Battler Mr Norman Wooland seemed to take a Stratford-
on-Avon view of Henry V. As a British Diplomat Mr
Thesiger put up a shrewd, sly, and mightily effective
performance. As the Judge Mr Wolfit did well in a part
which promised better than it performed. And as Begonia
Miss Eileen Beldon was in the unhappy position of having
to over-play a character that the piece would have been
better without.

Musicologists will not approve of Mr Priestley's *Music
at Night*. They will not approve because the author of
this play about a violin concerto, instead of telling us why
the composer wrote a disconcerting conglomeration of
B flat, B, D sharp, E, and A, concentrated upon the
hideousness of the chords struck by the concerto in the
hearers' memories. Let me dismiss the framework of the
play by stating with some bluntness that it is mere highbrow pretentiousness, and no more than a device for getting a dozen people to take it in turns to commune and
soliloquise while the others, whose turn is over or to come,
doze in the attitude of listeners to advanced music. They
are a rum lot, and the notion that more than, say, three
of them have a soul above rummy is the rummiest thing
about this very odd play. Does Mr Priestley really insist
that neo-César Franck would move gossip-writer, magnate,
and flibbertigibbet to more than a stifled yawn and a
polite thank-you ? But let us grant the framework ; after
all, plays have to be got going somehow. An elderly states-
man leads off with the remark : " I remember Ernest Newman saying that the slow movement in Elgar's 'Cello Concerto is the swan-song of a dying civilisation." Mr
Priestley's case is that the swan of humanity has turned
into the ugliest of Donald Ducklings, and in support of his
case he makes his characters evoke their dead selves, summon ghosts laid long ago, and behave generally as though

the play were an amalgam of *Dear Brutus*, *Outward Bound*, and *The Passing of the Third Floor Back*.

To go through the long cast one by one would take too long; let me choose three examples. First shall be the news-hawk or social-columnist, a callous, hard-bitten fellow with an expensive car and free access to the best restaurants and tailors. Are we to believe that when his dead mother appears to ask if all is well with her child this wholly successful vulgarian-with-a-niche would burst into tears? All that this means is that Mr Priestley is endowing the character with his own sensitiveness. Do we believe that this multi-millowner, whose betrayal of a confidence has led to a suicide, would start at a Banquo who has been in's grave these twenty years? Mr Priestley again. And the flibbertigibbet who is recalled by a long-lost sister to hankerings after early innocence? This is Mr Priestley's puritanism crying wanton.

The conclusion of the matter? That mankind is not happy in spite of wireless, picture-palaces, summer cruises, cheap motoring, long-distance flying, and gliders for everybody. The remedy? That Man should revise his notions of the real and the seeming, the nature of life and death, the meaning of existence. Up to now Man has held that to perfect himself is his highest duty. After the play, at my hotel, I took up Mr Laurence Housman's *The Golden Sovereign*, and almost at once came upon this passage in the study entitled *Echo de Paris*. The talkers are Mr Housman and Oscar Wilde:

L. H. Do you mean no artists are successful?

O. W. Incidentally; never intentionally. If they are they remain incomplete. The artist's mission is to live the complete life: success, as an episode (which is all it can be); failure, as the real, the final end. Death, analysed to its resultant atoms—what is it but the vindication of failure: the getting rid for ever of powers, desires, appetites, which have been a lifelong embarrassment? The poet's noblest verse, the dramatist's greatest

scene deal always with death ; because the highest function of the artist is to make perceived the beauty of
failure.

Mr Priestley in this play uses his function as a dramatist
to declare the unimportance of success and the futility of
personality.

> And many a thoughtful text around he strews,
> That teach the anxious modernist to live.

The important thing about a tree, he tells us specifically,
is not the individual leaf but the common trunk. So why
bother about whether you are a clever leaf, or a good-
looking leaf, or a leaf that rides the air more gracefully
than its fellows ? To which one can only reply that this
sounds all right for the trunk, but what about the leaf ?
Is it not the leaf's business to be the best leaf possible,
and trust either to the larger hope of some limbo in which
it shall live for ever, or believe that in sweetening the
summer it has achieved the purpose of its budding ? What
is the point of a tree going on producing leaves if the
leaves don't matter intensely ? Is what matters in Elgar's
Concerto not the piece of music itself, but the will to create
it ? But perhaps all this means no more than that Mr
Priestley has found himself up against the blank wall of
speculative questing. Is he, in arriving at this conclusion,
saying anything more than Kingsley's " Be good, sweet
maid, and let who will be clever " ? Do his spooks and
ghosts amount to anything more than the old adjuration
to hold death as the gateway to life ? Has the reader
found these ruminatings dull ? I can only plead that, for
me, they beguiled a last act of considerable tedium,
stressed rather than alleviated by the use of masks, Greek
chorusing, and other Bloomsbury wildfowl. Hereabouts
it became obvious that the author had been greatly
impressed.

And so, at least with regard to the second act, had been
the audience. Further, whether we accept or deny any

play's metaphysics is strictly not the point. Had this play's author given of his whole mind? Yes. Did this mind show itself as a fine mind? Yes. Had he done something to remove the old reproach that modern English playwriting is unworthy of serious attention? Yes. Had he written out of a complete disregard for anything except the dramatic clothing of something he vitally wanted to say? Yes. Had he interested his audience and dug a little below normal preoccupation? Yes. Had he trusted that audience to know a bold experiment from the timid compromise of commercialism? Yes. Had the experiment been worth while? Immensely! Except that too many of the actors insisted on being spiritual to the point of inaudibility, moving ghostly lips in soundless ecstasy, the acting was fair. But perhaps the whole thing isn't actable?

Mr Munro's *Coronation Time at Mrs Beam's* was all about Mrs Beam's at coronation time. This farce would have been much more amusing if it had been shorter by, say, an hour. It was extremely well acted, with Miss Jean Cadell again as the delightful Miss Shoe and with two brilliant cameos by Miss Phyllis Shand and Mr Cyril Wheeler.

The Malvern Festival (II)

ALEXANDER. A play. By Lord Dunsany. Thursday, August
4, 1938.

THE LAST TRUMP. A play. By James Bridie. Friday,
August 5, 1938.

ST JOAN. Revival of Bernard Shaw's play. Saturday,
August 6, 1938.

[*August* 14, 1938]

THE second half of the Malvern week began with Lord
Dunsany's *Alexander*, whose opening line is "At last,
Persepolis." Fatal word! Why did not the author of this
suave charade see that, in the language of the racing correspondent, Persepolis was the danger here? For alas!
Lord Dunsany is not a Marlowe, and though this is not his
fault it must, in the theatre, be our misfortune. We do
not start in our seats as we do when we hear, or should do
if we ever heard, Tamburlaine say:

> " And ride in triumph through Persepolis! "
> Is it not brave to be a king, Techelles?
> Usumcasane and Theridamas,
> Is it not passing brave to be a king,
> " And ride in triumph through Persepolis? "

To which Techelles answers:

> O, my lord, 'tis sweet and full of pomp.

Now this modern play about Alexander, while sweet to
ear and mind, has too little pomp both aural and visual.
A possible reason is that Marlowe, living centuries before
Tom Taylor, was a better disciple of that master-carpenter
than Lord Dunsany, who probably deems Taylor out of
fashion, pretends to be. Old Tom lays it down that the
whole secret of play-writing is to tell an audience what
you're going to do, do it, and tell the audience you've
done it. "Come now, my boys," says Marlowe's Tambur-

154

laine, " I'll have you learn to undermine a town, And make whole cities caper in the air." After which the cities duly caper, and, as a result of the capering, Tamburlaine enters drawn in his chariot by the uncapered kings of Trebizond and Soria, with bits in their mouths. How different is Lord Dunsany's play, where Alexander enskies his cities off-stage! The answer, of course, is that the object of the modern play is not spectacle, but philosophy. Still playing off Marlowe against Dunsany, I seem to remember a passage in *Doctor Faustus* which runs :

> Philosophy is odious and obscure. . . .
> 'Tis magic, magic that hath ravished me.

Alexander is short of magic.

Now there are two ways of producing a play deficient in magic. One is to pretend the magic isn't there; the other is to go out and buy a lot of magic and stick it on. (The half-and-half method adopted at Malvern seems to me to make the worst of both worlds.) Take this passage in which the author appears to covet perhaps not Alexander's ox nor yet his ass, but certainly his elephants and his camels :

COMMANDER OF THE ELEPHANTS. Upon what signal do the elephants march ?

PTOLEMY. When all hail him as the son of God. Where is the captain of the camel-guard ?

CAPTAIN OF THE CAMEL-GUARD. Here, Ptolemy.

PTOLEMY. When the elephants kneel by the throne the camel-guard goes by behind them at the walk, the musicians playing.

CAPTAIN. Yes, Ptolemy.

PTOLEMY. What music have you commanded them to play ?

CAPTAIN. The song that Marthos made in honour of God.

PTOLEMY. Ah, very good. On the golden trumpets ?

CAPTAIN. Yes, Ptolemy.

Could the composer of *Les Troyens* have demanded

better? I note that at the moment this country has neither a Berlioz nor amphitheatres like those at Arles and Nîmes for the proper exploitation of this pagan bombast. But it has a Coliseum and a Drury Lane, and I suggest that an Autumn Drama be made out of this play, with trumpet fanfares specially composed by Mr Louis Armstrong. Let elephants with jewelled howdahs and camels with pearl-cinct humps be the principal actors. As subsidiaries let Mr Donat and Mr Olivier, clad in gold armour, take it in turns to climb Alexander's throne by as many steps as the late Julian Wylie considered essential to a Palace Scene. Let Miss Dorothy Ward play the Queen of the Amazons by day, and Miss Phyllis Neilson-Terry play her by night. (I thought that Mr Donald Wolfit showed too much modern sensitiveness. For isn't Alexander's whole point his overweeningness and his despair at there being nothing more to ween over? I thought Miss Daphne Heard not at all bad as the Queen of the Amazons, while wondering whether not at all bad is good enough.) Let the scenery be by Chirico, with Xerxes' fallen statue looking like a piece of derelict Blackpool rock. Let Alexander's orgy be Cochranesque. Let everybody look about nine feet high. Let the chorus-gentlemen be rigged out in Mr Messel's beards, greaves, and shields, and let the chorus-ladies consult Miss Doris Zinkeisen. And if criticism can be more constructive I should like to see a sample of it.

"Your veins," said Tamburlaine's physician to his master, "are full of accidental heat. The humidum and calor now are spent; Which, being the cause of life, imports your death." All very much what, in Mr Bridie's *Last Trump*, Sir Gregory Butts says to the financier Buchlyvie. Only he puts it less poetically, though to our young moderns "arteries like a mouldering heap of rusty drain-pipes" is probably a very good line of poetry. The point is how to get Buchlyvie well. He is nervous about angina pectoris, and the idea occurs to Sir Gregory that one way to drive out a latent fear is to give the patient an active and immediate one. Wherefore it is pretended that the world is going to explode to-morrow morning.

The trouble with this play, as I see it, is that its major plot should explode twenty minutes after the curtain has risen instead of twenty minutes before it falls. But then Mr Bridie, except in his Biblical adaptations, never seems able to write one play at a time. On this occasion he has no less than three on the stocks at once. The first is as stated. The other two are concerned with the old question of destroying a countryside to make a town, and that old thing about whether young people in love should dispense with marriage. These two by-plays take up two-thirds of an evening which we should like to see wholly devoted to Mr Pettingell's financier and Mr Trouncer's physician. And, of course, we want to hear what Mr Bridie has to say on the question of world-annihilation-before-morning. Alas! he fobs us off with jokes—witty and entertaining, but only jokes. Why cannot Mr Bridie for once, like Matthew Arnold, be wholly serious? Why must he write little plays around big themes? Why does he write them as a snipe flies? Why does he commit the supreme mistake of keeping his best character out of his last act? Why, oh why, did not Mr Trouncer appear to trounce this dyspeptic world as he trounced that self-indulgent millionaire?

Why not turn Mr Shaw's *St Joan* into an opera? How Mozartian could be that trio for Warwick, Cauchon, and the Chaplain in Scene IV! Scene V contains a Verdi-ish sextet for Joan, Dunois, La Hire, Gilles de Rais, the Archbishop, and the Dauphin, all disposed about the steps of the cathedral. Why not a baritone and Rossini-like " Stogumber-here, Stogumber-there," followed by a bass aria on a familiar model, but this time on heresy? Joan's opportunities for *Una Voce*-ing are too obvious to need pointing out. Then how about a couple of Soldiers'

Choruses, one French, t'other English? And for Wagner-ish finale, a trio of Loire Maidens, a Warwick's Farewell, and a Closing Scene with Joan bel-canto-ing at the stake surrounded by a Meyerbeer-ish chorus. If any opera pro-ducer will trust me I will guarantee to do less harm to this great masterpiece than those balletomanes who would make Hamlet dance a polonaise round the body of Polonius.

"Motors at a quarter past eleven," said the Malvern doorkeeper. What an optimist! The performance was not over till the following week—to be exact, at five minutes past twelve on Sunday morning. Our weariness was not that of excessive vigil; the trouble was rather the play's failure to synchronise its dramatic and philosophic endings. In the theatre the piece finishes with Warwick's " I wonder." What a pity that Mr Shaw, whose prefaces are so helpful in explaining what we are going to enjoy, did not confine his Epilogue to the printed page, explain-ing what we have enjoyed! But, Epilogue or no Epilogue, the play remains one of the greatest glories of the English Theatre in this or any other age.

Are we to consider Miss Bergner's Joan as a perform-ance of Joan or just a performance? Think of all the things the preface tells us Joan must be. The most notable of Warrior Saints; the queerest fish of the Middle Ages; the pioneer of rational dress; the first Napoleonic realist; a Galtonic visualiser; a sane and shrewd country girl of extraordinary strength of mind and hardihood of body; a born boss. I do not think that the most indiscriminate of Miss Bergner's admirers would claim that her Joan is any of these things, and as a discriminating admirer I did not expect that it would be. That which I foresaw this ex-quisite little actress would achieve she did with miracu-lous, breath-taking beauty. She was like the six cherub heads in Reynolds's picture all rolled into one. She was like the Seraphim when they are not crying. In the early scenes she had a purity and a gaiety that brought the house to the verge of tears. She was mystical; she was rapt. In the trial scene she but half-listened to her tormentors, her ear still leaned to her voices. In short, I do not think I have seen an actress better fulfil what her physical means permit her to do than did Miss Bergner in the childish aspects of Joan. But bless me! as Charles Lamb would have said, how little she looked in her armour! How waif-like, how Tiny Tim-like—always provided that little tear-compeller was not too virile for Tiny Joan. Now one realised the secret of that inviolacy. Joan was the Luck of that French Roaring Camp. Her soldiers regarded her as Bret Harte's ruffians regarded their mascot. This was a Babe-in-arms as well as a Babe-in-armour. "There is a dangerous power in her outbursts," says the Archbishop. This was not true of Miss Bergner, whose outbursts had a pitiful and touching weakness. The point about Miss Thorndike's obstinate young woman was that she argued like blazes and made us think that blazes were an appropriate end. One felt that, given the century, the Thorndike Joan had nothing to complain of, whereas Miss Bergner made one want to rush upon the stage and rescue her. And Joan is just not rescuable.

The whole piece was, for a Festival, wonderfully well done, with excellent playing by Messrs Wolfit, Pettingell, Twiss, and Clunes. The way the last-named carried the piece through its first half was beyond praise. And for our special delight we were permitted to look again upon the quaintly humorous, pathetically wry, wholly Alice-in-Wonderland Dauphin of Mr Thesiger.

Two Views of Zola

THOU SHALT NOT—— A play. Translated from Zola's *Thérèse Raquin* by Alexander Texeira de Mattos. Playhouse Theatre, Wednesday, August 24, 1938.

[*August* 28, 1938]

A DISTINGUISHED critic has made three points of the greatest possible interest in connection with this revival. But first, in case people have forgotten Zola's play, let me run through the plot. The setting is a small draper's shop in a squalid corner of Paris, presided over by the strong-willed, doting Madame Raquin, whose weakling son, Camille, has married her niece Thérèse. The marriage is one of name only. Presently Thérèse takes a lover, who, with his mistress's connivance, murders Camille by tipping him out of a boat on one of those Sunday excursions by the Seine dear to the French *petit bourgeois*. A year later the guilty pair marry. But they cannot sleep; Camille's drowned face has murdered sleep. In the course of a quarrel they reveal their guilt to the old woman, who has a stroke. For a time she can neither speak nor write, and they live in daily fear of her recovery and that denunciation which they read in her eyes. One day it becomes obvious that she is getting better. Whereupon the pair take poison.

My eminent colleague tells us first that the play's attack, though magnificent, is not true. Second, that, though a woman is more than her crime, Zola writes as if the crime were all Thérèse. Third, that the story would have been more deeply moving if Zola " had permitted us to witness the longing and thwarted attempts of Thérèse and Laurent to love each other, if he had allowed them still to hope as men and women do; above all, if he had been able to communicate the truth that no murderer is, to himself, as other murderers are, but exceptional, pitiable, isolated by special circumstances, desiring appeasement as a child desires refuge from a storm!" "All this"—Mr Morgan goes on to say—"Zola misses and—let there be no mistake—deliberately sacrifices." I propose to show that there *is* mistake, that Zola sacrifices nothing because there is nothing to sacrifice. Indeed at this point I find myself wondering whether Mr Morgan can have forgotten that preface to the second edition of the novel specially written by Zola to make just this point of non-sacrifice. "This tragedy is not true," writes my colleague, "but it is magnificent." Zola's point is that his tragedy is sordid, but of intense reality.

The argument that Thérèse should be more than her crime brings up a matter that has been insufficiently probed—the aura of past impersonations by familiar players. Over and over again we have admired the subtlety of Miss Cathleen Nesbitt's creations—bloodless women without appetite, dependent on their nerves as a puppet on his wires, so many Hedda Gablers. But is Thérèse such a creature? I think not. Remember Zola's description in the novel: "One was conscious that beneath that apparent torpor were suppleness wholly feline, strong muscles, and a vast capacity for passion. . . . Beneath a purposefully calm exterior Thérèse concealed the fierce ardours of her nature. . . . To the outward eye she was calm and indifferent; her inner life was one of burning, uncontrollable desire." Miss Nesbitt wonderfully suggests this torridity of flesh, these damped-down bodily fires. But why must we draw the inference that Thérèse is a spiritual volcano? Why not be satisfied with Zola's statement that Thérèse's complicity in the murder is brought about by the frustration of her physical senses?

I am going to suggest that it is the miscasting of that admirable actor Mr Henry Oscar which has led Mr Morgan

to see in Zola's play more than Zola intended anybody to
see. Mr Oscar normally gives me more pleasure than
almost any other player. The best actor in the world for
suggesting compunction's natural prey, Mr Oscar is wildly
wrong as *un grand gaillard* possessed of broad shoulders,
the neck of a bull, hands to fell an ox—the build of your
all-in wrestler. It is just that quality of physical clum-
siness which, in Charles Bovary, so displeased Emma that
Thérèse finds enchanting. And Laurent's mind goes with
his physique. He is a healthy animal who takes Thérèse for
mistress because she will cost him less than the woman of
the streets. He murders Camille out of prudence, and after
the murder his trouble is not remorse, but the fear of
Camille's ghost. In what way, then, does Mr Morgan want
these two criminals to be more than their crime? Are they
to indulge in speculations on the nature of murder? But
they are not the speculative sort. Are they to explore that
apartness from other murderers for which William Bolitho
coined the phrase "demoniac Narcissism"? But they are
not aware of any such apartness.

Now Zola, while steadily refusing to give us more of
the criminal than their crime, expands that crime to include what comes after. I have no doubt the ultra-sensi-
tive school would like this to mean that Thérèse and
Laurent lie awake o' nights exchanging confidences of the
order of "The time has been, that, when the water was
in, the man was out," and "Who would have thought a
drowned man swelled so horribly?" But our couple have
long ago put all that behind them; their only fear is that
old Madame Raquin may recover. Except that after a
time Laurent becomes conscious of another fear. He has
begun to notice a change in Thérèse. She goes out more
than she used to. Can it be that her nerves are driving
her towards confession? Confession to whom? A priest?
The police? Laurent watches her and discovers that her
rendezvous is of the most ordinary. "But that's all right"

is his relieved comment. "A lover will keep her mind busy. What a bit of luck! No trouble with the police now." And he wonders why he has not thought of the same thing. After a bit he does think of it, and it is Thérèse who finds the money for his succession of mistresses. It goes without saying that none of this could have been put on the stage of the 'eighties, which, in Paris, was still glued to the old Dumasian ethics. In France, as everywhere else except Norway, the drama was fifty years behind the novel.

When Zola's book first came out there had been a howl of execration. The French reviewers, with their talk of *ordure et puanteur*, said the same things the English dramatic critics were presently to say about Ibsen. It is the old story of scenting moral implications where an author has merely nosed for facts. An ulcer, said Zola, is an ulcer, and for a demonstrator to point one out to his students is neither moral nor immoral: "I write as analyst pure and simple. I may be absorbed in putrefaction, but it is the absorption of the surgeon in his operating theatre." And now for the operative passage which so utterly demolishes any theory of a larger life for Zola's characters: "*Thérèse Raquin* is intended as a study not of character but of temperament. This is the whole book. I have chosen two persons entirely dominated by their nerves and blood-stream, knowing nothing whatever about free will, and whose every act is dictated by impulses of the flesh. Thérèse and Laurent are brutes in the guise of human beings, nothing more. I have tried to show, step by step, the way passion works in these brutes; how they are swayed by their instincts; how they cannot escape the mental deterioration which follows on the heels of nervous excitement. The love-making of my precious couple is the satisfaction of a need; the murder they commit proceeds from their adultery, and is looked upon by them as wolves look upon the murder of a sheep. Finally, what I have called remorse is no more than physical disorder, the protest of two nervous systems which have reached breaking-point. Soul is entirely lacking, I am happy to say, and principally because I have willed it so." Here, then, is the subnormal humanity of Mr James Cain. Thérèse and Laurent are the Cora and Frank of *The Postman Always Rings Twice* fifty years before their time.

Zola wrote his preface to remove any possibility of future misunderstanding. Alas for the vanity of human wishes! Either Mr Morgan or I have misunderstood him. My colleague says: " The dreadful consistency of Zola's work is at once its power as a theatrical onslaught and its defect as an interpretation of life." But how can that fail to be an interpretation which is not intended to be one? Zola ruled out interpretation when he wrote: " They are brutes, nothing more." " There is," says Mr Morgan, " in life, a certain moderation, an irregularity in the working of Fate; she plays her victims or, in Hardy's language, has ' sport ' with them." But did Hardy use sport in quite this sense? Isn't his sentence—I quote from memory— " The President of the Immortals, in Æschylean phrase, had ended his sport with Tess "? Meaning, surely, not that the god had finished playing Tess like a fish, but that the fun of cat-and-mouse with this particular mouse was exhausted. Perhaps Mr Morgan and I are not very far apart here. Where we differ is in thinking that high-souled Æschylus has any business in a galley of soulless brutes. What would Mr Morgan say if one set up Zola's soulless brutes as the standard by which to measure soulful adumbrations in a play by Mr Morgan?

I am in abstract discussion stepp'd in too far to get back to the material performance. I can only offer further apologies to Miss Nancy Price, Mr Bromley-Davenport, Mr Morris Harvey, and Mr Brian Oulton for their contributions to an evening of exceptional interest.

Mr Morgan's Play

THE FLASHING STREAM. A play. By Charles Morgan. Lyric Theatre, Thursday, September 1, 1938.

[*September* 4, 1938]

Her passions are made of nothing but the finest part of pure love.
                                                        Antony and Cleopatra

CAN a man embrace pure love—' pure ' in the exact opposite of Enobarbus's sense—as he embraces pure mathematics or pure poetry ?   I think the answer is to be found in Stevenson's remarks on the Permanent Possibility of Sensation. As it is within the area of conjecture that here and there a reader may be a little vague about those remarks, I permit myself to jog his memory. Philosophy's definition of life, says Stevenson, " is a Permanent Possibility of Sensation."   He goes on : " Truly a fine result ! A man may very well love beef, or hunting, or a woman ; but surely, not a Permanent Possibility of Sensation ! " How the author of our play must have shuddered at the trist anastomosis !   Then again : " As for caring about the Permanence of the Possibility, a man's head is generally very bald, and his senses very dull, before he comes to that."

But some of us have said much the same thing about the age a man must be to accept the definition of love as set forth in Mr Morgan's novels. Not to shift the blame on other shoulders, I remember a certain uneasiness with regard to that letter in *The Fountain* :

> I do not believe that the bodily delight of love is sin, but that it becomes a deadly betrayal wherever a human relationship is obsessed by the acceptance, or by the desire of it. Either you and I were by our discovery of each other made gods with power to create, in our

165

relationship, a perdurable essence, higher than ourselves,
independent of our delights, or we were animals caught
in a trap. . . . Our love was a predestined force that
would create of itself a personality—a hypostasis—more
beautiful and vital and lasting than ourselves, or it was
a sterile pleasure, no more.

In this, his first play, Mr Morgan has realised that
whereas disembodied ecstasy is feasible on the stage, bodi-
less ecstatics are infeasible. Wherefore his characters are
a flesh-and-blood lot, very much the people you and I
might meet at dinner. Which, again, does not prevent
them from talking out of full and firm minds. The hero of
this play makes the first full-throated statement of the
theme at which its author has often hinted: " A man's
love for a woman, though one of the expressions of it be
carnal, may be the very air in which his soul grows."
Novelists, explains Edward Ferrers to Karen Selby, are
wrong in their delineation of love as an arithmetical pro-
gression, passing from sentiment to sublimation through
a middle stage of passion. "Love is all things at
once," declares Ferrers, "a cake to eat and something
to worship." The theme once announced, every reed
and stop is pressed into service of this grand Morgan
Voluntary.

And now it is time to explain who these people are.
Commander Edward Ferrers, R.N. (Mr Godfrey Tearle), is
in charge of a naval experimental station on an island in
the Atlantic. He and four more officers are at work on a
torpedo which is to destroy enemy aircraft. Ferrers is a
mathematical genius, and as much in love with his science
as an artist with his art. His right-hand man, Selby,
dying, it is proposed that Selby's sister Karen (Miss Margaret Rawlings), also a first-class mathematician, shall
take Selby's place. Ferrers objects on the ground that an
equation is one thing and a personal equation another,
and that in properly conducted naval stations never the

twain shall meet. In the end he consents. Which brings us to the curtain of the first act.

In the second act interest is divided between the swaying fortunes of the experiment and the gravitation towards each other of Ferrers and Karen. The reader must now be told that this play is like some river rich in tributaries, creeks, and inlets—one of which is the discussion of the pure mind in the incontinent body. Also that, since it would be impossible to deal fully with this play at shorter length than the play itself, I shall confine what follows to the main stream. Ferrers, very much the conquering male, tells Karen that he is to be her god or nothing. This noways displeases Karen, who in the matter of subjugation to her lord is a pattern for Sultanas. But by ' god ' Ferrers means a mathematical god; his invention has to succeed or there will be no marriage. For, argues Ferrers, how can he remain a god who was once regarded as a mathematical genius but has been relegated by failure to the depths of schoolmastering and the heights of Swiss Cottage—a degradation known only to Viceroys declining from elephants with jewelled mahouts to a couple of housemaids in Kensington Gore? The experiment does in fact fail; there is much excitement in the tussle between an impatient Admiralty, playing into the hands of an Admiral's jealous lady, and mathematical theorists of genius denied sufficient time to perfect the practical workings of their gadgets. This brings us to the curtain of the second act.

Mr Morgan has confessed that in order to ensure an ending which should not disappoint he wrote his third act first. And I am to suggest to our playwright that the beginning of his third act is precisely the point at which Ibsen would have begun his play. How well one knows that opening, not at Swiss Cottage, but in some worm-eaten Nordic cot. John Gabriel Ferrers and Hilda Wrangle Selby have been married seven years; five children cluster round their four knees. Throughout three acts we learn of all that happened in the Atlantic eight or nine years before. We see the jealous, mischief-making lady, now in the guise of a nautical Thea Elvsted, turning up at Hilda's house carrying Ella Rentheim's melancholy valise. She is the senior wrangler of the two. From time to time we see Hilda going to a cupboard to take out a Vibrational Equation, pet it, and put it back as John Gabriel returns from the schoolhouse, takes off his goloshes, and draws from his coat that bundle of exercise books which he has brought home for correction. His impatient thrusting into the fire of some brat's discovery that two and two make five gives the clue to the ' total gesture ' of Ibsen's play, which is that a hypostasis by becoming unendurable ceases to be perdurable. But that is not the play Mr Morgan wrote, *and nothing will induce me, as a lover of pure criticism, to blame him for not having written it!*

No! Mr Morgan's way with this piece has been the Swan of Avon's way in *Antony and Cleopatra*, whose spirit has been hanging about ever since the curtain went up. It was not for nothing that Miss Rawlings made her first appearance in a veil or cloud exactly like the traditional headgear—called, I think, a nemis—of the Queen of Egypt. Now it is a fault in human nature, though an excusable fault, to imagine that the rest of the world is *au fait* with one's particular hobbies. Shakespeare's play is a critic's play, and I doubt very much whether anybody except a critic would be able to answer off-hand the question put by the First Lord of the Admiralty (Mr Felix Aylmer) to Karen: " What did Pompey say to Menas ? " The answer, of course, is : " In me 'tis villany ; In thee't had been good service."

Here is the point. The First Lord has said to Ferrers : " If you will admit to an error in your mathematics I will give you time to correct it. But if you hold by your mathematics I must call off your experiment, as it just doesn't work." To which Ferrers has replied : " Deny my mathematics ? Go back on the multiplication-table ? O Weederdee ! The scientist's pole is fall'n ; boy and girl mathematicians are level now with men ; the odds is gone." And so on and so forth, all in Shakespeare's best Egyptian manner. Whereupon Karen, who has been desperately recalling her High School lessons in English Literature, suddenly remembers the incident in Pompey's galley and starts a scene of excellent dissembling. She has been through Antony's calculations and has found a squiggly little error gnawing at the square root of one of them. " Excellent ! " says the First Lord. " Now you can have all the time you want to put your calculations right." And Ferrers overlooks the insult to the purity of his mathematics in the joy of getting enough time to make his gadgets work properly. After which Karen confesses her stratagem and is forgiven. Last we are to presume that the experiment is successful, that this country becomes immune from raiding aeroplanes, that Ferrers gets an earldom and a grant of cash, and that henceforth he and his Countess enjoy a hypostasis which has no reason for not being perdurable.

Well, this third act is exciting, though I confess a sneaking curiosity as to what would have happened to this pure passion if, after marriage, the couple had been unable to square the milkman's circle or box the butcher's compass. But, taking it for all in all, *The Flashing Stream* is a magnificent play, at once subtle in thought and downright in exposition, swift in action and noble in expression. It is a compactom of philosophy about passionate truth and impersonal passion. Every sentence, every word, has the thing which matters most in a man, a horse, a piece of writing, or work of any sort if it is only laying one brick on top of another—quality. Mr Morgan has dug his play out of a marble quarry with a pickaxe of gold tipped with witty steel. For his play, while being intensely serious, takes care to be immense theatre and good fun as well.

Mr Tearle magnificently suggests the artist consumed by his own flame, the man of science to whom scientific truth is this world and the next. Miss Rawlings matches this fine performance with a lovely sweep of passion in all its manifestation—physical, spiritual, maternal; in short, the *ewig weibliche* in full tide and spate. Not a word wrong, not a movement out of place. Grandly they sing and act the love-duet from *Tristan*, while poring over blue-prints of rhomboids and parallelopipeds. Grandly sine calls to cosine; passion, constant, declines to go off at a tangent. Will Mr Morgan forgive me if I say that he will not know what he owes to this superb pair till he sees what Hollywood makes of his " impersonal passion " ? I trust his answer will be Lear's: " Never, never, never, never, never ! "

There are contributory performances of great skill and charm by Miss Marda Vanne, Mr Aylmer—a delicate piece of acting, this—Mr Leo Genn, Mr Anthony Ireland, Mr H. G. Stoker, Mr Desmond Roberts, and Mr Roger Maxwell. Mr Peter Creswell's production is impeccable, and the house on the first night received the piece with so much enthusiasm that I can almost predict a Possibility of Sensational Permanence.

Shakespeare Comes Home

HENRY V. Revival of Shakespeare's play. Drury Lane Theatre, Friday, September 16, 1938.

DEAR OCTOPUS. A play. By Dodie Smith. Queen's Theatre, Wednesday, September 14, 1938.

PAPRIKA. A musical comedy. Book by Eric Maschwitz. Music by George Posford and Bernard Grün. His Majesty's Theatre, Thursday, September 15, 1938.

THE LAST TRUMP. A play. By James Bridie. Duke of York's Theatre, Tuesday, September 13, 1938.

[September 18, 1938]

THIS play,'' once wrote Mr Beerbohm of *Henry V*, '' should be done brilliantly, splendidly, or not at all. Only the best kind of acting, and the best kind of production, could make it anything but tedious. Except a few purple patches of poetry, it contains nothing whatsoever of merit. It is just a dull, incoherent series of speeches, interspersed with alarums and excursions. As a spectacle, it might be made much of. Mimes might, by exercise of much imagination, make the speeches interesting and impressive. With a very keen sense of character, they might give life and individuality to the puppets.''

Granted these premises, I must conclude that the production at Drury Lane would entwine itself round that fastidious organ which is Mr Beerbohm's heart. As a spectacle the play is made much of. The scene is gay, and shows the Middle Ages not as the dingy, snuff-coloured thing they probably were, but decked out in brilliant blues, yellows, and crimsons, pageant-wise. And since no piece can be always gay there is here and there a hint of grave, realistic, and even modern beauty. Picardy, for example, looks like the Picardy that the English recently knew—featureless hillsides sloping to a dull river, whose banks are dotted with pollard-willows. This is not a back-cloth excitedly seen from a stall, but a panorama patiently gazed at from a box marked " *Hommes* 40, *Chevaux* 8." Or was the order the other way about? How dim these memories grow!

Yes, I think this is the right way for this theatre to make much of Shakespeare's play. For Drury Lane is in a peculiar position. Shakespeare, in this theatre, is not a man wooing a new mistress, but an old mistress trying to creep back into favour and decking herself with forced and absurd coquetry. Does the brave tune, which bands on- and off-stage play a trifle too often, court too many worlds? Does it try to be Elgarish, Hope-and-Gloryish, and at the same time not lose touch with the modern theme song? Of course it does. But is anybody going to tell me that Drury Lane's customers of to-day pine for the skirling of fifteenth-century pipes, or whatever instrument the fifteenth-century equivalent of *Tipperary* was played on? Does there hang about the stage the faint suggestion that the piece should have been called *Sanders of the Channel*? For the life of me I can't see why not. Even so, I do not agree with the theory that Shakespeare would have approved these marvels of modern production because of a seeming yearning for production indicated in this play's prologue. All sensible people have always regarded that prologue as a mere poetic *façon de parler*. Shakespeare knew perfectly well that the "vasty fields of France" would be too vast for his, Marlowe's, or anybody else's mighty line. The actor has never lived who could make Henry's speeches effective if delivered in Wembley Stadium, or even the stadium at Harringay. Even Drury Lane is a very near thing, though in the past it was not so. But then the old actors were expected to have voices, whereas in your modern actor voice, when it exists, is thrown in as something over and above the bargain.

Now Mr Novello has a voice, and though a little light in timbre it will do. He comes on to the stage helped by his enormous popularity, yet in a sense hindered by it. Harry's growing indignation with which this play's war begins—can we quite distinguish this from the note of fracas sounded at the end of Mr Novello's plays about parties? Well, if we can't we are bad playgoers. And, since the scenery has already made the " centuries kiss and commingle," why should not the acting do the same thing? After all, King Henry has only just stopped being Prince Hal, and I do not think it is wildly un-Shakespearian to suggest that the scapegrace companion of Falstaff had a good deal in common with to-day's man-about-Mayfair. This may not be the whole of the character, and I recommend Mr Novello to study, if he does not already know, Montague's " Shakespeare's Way with Agincourt." But it is one side of Henry, and if Mr Novello can deepen it a little he will end by being a very good, complete Henry. He has fire where fire should be; the prayer before the battle and the reading of the list of the dead are movingly done; and the soliloquy beginning " Upon the King . . ." has an entirely admirable cogency. It may be that Mr Novello is not yet a sufficiently experienced Shakespearian actor to hold the house with a bare stage. But he is not asked to. He is asked to persuade playgoers to flock to Shakespeare on a crowded stage. And he has responded nobly. An excellent cast gives him excellent support.

A letter received :

DEAR MR AGATE,

As I sat in my lofty perch at the Queen's Theatre to-night and watched the back of your head sauntering resignedly back to its stall after each interval, I found myself reflecting : " Ah, yes, Mr Agate, you'll tell us next Sunday that *Dear Octopus* is just another commercial success

without any artistry about it ! " What I do honestly want
to know is why you rave about a play like Tchehov's *Three
Sisters* and pooh-pooh what seems to me to be its English
equivalent. If Miss Smith had devised a hoax and called her
family not the Randolphs but the Randolovs, with Marie
Tempest and Leon Quartermaine still at the head of it
holding a Russian golden wedding, with the children im-
personated by John Gielgud, Valerie Taylor, Madge
Compton, and Nan Munro, renamed Nikolai, Nina,
Natalia, and Nadya—in this case, will you please tell me
what would prevent you from being taken in ? Say, too,
the nursery was full of Russian toys, and that Angela
Baddeley's part was rechristened Dunyasha ? How, again,
is the timbre of the stable-clock heard by the grown-up
children inferior in melancholy to Tchehov's distant
noises ? Do answer this, I honestly want to know.

Yours,
GALLERYITE

And here is my reply :

DEAR GALLERYITE,

I am afraid you do not read my writings as sedulously
as you should. You see, I have been before you in spotting
Miss Dodie Smith's resemblance to Tchehov. If you will
turn up the *Sunday Times* for November 17, 1935, you will
find in my article on the Old Vic revival of *Three Sisters*
the following : " If, like Bunthorne, you are fond of touch-
and-go jocularity, Tchehov is the shop for it. Now is there
or is there not an overtone in the phrase ' touch-and-go ' ? "
You realise, of course, that Miss Dodie Smith, under the
name of C. L. Anthony, had just written a play called
Touch Wood. My article went on : " It occurs to me that
Three Sisters is a purely arbitrary title, and that Tchehov
would have been just as pleased to name his piece *Call It a
Lifetime*. Between you and me, reader, I have always
suspected this dramatist of being the lightest of his kind,

174

the C. L. Antonovich of Russia!" You also realise that
another of Miss Smith's plays was named *Call It a Day*.
And here, perhaps, if I were in a lazy mood I might leave
the matter, though with an uneasy suspicion that your
letter is still not fully answered.

But this is too early in the week for laziness, and the
explicit challenge of your letter does, perhaps, deserve a
more explicit answer. There are two incidents and four
characters in Miss Smith's latest play which are pure
Tchehov. The first incident is the striking of the stable-
clock, which you have already spotted. The second is that
something which brushes Miss Nan Munro's forehead, and
may be the touch of a departed hand or merely a moth.
Both incidents could go into any Tchehov play and not
appear out of place. Two of the four Tchehovian characters are the daughter who comes home after an unhappy
love affair abroad, and the little girl who finds her dead
mother in her aunt—the relationship here is left quite
exquisitely unexplained. The quartet is completed by
Nanny, the overworked companion who might be any
Russian serf in love with her young master, and by Hilda,
whose compulsional neuroses might be part of the make-
up of the German governess in *The Cherry Orchard*.

But, dear Galleryite, note this. A Tchehov play is all of
a piece; it is one lot of soil out of which everything grows
naturally. Whereas Miss Smith's play is like a bed in
which the gardener has stuck a few choice plants. There
are whole characters and incidents in the play which not
only do not belong to Tchehov, but hardly belong to Miss
Smith. Take the old lady who rules this family. Do you
not perceive that this is not a character at all, but something that exists solely by virtue of an actress's poise,
attack, verve, and those fifty years of consummate
artistry which have enabled this particular actress, Dame
Marie Tempest, to create life where no life is? Consider
the part of that other old lady, her sister. Do you not

perceive that this comes out of the stock-pot of late Victorian drama, and might be a figure in a play by Jones, Carton, Davies, Lonsdale, almost anybody ? Here again the playwright owes her success entirely to the ageless glitter of Miss Kate Cutler. Then take the male head of the family, and compare that shadow of a shade with a creation of such intensity and fullness as Tchebutykin; I thought it ingenious of Mr Leon Quartermaine to send on a velvet jacket to deputise for him in this part. Consider the son of the house who, just because Miss Smith wants a happy ending, discovers a belated passion for the companion, so that we must suppose him to settle down in life like Clement Hale with Sweet Lavender. Here the abstracted look in Mr Gielgud's eye was a mute appeal to the house to pretend that he had left the cast and that somebody else was winding up the play for him. There was one more grown-up male character. Did not nature abhor a vacuum I should say that the part played by Mr Felix Irwin was it. To put it bluntly, there is not a line in the play to suggest that Miss Smith can draw a male character.

I must not bore you with any further tale of divergences. Let me conclude by saying that though this play is immensely entertaining, the author of *Autumn Crocus* has still a long way to go to justify comparison with the great Russian's October gardens and November woods.

Yours sincerely,

JAMES AGATE

Mr Maschwitz, who presents his—to put it mildly—non-success, knows what the British public demands in its inanities. First, the outlay of a sum large enough to endow with a permanent repertory theatre a town the size of Taunton or Kettering. Second, a pseudo-Viennese score totally indistinguishable from any other pseudo-Viennese score. Third, a plot so drivelling that the spectator must go on looking straight in front of him since shame will not let him look at his neighbour. Fourth, an utter absence of wit. Fifth, the engagement of a number of distinguished artists who appear in the first scene and then retire to their dressing-rooms to pat shirt-fronts and fiddle with bracelets until, in the last scene, they come on again.

Mr Maschwitz has lavishly carried out these behests. £30,000 has obviously been spent on the scenery and clothes. The near-good music might be by any near-good composer. In the foyer, between the acts, friends stood back to back lest, face to face, they might be tempted to discuss the plot. There was not a line out of which the combined geniuses of Arthur Roberts, Pélissier, and Grock could have got a laugh. Artists like Miss Helen Haye and Mr Malcolm Keen put one in mind of the epitaph for an infant dying young:

> If so soon I must be done for,
> I don't know what I was begun for.

Mr Maschwitz did more. He threw in some graceful quotations from earlier masterpieces in this genre. The scene in the café recalled a similar scene in *Bitter Sweet*, with Mr Austin Trevor threatening a peasant girl about to sing in grand opera with the extremest rigours of Magyar jealousy.

But Mr Maschwitz forgot one thing, which is that all shows of this kind must be built up and round a talent. It doesn't matter much what kind of talent, so long as it is genuine and there is a lot of it. It may be the voice and artistry of an Evie Greene. It may be the nimble feet and dancing brains of a Binnie Hale. It may be the sheer likeableness of a Peggy Wood, the generosity of spirit of a José Collins, the charm of a Gertie Millar or a Lily Elsie. It may even be the uncomplicated good looks of a Marie Studholme or an Edna May. Whatever it may be it must exist without disputation. And, alas, Mr Maschwitz has not built his show up to, or round, any comparable talent ! But for the grace, poise, and period sense of Miss Stella Arbenina as the Empress of Austria, the evening would have been entirely embarrassing.

Mr Bridie's Buchlyvie is a monument to unlikeableness. Sir Seymour Hicks is a mountain of charm. How bring the two together ? Obviously by making each go half-way. Sir Seymour is ready with his half, but the monument, alas ! won't budge. Now in going half-way this beautiful actor has done more than could be expected of him. He has stuck putty on his nose. He has betrayed the world's wittiest upper-lip by hiding it under a hirsute horror, to wit, a moustache. But the twinkle in the eyes remains, and monuments, alas ! do not twinkle. Monuments do, possibly, pause, though not as often as Sir Seymour. Perhaps I am making an unnecessary fuss about what was merely first-night preoccupation. But the too-long pauses did suggest that Buchlyvie was not Buchlyvie, but Macready sitting on a monument smiling at the notion of drying up.

Waggery at Westminster

TROILUS AND CRESSIDA. Revival of Shakespeare's play. Westminster Theatre, Wednesday, September 21, 1938.

THE CORN IS GREEN. A comedy. By Emlyn Williams. Duchess Theatre, Tuesday, September 20, 1938.

GOOD-BYE, MR CHIPS. A play. Adapted by James Hilton and Barbara Burnham from the novel by James Hilton. Shaftesbury Theatre, Friday, September 23, 1938.

[*September* 25, 1938]

THE managements at the Drury Lane and Westminster Theatres seem to me to be faced with the same difficulty, though with an important difference. Drury Lane's difficulty is to persuade people to come to see a popular play; that of the Westminster is to induce them to see an unpopular play. Then why in heaven's name does the Westminster make it more difficult by calling itself the London Mask Theatre? Call a theatre a theatre, a play a play, a management a management, and the average man will be, in the vulgar phrase, all for it. He will at least go with an open mind. But to tie round your venture's neck a label like " Mask " or " Cothurnus " or any other highbrow appellation is like presenting a nervous, untrained horse with the stuffed dummy of a policeman. The horse shies, I shy, and the public shies. And this may be very unfair to the venture. Now let's change the subject.

Is it fair or unfair to this difficult play to present it in modern dress? Mr MacOwan, the producer, tells us in a prefatory note on the programme that much of what Shakespeare wanted to say can only be seen clearly by relating it to contemporary experience. Very much, I suppose, as the boys of Dotheboys Hall could only get a clear vision of spelling by relating it to practical experience, cleaning windows and the like ! What Mr MacOwan is really trying to say, though he does not quite dare, is that he believes the only way of getting people to see a piece they are not inclined to is by giving them something else of the same name that they have more mind to ! The matter of this new-fangled dressing is really very simple. The Elizabethan playgoer, attending an Elizabethan play, heard language that his ears were attuned to, while looking at costumes to which his eyes were accustomed. There was no discrepancy. I suggest that two minutes after the performance had begun the Elizabethan playgoer entirely forgot all about costume, and had his whole attention centred on what the actors were saying. Now, dress up a Shakespeare play in to-day's costume, and what happens ? First, there is a colossal discrepancy between dress and speech. Second, you never stop thinking about the costumes, with the result that you have less attention to spare for what is being talked about.

At this point of the argument the reader will want to know why I should object to Mr MacOwan's discrepancy when I don't object to M. Giraudoux's. In the case of *Amphitryon 38* we heard new speech wedded to old costume, which is the opposite of old speech and new costume. But the point in M. Giraudoux's case was that the mythological costumes were more or less what one expected mythological people to be wearing. Wherefore, having spent two minutes in appraising the costumes, we thought no more about them. Wherefore discrepancy vanished. But it doesn't vanish at the Westminster. I defy anybody not to go on being intrigued by the costumes. Then wasn't the room placed by Pandarus at the disposal of the lovers exactly like your shop-window advertising a bedroom-suite for forty shillings down and the balance spread over forty years ? Wasn't Pandarus exactly like the regretted Mr Dulcimer ? Wasn't his bringing of the morning tea exactly like a Shakespearean skit in a

revue by Mr Farjeon? Wouldn't the song he sang at the
piano admirably suit Mr Rex Evans? How did the soldiers
of old tell the rank of their officers, since they didn't seem
to be wearing badges? What were the wars, prior to the
Trojan war, in which they won so many medals? How
could any horse drag Hector's body through that field of
barbed wire? Didn't Thersites' deplorable suit and fag
never out of his mouth exactly suggest a Hyde Park
orator in one of Mr Sean O'Casey's essays in London
sociology? Was not Ulysses' " since things in motion
sooner catch the eye than what not stirs " the forerunner
of the winking sky-sign?

Yes, there were a lot of things in Mr MacOwan's production to attract and hold the attention. But so far as
I was concerned—and I cannot speak for anybody else—
they attracted and held the attention *away* from Shakespeare's tragedy. Of course, there are things in this play
that no monkeying with the manner of its presentation
can spoil. Every line spoken by Mr Robert Speaight's
Ulysses was the purest gold; every word spoken by Mr
Stephen Murray's Thersites was the shrillest vinegar.
Helen, as Mr J. B. Bergel has beautifully pointed out, was
any film star. About Miss Ruth Lodge's Cressida one feels
inclined to repeat the late Grant Allen's remark about
Hedda Gabler—that he took her in to dinner every night!
That Cassandra was just a bore in black velvet was not Miss
Rosanna Seaborn's fault; she is a bore anyhow. Troilus is
inclined to take on wordiness unless there is a Swinley to
speak the verse. Mr Robert Harris tried nobly, but it
wants more than a noble trying to put up with Troilus's
interminable maundering. Men were let down by witchery
long before this young Trojan, and have not made so
much fuss about it. Was Hector quite so lackadaisical a
youth as Mr Colin Keith-Johnston made him? And could
anybody have played Pandarus better than Mr Max
Adrian?

This array of questions shows that the evening was not beggarly, though one didn't feel it had enough to do with Shakespeare to provoke one to a discussion of the play. At least I am not so provoked. I was too much entertained by the modern dressing to think about anything else. And I despised myself for being so entertained.

That *The Corn is Green* is a good little play, and what this good little play is all about, and who acts in it, and how they fare—all these things were the talk of London's smartest grill-room half an hour after the curtain fell, and were doubtless bruited all over the country by breakfast-time next morning. *The Corn is Green* is a simple little story about how a noble-minded woman—who incidentally isn't a fool—decides to bring education to a remote Welsh mining village. Discovering a genius, she grasps her nettle and brings it to flower, fruit, or whatever it is that nettles do. The evening, then, belongs to Dame Sybil Thorndike, who gives one of the sincerest and tenderest performances of her career, and to Mr Emlyn Williams, to whom, as author and actor, must go the credit of staging a man of genius whose genius is manifest and unquestioned. The simplicity of the story can be relied on to throw the spectator into a mood of acceptance of make-believe, from which he need make very occasional sorties to admire this bit of pathos pressed home but not too far home, and the skirting of that bathos which, ever round the corner, never arrives. For this Mr Williams has to thank a sense of wit and humour which is as uncanny as Miss Dodie Smith's sense of how to make characters move naturally among tables and chairs.

It seems to be a rule with Mr Williams that the smaller the part the sharper must be its outline. The piece is full of clever little character sketches, including the usual one for Miss Kathleen Harrison, and one big character sketch. This is the part of the village hussy, faultlessly played from start to finish by Miss Betty Jardine. Miss Jardine will, some day, play Cressida. But what nonsense I am

talking! She plays it brilliantly now, and in this piece.
Modern dress and all. If anybody should want to know
whether I really enjoyed this play I can only say that Mr
Williams, aided by Dame Sybil Thorndike, scored, so far
as I was concerned, two lumps-in-the-throat and a half
lump. And I suggest that this is a very fine score indeed.

Sticklers for dramatic propriety will insist that *Good-
bye, Mr Chips* is not a play at all. Where is the clash of
something or other which betokens something else? Well,
it just isn't there! Is there anything dramatic about
bereavement, or growing old, or falling asleep over the
fire? But a very pleasant evening may be spent in watching this undramatic parade, full of nostalgia to suit every
age. Some wit said the other day: " The English enormously admire any man who has no talent and is modest
about it." In that flash is contained the whole of Mr Chips.
We first see him as a young and shy schoolmaster with a
Number One inferiority complex. Every half-hour or so
marks the passage of ten years, and though his shyness
wears off a little the inferiority complex remains unimpaired. Life passes Mr Chips by, as it passes by any
cog in a wheel which goes on doing the same thing until
it wears out. When Mr Chips wears out it is time to go
home. Does this sound a little dull? I don't think it is.
The evening is rich in studies of school life, and at least
the play moves on a plane on which one can respect it,
which is more than can be said for some of the plays about
schools.

Mr Leslie Banks has followed his authors in presenting
Mr Chips as a placid stream whose strength is its fullness,
and has very cleverly realised that the point about
placidity is not excitement. He lets Mr Chips tell his
own tale, and in the end we have grown to like Mr Chips,
perhaps even a little more than like, and to be able to
place him in the English scene. There are good performances by Miss Gillian Lind and Miss Ann Wilton, by

Messrs Michael Shepley, Godfrey Kenton, Hubert Harben, and Robin Maule, by a crowd of clever schoolboys, and by the furniture. But I beg to inform the producer that in 1878 drivers and brassies did not boast ivory faces! For older playgoers the most beautiful thing in the evening was the playing of Miss Constance Cummings. This had some of the fragrance and pathos, sensitiveness and radiance, of the great actresses of our youth. What I want to know is where Miss Cummings has found the model for acting at once so uncommon and so little common.

Mr Morgan's Play Re-examined

[*October* 2, 1938]

Severe asceticism operates differently on different natures,
and, while there are some whom it does but discipline and refine,
there are more whom it tends to coarsen and to brutalise, even
apart from the many whom it is apt to affect with morbidness,
if not actual insanity.   *Encyclopædia Britannica*

THIS week I propose to attempt the difficult feat of
reconsidering Mr Charles Morgan's *The Flashing Stream*
in the twofold light of my reaction to the play at the time
of its performance at the Lyric Theatre, and as I now
think of it after reading the newly published preface. I do
not suppose there is any power on earth which would
persuade this fastidious spirit to believe that *in the
theatre* the love of Edward Ferrers for Karen Selby is a
high-falutin' interloper, and that, sitting in one's stall,
what one is really anxious about is that aeronautical
experiment. I did not say this in my notice, for the reason
that the play seemed to me to be of that quality which
calls for unmitigated trumpeting, without asides. Con-
frontation with this preface is another matter.

Let us consider that passage which sets forth the
astonishing theory that singleness of mind, which is the
subject of this play, cannot co-exist with a sense of
humour :

> " Blessed are the pure in heart, for they shall see
> God," said Jesus. He had no gift of denigration, no
> joy in derision, no ' sense of humour.' Shakespeare
> had none. Wit and mirth he had, but not the sense of
> humour that is for ever blunting the edge of spiritual
> truth. He who wrote the Sonnets, or Hamlet's bidding
> to Ophelia, or *Troilus and Cressida*, or Cleopatra's scene
> with Mardian had no moderation, no smell of the sixth

form, no sense of humour. Milton had none; Wordsworth none; Shelley none; Nelson none. . . . The sense
of humour by which we are now ruled avoids emotion
and vision and grandeur of spirit as a weevil avoids the
sun. It has banished tragedy from our theatre, elo-
quence from our debates, glory from our years of peace,
splendour from our wars. . . . One by one it has
damped the sparks of life—art, love, duty, faith—until
the Bible has begun to vanish from our language and
Romeo himself speaks to Juliet as if he were a dumb-
waiter offering her an ice. It is talent's sneer at genius,
in whatever form genius appears. It is mediocrity's
hatred of the Spirit of Man, a blanket on vision, a yelp
at saints.

I cannot see in this passage anything except a desire to
make a virtue out of a shortcoming. None of the damping
acts which Mr Morgan rightly condemns proceeds from
anything anybody else except Mr Morgan would recognise
as a sense of humour. That a Romeo cannot declare his
love to Juliet with the ring of real passion is not because
a great actor has too much sense of humour, but because
a little actor has insufficient sense of acting.

Then, again, how can Mr Morgan be so sure that Jesus
had no sense of humour? There is evidence, I think, that
behind the extreme carefulness of every recorded statement lay that sense of balance, that capacity to see all
round things which is part and parcel of the saving grace
of humour. It is never quite sufficiently remarked that in
the incident of the young man who had great possessions
it is not Jesus who seeks an opportunity to condemn
wealth, but a wealthy young man who approaches Jesus.
And that Jesus, being so approached, confines himself
with maximum strictness to the terms of reference laid
down by the young man: " Jesus said unto him, If thou
wilt be perfect. . . ." How can Mr Morgan be certain that
" If thou wilt be perfect " was not a good-humoured
rebuke at the presumptuousness of aiming at an ideal
beyond human capacity? Is it not lawful to connect this

with the words of that other preacher : " Be not righteous over much ; neither make thyself over wise : why shouldest thou destroy thyself ? "

In any case, what is a writer doing discoursing of a sense of humour who in his work shows himself to possess less of that quality than even the late William Archer ? Do I set up to write plays about St Simeon Stylites ? The trouble, of course, is the old one of the confusion of terms. When Mr Morgan writes " humour " he means something else. Singleness of mind may include, and is all the better for including, a sense of humour. What cannot go with singleness of mind is *vulgarity* of mind. Careful readers will have noted the words : " The sense of humour that is forever blunting the edge of spiritual truth." This is flat nonsense. To a full man the possession of humour does not blunt spiritual truth ; it throws it into relief. I am not concerned with what humour does to a recluse, who is not a full man.

Oddly enough this preface reveals that what the play is essentially about is the twelfth verse of that nineteenth chapter of St Matthew from which I have been quoting ! Indeed, Mr Morgan quotes the verse. The play, then, is a re-examination of what is a sane attitude towards sex, from which it emerges that there is a time to enjoy and a time to abstain, and that neither abstention nor non-abstention is more ' moral ' than the other. Consider the view taken about sex in the Dumasian and post-Dumasian theatre—I refer, of course, to the younger Dumas—whose ethics governed our own stage until the coming of Ibsen and Mr Shaw. All good playgoers must remember Montague's passage about the Dumasian half-made woman, " the obtrusively weaker vessel, ' thither all dewy from a convent fetched,' and as breathless with aghast innocence as if she had run all the way." In the Victorian theatre marriage, to such a creature, postulated a violation, a pleasureless sacrifice to the instincts of the grosser male.

Even in Ibsen the woman's share in the companionship is blighted with spirituality, while in Shaw the relationship has the Life Force for ' alibi ' !

Mr Morgan will have none of this. He very finely writes :

> Karen says openly what has, I think, not been said in the theatre for over a hundred years and not by an honourable character since the Elizabethans—that she desires men; and by this she means not that she is indiscriminating or self-indulgent—for evidently she is neither—but that the experience of sex is, in her case, what Nature intended it to be and what in women not aversionists it is—a delight, and not an act of self-sacrifice.

So much for non-abstention. But Mr Morgan's idea is not wholly revealed unless we accept his play as an exemplification of his theory of total denial :

> A writer at a crisis of his work, a priest at grips with his faith, a man of science at the height of his problem, may see before him a time in which his singleness of mind can be safeguarded only by renouncement of the act of sex. . . . A man must learn to quit a woman as a seaman his country, remembering her beauty without enslavement, and this he teaches himself to do not by rejection of her, but by devotion to his voyage.

In other words, the artist must go into training like the athlete. But hold on a bit ! Is Mr Morgan's " singleness of mind " anything more than the old " drive " ? And had Balzac, plying pick and shovel (R. L. S.'s phrase), no such quality, no singleness ? To Mr Morgan's Milton and Wordsworth I oppose Dickens and the elder Dumas. If these in their work had singleness of mind—and it would be idiocy to deny it—then there must be other brands of this virtue besides Mr Morgan's pale and negative one. There must be a brand for the masters of gusto who work best with the noise of the crowd surging in their ears and the blood pulsing in their temples. Mr Morgan has been honest about Karen. Why is he not equally honest about Ferrers? There are great artists for whom discipline of the body, instead of clarifying the mind, clogs it. The author of *Virginibus Puerisque* was as pure of heart as living in this world comports. Yet we find him writing:

> In a man who finds all things good, you will scarce expect much zeal for negative virtues: the active alone will have a charm for him; abstinence, however wise, however kind, will always seem to such a judge entirely mean and partly impious. So with Dumas. Chastity is not near his heart.

Does Mr Morgan pretend that *The Three Musketeers* would have been a better book if Dumas had never had the mania for being photographed with Adah Menken on his knee? I know his answer. It is that I must only interpret singleness of mind as " drive " if and when the horse's head is turned in an abnegatory direction.

But now comes my point as a dramatic critic. If the immediately foregoing is Mr Morgan's play—and from the preface it appears that it must be—why on earth does it bother about aeronautical experiments in mid-Atlantic? It may be answered that the aeronautics are introduced to show " the man of science at the height of his problem." To which I retort that if Ibsen had written this play he would have made the aeronautics happen before the curtain rose, and staged the whole piece in some dingy lodgings with Karen and Ferrers going at it hammer-and-tongs like Rita and Allmers. I have cited Ibsen because it occurs to me that Mr Morgan has fallen into the trap into which the Great Man himself fell when he made the mistake of supplying *Little Eyolf* with a first act which was too exciting for what was to follow. Shakespeare, in *Antony and Cleopatra*, knew better. In that

189

study in non-abstention he did not distract our mind by any detailed account of naval tactics at the Battle of Actium! Nevertheless, and when all is said and done, I reiterate that in the theatre of imaginative vision this is the best play we have had since Mr Huxley's *The World of Light.*

English and Russian

THE WHITE GUARD. A play. Adapted by Rodney Ackland from the Russian of Bulgakov. Phœnix Theatre, Thursday, October 6, 1938.

ON BORROWED TIME. A comedy. By Paul Osborn; adapted by Ian Hay. Haymarket Theatre, Tuesday, October 4, 1938.

BOBBY GET YOUR GUN. A musical comedy. By Guy Bolton, Fred Thompson, and Bert Lee. Music by Jack Waller and Joseph Tunbridge. Adelphi Theatre, Friday, October 7, 1938.

[*October* 9, 1938]

WHAT a lot of trouble it would save the critics of the drama and the cognate arts if only they could lay down a few axioms which everybody would accept! There would be no difficulty with the axioms; the trouble would be with their acceptance. For example, any German music is better than any French music of the same kind. Any French actor is better than any English actor of the same type. Any Italian opera-singer is better than any sort of English opera-singer. Any Russian playwright is better than any English playwright without any reference to kind. Different reasons may be given in support of these axioms, and please will nobody write to say that an axiom should be self-supporting! The reason why any German symphony is better than any French one is because there aren't any French symphonies. The reason that French actors are better than English is that in the English view pantomime, which is the essence of acting, is simply ' not done.' Now about opera-singing. Is it decent for an Englishman to clap trunks on his thighs and his hand on ·his heart and serenade his beloved in the greasy accents of a pastrycook? About Russian playwriting I shall take

191

leave to be a little more serious. The reason for superiority here is that your Russian dramatist writes for adults, whereas your English playwright sets out merely to amuse adolescents !

Looking through the list of modern plays now happening in London, I perceive only one—*The Flashing Stream* —whose intellectual content demands that the spectator shall have come of age. I have not included *Glorious Morning* in the adult category because I have already proved once, and am prepared to prove again, that intellectually this play is on the same level as *The Sign of the Cross*, though in other respects less amusing. As for *Good-bye, Mr Chips*, I see nothing in it which one of Mr Chips's fourth-form pupils could not have written, nothing in the charming *The Corn is Green* that Mr Emlyn Williams could not have thrown off when he was seventeen, and nothing in Mr Ervine's *Robert's Wife* which my distinguished colleague could not have written with his left hand while penning dramatic criticism with his right. As for most of the others, are they or are they not all about what is considered good form on the dance floor of the Harringay-cum-Tottenham Lawn Tennis Club?

M. Bulgakov's play is concerned with the things which occupy the adult Russian mind—things like getting drunk, making love, philosophising, sacrificing life to that which even in the moment of sacrifice is seen to be futile, getting drunk again, maundering, resolving to commit suicide, bungling that same, commuting the dross of everyday life into the gold of music and poetry, braggadocio, melancholy, and a general mood of exaltation-cum-hangover. If this be a true presentation of the Russian attitude to life then it would seem that the Russians live more fully than the English, whose sole concern with life is what part of it is good form and what isn't. Shall Tom marry a chorus-girl? Shall Mabel accept the risks of being a mannequin? In both cases Father threatens disinheritance in spite of Mother weeping over her knitting-needles. Both children are turned out of doors, but Aunt Edith surreptitiously lends them money until Father, who is threatened with apoplexy, forgives them as much for his sake as theirs. I see that play twice a week !

One of the reasons why Russia's plays are better than England's is that her plays are written by her best minds, whereby Russian plots are reflected in the " intenser day " of greater art than ours. Also, what I have already written shows that the wave of sensibility in which the Russian theatre is immersed has more to reflect, since more passes through the head of a young Russian in ten minutes than through the corresponding British cranium in ten years. Now just as all English plays are the same play, except that Tom and Mabel become Dick and Gladys and Aunt Edith turns into Aunt Edna, so all Russian plays appear to be the same play, which is one of the reasons why all modern Russian playwrights are foolishly assumed to crib from Tchehov. Now this is like saying that all English playwrights crib from Miss Dodie Smith, whereas nothing could be further from the truth. Mr Jones's comedy about Harry and Phyllis who get into a scrape and are rescued by Aunt Ethel is not a plagiarism from Miss Smith; it happens because Mr Jones thinks along Miss Smith's lines. So, apparently, every Russian dramatist since Tchehov has thought along Tchehov's lines.

The first act of *The White Guard* takes place in any Tchehov parlour. People drop in and out, get drunk, make love, philosophise, get more drunk, maunder, attempt suicide, bungle it, sing and poetise, boast, drool, and explore heaven and hell simultaneously. The peg ? Not, as you might think, some cherry orchard or journey to Moscow, but stirring events in the Ukraine in 1918. Assiduous application to the programme might tell one what is going on. All I realised from the middle act was that the Ukraine in 1918 was a very noisy and bangy place. And then, in the third act, back we were in that parlour— I never quite gathered who owned it—and everybody resumed getting drunk, making love, philosophising, etc. And in the end they ran away from defeat and discarded their uniforms in exactly the same mood of intellectual detachment with which they had put them on and gone forth to victory.

The piece was brilliantly acted. Mr Michael Redgrave as leader of a forlorn hope had real passion. The others, notably Mr Stephen Haggard and Mr Glen Byam Shaw, took their cue from him admirably, and Mr Marius Goring deserved very great praise for travelling so far from his usual self. But you may travel a long way from St Pancras without getting to St Petersburg ! Mr Goring's study of the third-rate opera-singer, who is also Shakespeare's Mercutio turned volunteer in the White Army, struck me as probably as near to a character wholly foreign to him as a French actor's Hibernian character-sketch would get to Mr O'Casey's Paycock ! In the middle of all this entered Mr George Devine, whereupon the pretence that anybody else was Russian completely vanished. For this ingenious actor made us realise that, to a Russian, pouring out vodka into tumblers, mustard into a footbath, and his blood for his country are equally important manifestations of the poetic spirit ! Also, he *looked* Russian. Miss Peggy Ashcroft gave an exquisite performance of something which got no nearer to Russian than the handbag department at Harridges. At least I couldn't believe that this fragile, spiritual creature would ever have married that clod of a husband (a good performance by Mr George Hayes), or run off with that manifest charlatan (Mr Goring). Nor did I believe this Yeliena when she said : " Room full of smoke, men drunk all over the place, table not cleared, dishes unwashed, all the lights on—what a time to make love ! " I believed that Yeliena, as Miss

Ashcroft played her, would have got up from that sofa and left the room ten minutes earlier. All of this does not deny the performance beauty in intention, and even in realisation within the actress's physical means. It only remains to say that the production by M. Michel Saint-Denis was superb at every turn.

When I came back for the second act of *On Borrowed Time* I expected to find the audience gone. Instead it had borrowed a little more time and stayed. Now let's be sensible about this extraordinary play, whose main fault was that it was at the wrong theatre. To this day Paris has a respect for these matters. One knows exactly the kind of drama which will be put on at the Châtelet or the Odéon, and the difference between a tragic actress at the Porte St Martin and the same thing in the House of Molière. The French grade their theatres just as we English in our motoring-guides grade our hotels. Before the war London did the same thing, and this little fantasy could have been safely confided to some sentimento-farcical little cubby-hole like Terry's Theatre.

Continuing to be sensible, let it be realised that American and English notions of what is tear-and-laughter-compelling may reasonably differ, and that the difference is no ground for obloquy. It may be that Texas or Arizona would not make much of a play in which, after a dinner-party and at the bidding of their host, guests in evening-dress go out through French windows into a wood and engage in sentimental conversation with children they have never had. Leaving prejudice on one side, is this more absurd than coaxing Death to climb an apple-tree, and keeping him there until your little grandson who has had an accident needs Death to come down from the tree and rescue him? Is it argued that *Dear Brutus* was the product of a sensitive and imaginative mind, and that *On Borrowed Time* seems to be the product of an insensitive and clodhopping one? Agreed! Then you must find some insensitive and clodhopping theatre to house the American play. There's a propriety in these matters. If you must go to the Haymarket you will be amazed by Mr Frederick Leister's rich performance of somebody called Gramps, and by Master Geoffrey Atkins, who is extremely good as a small boy called Pud.

For the Adelphi production tiaras had been re-set. Eight-cylindered Sedancas-de-ville had been re-bored. Dramatic critics, who rarely dress, dressed. There was an air of expectancy which in Paris would have been excessive for a new Sardou with Sarah, and in Rome for a new D'Annunzio with Duse. Social, intellectual, and artistic London was agog. Grave issues lost their gravity. Questions of armament and re-armament were banished. Bobby was going to get his gun. After he had got it salvo succeeded salvo, and at the fall of the curtain cannonades of applause saluted this idiot's delight.

A lot of it was very funny. There was a scene with penguins which Anatole France would have relished. There was buffoonery on and under a bed. There was a jolly song called *The Captain Hates the Sea*. There was a burlesque of *Antony and Cleopatra*, with Cleopatra saying : " The torch is out ! " whereas admirers of Miss Gertrude Niesen, of whom I count myself discreetly one, know that the torch is very much in. But why does Miss Niesen play so many tricks with her torch-singing that you cannot recognise the melody's shape. It is as though some one had sat on a blancmange. Or, since the passion is negroid, a chocolate mould. Whenever Miss Niesen desisted, Miss Bertha Belmore, Mr Wylie Watson, Mr David Burns, and Mr Bobby Howes bobbed in and out. And duchesses, putting their tiaras together, were heard to pronounce the show a bit of all right !

A Merton Hodge-podge

THE STORY OF AN AFRICAN FARM. A play. By Merton
   Hodge; based on the novel by Olive Schreiner. New
   Theatre, Wednesday, November 30, 1938.
TWELFTH NIGHT. Revival of Shakespeare's comedy.
   Phœnix Theatre, Thursday, December 1, 1938.

[*December* 4, 1938]

WHY do they do it? People don't eat with paper-knives
or comb their hair with forks. Then why this passion for
musical and dramatic transubstantiation? For years I
have been listening to those cinema organists, those male
Venuses who, rising from what was once an orchestral sea,
proceed to spray the audience with Chopin's E flat Noc-
turne, Thaïs's "Méditation," Saint-Saëns's "Dying
Swan," Bach's G string Aria, Wolfram's "Star of Eve,"
and the Pizzicato from Delibes's "Sylvia." Everything, in
a word, that has ever been written for any other instrument!
The same blight affects the theatre, where adapters and
transcribers and monkeyers of all sorts can never be persuaded that a writer, when he chose to tell a story through
the medium of the novel, knew his own business best.

There is a case, I suppose, for the set of happenings
which make as good a plot in one medium as in another.
And one could cite old things like *La Dame aux Camélias*,
The Only Way, and *East Lynne*, and some new ones like
The Constant Nymph, which have done as tear-compel-
lingly in one medium as in the other. But that is a very
different thing from putting on to the stage novels whose
effect is achieved by the way the words lie on the page.
Your transmogrifier can never see that reading *in* a book
is an intenser thing than looking *at* a stage. Let me give

197

an example. A lady asked me the other day what I should think of a play made out of the magnificent short novel called *Sailor Town*, by Mr Paul Hervey Fox, the whole point of the story being a six days' debauch by a drunken sailor on an island off the beaten track. Apart from whether or not a nice-minded lady can enter into the feelings of a nasty-minded sailor, I begged the intending dramatist to realise that, whereas in the novel we are made to see the universe through reeling eyes and end by being ourselves intoxicated, in the theatre we should do no more than behold that very different thing, a reeling actor, and end by being bored.

Every intending adapter should ask himself whether his story can go straightforwardly from one medium into the other, or must, like the example I have given, necessarily suffer a fatal transposition, like a dish-cover slipping off a dish. Can you clamp the play to the story, and will it fit if you do? If not, the result must be unhappy. In adapting Olive Schreiner's story Mr Merton Hodge had two difficulties. The first was the one at which I have already hinted, that of getting a yellow disc, some holes cut in paper, and some painted rocks to convey the sentiment of the South African moon, stars, and veldt. And as a practised dramatist he must also have realised the extraordinary difficulty of getting young ladies with Kensington accents to sound like the daughters of South African farmers. Still, Mr Basil Dean is a wonderful producer, and Mr Hodge may well have had him in mind for the overcoming of Difficulty No. 1.

What I cannot understand is Mr Hodge's attitude when it came to Difficulty No. 2, especially as the difficulty was of his own making. Why did he insist on making an effectively sentimental theatre-piece out of this strange little masterpiece of twisted Brontesque, pre-Freudian psychology? The key to the book is the character of Lyndall, who in mind and spirit is too big for her environment. In

Lyndall's life there are three men. There is the Stranger
to whom she gives herself for experience' sake and who is
the father of her baby. There is Gregory Rose, amorist-
cum-charlatan, who likes dressing up in women's clothes
and, having written a love-letter, is capable of reading it
over with approval. And last there is Waldo, described
by Gregory as " only a servant of the Boer-woman's, and
a low, vulgar, uneducated thing." Rightly this book
should have been called *The Tragedies of an African Farm*,
for Waldo is as tragic a figure as Lyndall. It is to Waldo
that Lyndall reels off her woman's creed, and we should
remember here that the date is 1883 :

> " Power ! " she [Lyndall] said suddenly, smiting her
> little hand upon the rail. " Yes, we have power ; and
> since we are not to expend it in tunnelling mountains,
> nor healing diseases, nor making laws, nor money, nor
> on any extraneous object, we expend it on *you*. You
> are our goods, our merchandise, our material for opera-
> ting on ; we buy you, we sell you, we make fools of you,
> we act the wily old Jew with you, we keep six of you
> crawling to our little feet, and praying only for a touch
> of our little hand ; and they say, truly, there was never
> an ache, or a pain, or a broken heart but a woman was
> at the bottom of it. We are not to study law, nor
> science, nor art ; so we study you ! "

Note, too, the rider to this, which is here slightly condensed :

> " They say women have one great and noble work
> left them, and they do it ill. That is true ; they do it
> execrably. It is the work that demands the broadest
> culture, and they have not even the narrowest. The
> woman who does woman's work needs a many-sided,
> multiform culture ; the heights and depths of human life
> must not be beyond the reach of her vision ; she must
> have knowledge of men and things in many states, a
> wide catholicity of sympathy, the strength that springs
> from knowledge, and the magnanimity which springs
> from strength. *We* bear the world, and *we* make it.

And yet some say, if a woman can cook a dinner or dress herself well she has culture enough."

I find that Mr Hodge has betrayed Olive Schreiner's work in letter and in spirit. I find the betrayal of the spirit in the fact that there is not one word in the whole play which hints at Lyndall's strength, that astonishing mixture of Hilda Wangel's audacity and Jane Eyre's circumspection. Instead we are presented with a nice little girl who goes away, has a baby, and dies. I find the betrayal of the letter in the fact that she dies in the arms of the wrong man, to wit, the Stranger. Whereas in the book it is the womanish Gregory who, donning nurse's costume, deceives Lyndall's failing eyesight, tends her, and is with her at the last. Mr Hodge may justly have deemed this Lady Isabel business impossible in the sophisticated nineteen-thirties, and perhaps it is the least convincing thing in the book. But even the flaws in a masterpiece are still part of that masterpiece, and the impossibility of keeping to Olive Schreiner's story was the best reason for leaving Olive Schreiner's story alone.

In the novel nearly as much space is given to Waldo as to Lyndall, and the result is a close study of the uneducated and inarticulate artist. It is with Waldo's death that the book, in fact, ends. Yet in the play we are given nothing of this, and almost nothing of his artistry, the character shrinking to that of an amiable, ill-treated, and unexplained oaf. And both letter and spirit are betrayed together when the main interest of the play is shifted to Tant' Sannie and Bonaparte Blenkins. Here the balance of acting capacity is all wrong. Their enactors could not make much of the Waldo and Gregory because they were not allowed to, and Miss Curigwen Lewis, while under a similar disability, did not give us the impression that she could have accounted for more than she was allowed. As against players handicapped this way and that, Miss Mary

Clare as Tant' Sannie was given scope for a portrait of great vigour, while Mr Aubrey Dexter as Blenkins had room to put up a magnificent show of oily, comic villainy something after the manner in which Ambrose Manning used to play Father Christmas in *The Silver King*. Miss Clare and Mr Dexter were wholly justified in all that they did. The point is that the rest of the play lay down and died under them. It is pleasant to record the unqualified success of Miss Alexis France as Em. In this character and in its placing Mr Hodge was entirely faithful; he was beautifully seconded by an extremely clever little actress. All producers given an inch take an ell, and it would have been inhuman to expect Mr Dean not to make much of that Boer wedding. This resolved itself into a cavalcade of Spy's cartoons, the stage being filled with replicas of Oom Paul and the contemporary Marquis of Hartington at their most bearded and top-hatted. On the whole, a pleasant evening. But why drag in Olive Schreiner?

Twelfth Night was C. E. Montague's favourite comedy. Which is not surprising, since it is everybody's favourite comedy. It had better be, for there is no getting away from it. If anybody thinks of staging Shakespeare in an aquarium or on the top of the Wrekin, *Twelfth Night* will be the comedy chosen. The play occupies the same relation to the classical drama that Beethoven's Fifth Symphony does to classical music. Do foreign conductors coming over here treat us to something unfamiliar—Mahler's Ninth? No! For the good reason that in the English concert-hall unfamiliarity breeds contempt, wherefore we get a ' new reading ' of the old No. 5, which means a demisemiquaver an hour slower or faster. And, of course, the hall is filled, and the musical critics trying to escape get jammed in those amiable doors.

In the theatre the reverse happens. Let a foreign producer attempt a new and strange work, and the critics eager to get in are trampled underfoot by a public anxious

201

to get out. M. Michel Saint-Denis's recent experience with *The White Guard* proves this up to the hilt. For his second venture he has taken no risks, preferring to play the safest card but one in the entire Shakespearean repertory. Which brings me to my point. Let me say that I will never, except under compulsion or because of the presence of a new, guaranteed great actor—the age of the guarantor to be at least sixty!—see *The Merchant of Venice* again. And that I attend performances of *Twelfth Night* under protest. This malady of too much masterpiece has, of course, nothing to do with the quality of that masterpiece. Say a word over to yourself often enough and it ceases to have any meaning, even if it be the most beautiful word in the language. The French have a phrase for this critical malaise—they talk of *toujours perdrix*. To drive the point home, what about that clause in every Norwegian domestic servant's contract, the clause that he or she shall not be obliged to eat salmon, that most delectable of fish, more than once a week?

The result of enforced attendance at a play which has lost its meaning for one must be a mere allotting of marks, like a schoolmaster correcting his form's exercises. Rating Miss Jean Forbes-Robertson's Viola at 90, I place Miss Peggy Ashcroft's at 84. If Miss Vera Lindsay, like all Olivias, languishes in the 70's, it is Shakespeare's fault for having created a great lady instead of a great character. Miss Lucille Lisle's Maria giggles so excessively that the mercury jumps about too much to be read. I think I shall forget what my thermometer registered about Mr Esmond Knight's Orsino, Mr Warren Jenkins's Feste, and Mr George Devine's Sir Toby. None of these players is the actor for his part. But enough, perhaps, of this nonsense. Two performances stand out. These are the superb Malvolio of Mr George Hayes and the glorious Aguecheek of Mr Michael Redgrave. And I must not forget that Mr Thomas Heathcote contributes an agreeable note on Fabian. M.

Saint-Denis produces in the now fashionable manner, suggesting that all the characters are taking part in a fancy-dress ball. Whereas Shakespeare's Illyria is, as everybody knows, a thoroughly grubby country smelling of musty velvet curtains, orange peel, and the kerosene lamps of the Waterloo Road.

Mr Odets Goes Highbrow

PARADISE LOST. A play. By Clifford Odets. Stage
Society, Sunday, December 11, 1938.

WINDFALL. A play. By Howard Irving Young and
Jeffrey Dell. Apollo Theatre, Thursday, December 15,
1938.

[*December* 18, 1938]

PERHAPS it will clear the ground if I say that this failure
is better value for money, dramatically, emotionally, and
in the scale of pure entertainment, than all of London's
current successes put together, bar two plays that I have
seen and one that I haven't! Watching this piece, any
knowledgeable playgoer must say to himself : " The
fellow's a born dramatist!" at least once every five
minutes, whereas your fashionable authors might just as
well have been shopwalkers, toastmasters, or shoemakers
who have wearied of their lasts. When Mr Odets's *Golden
Boy* was produced a well-known English novelist and playwright wrote to me protesting that this was a hokum play
without integrity : " Practically every scene is jazzed up,
given more punch and excitement and noise than it should
have, without reference to reality at all." Now it was
Ibsen's way, when told what message he ought to have
preached instead of the one he actually did preach, to write
his next play according to the prescription enjoined upon
him, and to disgruntle his audience more than ever. I am
not very clear about the dates of Mr Odets's plays. But of
this I am sure : either *Paradise Lost* was written to confound
the detractors of *Golden Boy* or vice versa. And my impression is that vice versa wins. The whole atmosphere
is one of complete integrity. There is not an inch of
intentional hokum to be glimpsed, and every scene, and
every line of every scene, has its reference to reality.

204

Indeed, there are so many references to reality that the poor thing is buried beneath them.

At this point I have to put the vulgar question—what, in this piece, is Mr Odets getting at? The answer would appear to be—social conditions in a Capitalist state, the method used being the old one of faulty analogy. Now we know that the strength of a chain is its weakest link, the speed of an army the pace of its slowest footslogger, and so forth. But we also judge the height of a mountain-range by its peaks, and the genius of a Beethoven by his symphonies and not his Turkish Marches. Is an economic system to be judged by its successes or by its failures? I suggest that both tests are wrong, and that the test of a civilisation is not its tyrants or its slaves, but the general run of happiness among its wage-slaves. The cross-section of society which Mr Odets has chosen to show us is a miasmatic welter of failure, decay, and death. Mr Odets, an American, tells me that the home of the Gordons is what you may expect under a Capitalist régime. I, as an Englishman whose acquaintance with America is limited to a three weeks' visit to New York, tell Mr Odets (a) that he cannot produce such a home, and (b) that if he can, the life contained therein would be equally catastrophic under Socialism, Communism, or any other 'ism.' These people are without virtue, and their faults cry to heaven. What's the good of blaming Capitalism?

Let us look briefly at the weird collection which Mr Odets has pinned to his stage as a butterfly is pinned to a showcase. Leo Gordon is a spineless, nostalgic, vapourising manufacturer who would lose money on a tobacco kiosk. He has been for some years in partnership with a Mr Katz without discovering that his partner has the soul of a thug and the mind of a fire-raiser. Katz would also be a hundred per cent. sadist if he were not also a hundred per cent. coward, and, moreover, the victim of some obscure disease. Gordon has three children. Ben is an

amateur sprinter with the mind of a professional gigolo.
He marries a wanton and joins in partnership with his
wife's lover, who is a taxi-driver turned gangster. The
second son is dying of sleeping sickness, and there is a
sleepy daughter who, by giving music lessons, appears to
earn the only money coming into the house. Her heart is
broken because some down-at-heel young man, who ought
to be behind a counter selling gloves, wants to be an
orchestral conductor, but, finding competition with the
Toscaninis and the Barbirollis too keen, mooches off to
Chicago. Lastly, Gordon has a wife, a self-complacent,
detached creature who wears delightful silk stockings and
goes out to play bridge. I do not believe that any American middle-class family, under Capitalism, Communism,
or any other ' ism,' boasts or is going to boast a kettle of
fish quite so unpretty as this one.

Now let us be fair to Mr Odets. It is a first-class mistake in criticism to dislike the whole of a piece because
there are aspects of it with which one is unfamiliar. *This
play is American*, and we must not be put off because it is
not English. The set, designed by Mr Hamish Wilson
and passed by Mr Guy Glover, the producer, suggests to
the English eye the hall of some noble mansion behind
whose folding doors footmen preening their calves prepare
to announce the Duchess of Road and Lady Agatha
Mender. The English playgoer is necessarily a little at
sea when into this magnificent apartment, alleged to be
the living-room of the Gordons, irrupt without waiting to
be announced a boiler-stoker and a queer little piano-
tuner who seems to be a mixture of Quilp and Little Nell's
grandfather. The latter character, who has the biggest
part in the play, is always cropping up in American
comedy, one of the variants being Grandpa in *You Can't
Take It With You*. He is a master of foolish saws and
antique instances, all of them disconnected. When, then,
the stage is cleared for this odd creature who has spent all

night in gaol, the stoker in dungarees, and the dying boy, who has now exchanged a dinner-jacket for a silk dressing-gown, the English playgoer may be excused if he finds that his finger is not, so to speak, on the American social pulse. This, however clearly one may recognise the fault as that not of the patient but of the pulse-feeler, does make it difficult for us.

Despite this difficulty three things emerge from this play. First, that Mr Odets holds the attention of the spectator with every word he writes and every pause he enjoins. Second, that he is a born dramatist whom no amount of pretentious thinking can make into anything else. Third, that what he has tried to say in this play is complete nonsense. In the end the ruined manufacturer, whose furniture has been piled on the sidewalk, has a lyrical passage in which he expresses his conviction that in the failure of the individual is to be read hope for the nation as a whole. Which, of course, is bunk, and pretentious bunk. Why, then, do I say that this play is better than all London's commercial successes? Because it is brainy nonsense about things worth thinking about. Because this doesn't bore me and those do. Because I prefer sitting up in protest to lying on my neck yawning a hole in the ceiling.

The piece was brilliantly acted by an assemblage of players relying on their talents rather than their reputations. So faithfully and sensitively acted that apologists for Mr Odets must not try to ride off on the plea that his play was insufficiently interpreted. I shall select for special mention Messrs Noel Howlett, Alan Wheatley, Christopher Steele, Gordon Brown, Guy Glover, Alan Keith, and George Benson, and Mesdames Barbara Couper, Nell Carter, and Ilona Ference.

Windfall is a perfect example of the stuff which, after Odets, is unbearable. I refuse to write fully about this play because, in my opinion, not any of it should have been produced. It is a mixture of thriller and that old sentimental business about the wife who takes back her husband who has very nearly erred but didn't. The halves do not fit, which might not matter if each were a good half to a good whole. But it isn't, and the whole isn't, and nothing is, and this is nothing. No blame on the first night attached to a good cast, which would, I think, have thrown up the sponge if the theatre had contained a sponge. But it didn't, except of course the one with which my colleagues could be seen actively wiping this misadventure from their memories.

Hanging Matters

[*January* 22, 1939]

MANY years ago there was a great fuss in Manchester. The Hallé Concerts had made a loss on the year, and the rumour had gone round that the guarantors might be called upon. At once the air was blue with missives of protest, many of which appeared in the columns of the city's august newspaper. The correspondence was ended violently and abruptly by a letter from a witty schoolboy of my acquaintance: " Sir,—I submit that the function of a guarantor is to guarantee."

Similarly I submit that the function of an experimental theatre is to experiment. The question immediately arises: Experiment with what? And here very tentatively I put forward one or two opinionettes, meaning something less than settled convictions. In my view a repertory theatre should not trot out old pieces which have had their day in every country but this, and would have had it here but for censorship nonsense. Whether the ban has or has not been removed from Maeterlinck's *Monna Vanna*—I can never remember these petty vetoes—there could be nothing experimental now about producing a piece embodying the thought of a past decade. There is nothing experimental about producing the minor works of major dramatists, and the example I will give here is that piece

209

of Galsworthy's in which a mob breaks windows to enable a pigeon to escape to the roof! There is nothing experimental in reproducing twenty-year-old plays in order to see if they are as dud now as they were then.

The proper play to experiment with is one whose quality cannot be determined till the experiment has been made. Fifteen years ago I wrote in these columns an appreciation of a play called *The Seven who were Hanged*, by Andreyev. This was acted in Yiddish, of which I don't understand a word. Yet the piece made an impression on me greater than any play written subsequently, with the exception of the best work of Mr O'Casey. For fifteen years I have been talking about this piece to anybody and everybody who could conceivably produce anything anywhere. This five-act drama consists of an attempted crime, and the trial and sentence of five anarchists to whom are joined a half-witted vagrant and a brigand. I wrote:

> Take the Cabinet Minister; at the beginning a figure of farce as the elder Guitry might conceive farce, scenting his waistcoat, hands, and the tufts of hair surrounding his little piglike ears, then changing to a figment of Grand Guignol with his horrible, stertorous death-agonies. Yet behind this comic monstrosity generation after generation of oppressors loom.
>
> In the police-court our sympathies are not maudlinly invoked. We deplore the crime, and are not invited to side with Anarchy. We feel pity, not for the individual prisoners, but for that spirit which would not hurt a fly yet knows no ruth in the cause of revolution. When the five learn that their request—to be hanged together—is granted, their tribulation turns to ineffable joy, and with faces transfigured and shining they chant the revolutionary's creed. The leave-taking scene in the prison has a purely human quality of pathos, and as it is played at the Scala is almost beyond bearing. I do not imagine that a single eye can have remained dry throughout this act. The scene in the train is an essay in brotherhood.

But it is in the last act that the theatre is used at its best. It could be sensational, harrowing, ' effective ' in the commonplace way. It is, however, none of these, but draws the piece to a grave liturgical close. It remains in the mind like music.

It is no use telling me that this play cannot be got hold of. It can, by anybody who wants to get hold of it. The Yiddish Art Theatre has not vanished into thin air; or if it has, not all its actors have. Somewhere a copy of this play exists. It is no use telling me that the piece is not translated. There are such things as language-schools who will furnish a literal translation from the Chaldean or the Choctaw. *And I would rather listen to the worst possible English of this play than to the best possible English of any living playwright.*

Whether the play can be acted is another matter. There are eighteen magnificent parts, and for seven of them I should require Mr Charles Laughton, Mr Robert Harris, Mr Michael Redgrave, Mr Wilfred Lawson, Miss Flora Robson, Miss Beatrix Lehmann, and Miss Peggy Ashcroft, and my ideal producer would be M. Saint-Denis. It may be that such a company could not be assembled except on a Sunday evening. But what is there so infeasible about Sunday evenings? Has no play ever been produced on Sunday evening? I have made all the points contained in the foregoing to every West-End manager times without number. None has taken the slightest notice, and the fact that the play is ten times more apt to world conditions than when it was written merely makes them more adamant.

In the meantime *Adults Only* is exactly the sort of little play which ought to be presented by an experimental theatre, if only for the fact that performance reveals two things. First, that the authors have some talent for play-writing and, second, that at present they are doing everything wrong. They are diffuse and repetitive. They insist on unimportant detail. They put the sting of their play into the very tip of their play's tail, so that you only know what it has all been about when it is all over, and are quite likely to leave the theatre without being stung at all. But there is no doubt that the authors can, if they want, become playwrights. They were greatly helped on Sunday by Mr Bernard Lee, Miss Eileen Beldon, Miss Edna Best, and Miss Joan Harben. There was a very large supporting cast.

They Walk Alone failed with me for three reasons. It was too much talked about beforehand, it was too long, and in the matter of the plot there were more holes than sieve. It was known that a sexual-homicidal maniac invariably prefaced his or her stranglings by an organ recital in the chapel next door to a farmhouse. Three murders had happened, and a fourth was imminent. It was one in the morning and three hefty young farmers were sitting in the kitchen waiting to see if the organ would play. It did. Did the three young men rush into the chapel and secure the organist? No, because their womenfolk forbade them! This occurred in the second act, and the play, so far as I was concerned, came to an end.

It was acted well, if unevenly. Miss Carol Goodner's performance of the farmer's wife would have been admirable if it had remotely suggested a farm, and I didn't believe that Mr Alastair MacIntyre as the farmer knew a horse from a cow. I have lived on farms and have never met a West Kensington accent. Young Mr Jimmy Hanley was excellent, and if his accent was Cockney rather than Lincolnshire it was at least an accent. But the only character who had obviously fed pigs was Mr Peter Standfast's Saul. This was good acting because we never saw him go near a bucket. But even through his Sunday clothes the young man gave the right impression. Which is acting. Miss Lehmann's farm servant would have wrung horror from a dishclout. It was, perhaps, not this brilliant actress's fault that Emmy would have been dismissed as soon as Miss Goodner saw her put her hands round a teapot. The author had obviously said, " Let 'em have it ! " and Miss Lehmann obeyed. There was an incredible scene after curtain-fall when flustered gentlemen appeared from here, there, and everywhere and distributed credit for everything to everybody.

Except for one or two changes in the cast and the addition of a song or two, I see no difference whatever between the first and second eruptions of the Magyar volcano. There are the same plot, the same dialogue, the same fearsome stretches of humourless clowning, the same glittering costumes, the same handsome scenery, and the same thimbleful of music eked out with a quart of orchestration. The interpolated song about which so much fuss has been made, " Music for Romance," is that old hymn to necking with which every prima donna in this kind has regaled us. People in the foyer were saying that this is another *Tale of the Vienna Woods*. Don't you believe it ! This is a tale to be told *to* the Vienna Woods. It is a rosered tale, half as old as waltz-time.

There came a moment when Miss Stella Arbenina as an Empress in riding-costume proposed, after an exquisite little bit of acting, to quit the scene. Shades of Hortense Schneider, and poor Offenbach, and wander-witted Meilhac and Halévy ! Cretins that by modern taste these must be held to have been, none of them, including Hortense herself, would have allowed an Empress *en amazone* to go off without a song !

The graver thought here comes to me that the males of our nation must have lost their voices. If not, why had the management to go to France to find a singing hero ? Why had the makers of *The Mikado* film to go to America to find a Nanki-Poo ? Yes, there was food for thought— when Miss Binnie Hale was not on the stage ! When she was she did the thinking for us. For here is an actress who can transmute witlessness into something which will pass for wit, who can make us believe that the dreary accidents overwhelming this play's little opera-singer are happening to a real person for the first time. Here, even, is almost a voice, and used with a bravura which would quell a sterner musical critic than I can pretend to be! Here, in short, is talent which would have been recognised as talent by the geniuses who in the 'sixties provided the Bouffes Parisiens with their intoxicating little master-pieces. Miss Hale belongs to the dimension of great art in little space. The rest of this show is a mass of glitter and pretence, a costly wilderness in which nothing grows.

Mr Coward Upside Down

DESIGN FOR LIVING. A comedy. By Noel Coward. Haymarket Theatre, Wednesday, January 25, 1939.

THE PLAYBOY OF THE WESTERN WORLD. Revival of Synge's comedy. Mercury Theatre, Friday, January 27, 1939.

[*January* 29, 1939]

> Trois pigeons s'entr'aimaient d'amour tendre!
> *The New La Fontaine*

THIS play, which might have been an airy, debateless excursion into Cloud-Cuckoo-Land, is an elaborate and painstaking examination of the case for cloud-cuckoos. This being so, one cannot make for the play the excuse that Lamb made for Restoration comedy—that it all happens in an amoral world in which the moral sense cannot be offended because it does not exist. "Of what consequence is it to Virtue," asks Elia, "who is the father of Lord Froth's or Sir Paul Pliant's children?"

Hear now Mr Coward's chamberer:

> We're not doing any harm to anyone else. We're not peppering the world with illegitimate children. The only people we could possibly mess up are ourselves, and that's our look-out.

And what is that look-out? To answer we need only put to Otto one of Elia's questions. Would Otto's principles universally acted upon reduce the frame of things to chaos? It is the second of this play's chamberers who supplies the answer: "We all love each other a lot, far too much, *and we've made a bloody mess of it!*"

For Mr Coward sees as clearly as the sternest moralist could wish that flouting convention is a form of parasitism. "The passion to *épater le bourgeois*," wrote Montague in his essay on Wilde, "to knock the stupid party

215

all of a heap each time you open your mouth, is itself a
form of parasitism: for where would you be without the
bourgeois to keep you going with his horror?" Whence
do parasitic Otto and Leo and Gilda imagine they are
going to draw their sustenance when, having cut themselves off from normal society, they have exhausted themselves as sources of entertainment? Here Mr Coward uses
his moral as dagger and turns it in the wound. Otto
goes on:

> Our lives are diametrically opposed to ordinary social
> conventions; and it's no use grabbing at those conven-
> tions to hold us up when we find we're in deep water.
> We've jilted them and eliminated them, and we've got
> to find our own solutions for our own peculiar moral
> problems. . . . There's no sense in stamping about and
> saying how degrading it all is. Of course it's degrading.
> . . . Therefore the only thing left is to enjoy it thor-
> oughly, every rich moment of it, every thrilling
> second. . . .

Until, of course, the seconds cease to be thrilling and the
moments rich. And now comes the dramatic point: can
those solutions be found, and is it good fun sitting in the
theatre while the characters find them?

The play might make easier watching if Mr Coward,
normally so nattily minded, were less vague in his use of
the word ' love,' to which he gives a plurality of meanings.
It is as though Dickens had employed the same word to
cover Mrs Nickleby's affection for her spouse, Sir Mulberry
Hawk's eye for her daughter, Mr Crummles's emotion on
first beholding Mrs Crummles inverted on her spear, Mr
Mantalini's adoration of Madame, the altruistic fervour
of the Brothers Cheeryble, and the friendship of Nicholas
for Smike. Is this far-fetched? I think not. Hear Leo:
" I love you. You love me. You love Otto. I love Otto.
Otto loves you. Otto loves me." This is where Leo and
Otto and Gilda make their mistake. Nobody in this play
loves anybody. For to love in any grown-up sense you must

be grown up, which Leo and Otto and Gilda are not. They are vicious babies occupying the same perambulator and sharing a bag of sweets which they snatch from one another.

Does this make an entertaining evening, or does it not ? For me, not. If I am interested in that triangle which was Von Bülow, Cosima, and Richard Wagner it is because one of them was a Wagner. Put that on the stage, and even then what I want to see is the curtain falling on the first night of *Tannhäuser* in Paris. Contrariwise, if that on which the dramatist raises his curtain is nothing more than the trio's sleeping arrangements, why, then I go to sleep myself ! In Mr Coward's play there is perfunctory talk of Otto being a painter, Leo a playwright, and Gilda an interior-decorator. But I do not believe this. The play has but one interest, the plot but one aim, and the wit but one point, and to these three things, which are but one thing, Mr Coward sticks with the single-mindedness of a sleeping-car attendant. *Et c'est moi qui dors !*

How is the play acted ? I am reminded of a story about Oscar Wilde who, during a heat-wave in New York, was seen on Fifth Avenue in heavy boots, a mackintosh, and carrying an open umbrella. Being asked for an explanation, he replied : " They tell me that it is raining in London ! " Similarly I shall say that the present play was magnificently acted—in New York ! But there Miss Fontanne and Messrs Lunt and Coward had the easy task of exploiting their own genius for the tart, cynical, and impish, for presenting human beings as gargoyles. The task before Miss Diana Wynyard and Messrs Anton Walbrook and Rex Harrison was quite other, and one reflected that honey can never suggest vinegar. The note of Gilda, however you try to disguise it, is, in the last resort, an elegant sluttishness. Valiantly though Miss Wynyard attempted this, she achieved only elegance, and the result was like St Cecilia in full blast on her organ failing to swing it on the voix-celeste. Mr Anton Walbrook and Mr Rex Harrison tried very hard. But trying was not enough. We felt that at heart both Otto and Leo were decent fellows.

Tragic acting, it has been said, should set you a-tingle with its first line. You cannot tell why, except that virtue has gone out of the artist and possessed the spectator. It should have been so with this play's comic acting. Vice should have proceeded out of these vicious babies, and possessed us. It did not. Mr Coward's message to his characters was obviously : " Destroy yourselves and like it ! " Which, of course, made it a moral play. His English cast lets him down by its very niceness. Otto and Leo and Gilda have no notion of destruction. They flit before us neither in Lamb's " palpable darkness," nor even in his " privation of moral light." They pretend that the day is sunny, and ask us to join in their basking. Which makes it not at all the moral play that Mr Coward intended.

If there is one thing more contemptible than a half-hearted gambler it is a half-hearted quoter ! I began this week with Lamb, and I shall stick to him : " Amidst the mortifying circumstances attendant upon growing old, it is something to have seen the School for Scandal in its glory." Amidst the mortifying circumstances attendant upon being an ageing dramatic critic, it is something to have seen *The Playboy* in its glory. The snag is the danger that one may be unfair to later presentation. But there is one shimmer of the sun and another of the moon, and Miss Pamela Gibson may be said to play Pegeen Mike quite nicely. It goes without saying that whoever saw Maire O'Neill in her first radiance play this part knows that he will never see it played again. To-day Miss O'Neill plays the Widow Quin, and this leads us straight to Shakespeare's fifth sonnet. For in this gracious player there still remains summer's distillation :

> And flowers distill'd, though they with winter meet,
> Lose but their show; their substance still lives sweet.

And since Shakespeare has turned up let me beg **Mr Cyril Cusack** to restudy Christy Mahon and reform him not altogether but in part. There should be Pistol as well as Romeo in this Irish lover, and the master of braggadocio as well as the wistful wooer. No young actor living could give more exquisite delivery of " Let you wait, to hear me talking, till we're astray in Erris, when Good Friday's by, drinking a sup from a well, and making mighty kisses with our wetted mouths." But Mr Cusack takes insufficient note of " to hear me talking." " And are etceteras nothing ? " asked Pistol. Mr Cusack must give us the etceteras. But it was a great evening all the same.

The Dating of Plays

THE IMPORTANCE OF BEING EARNEST. Revival of Oscar
    Wilde's comedy. Globe Theatre, Tuesday afternoon,
    January 31, 1939.

NORA. Revival of Ibsen's play. Duke of York's Theatre,
    Friday, February 3, 1939.

GAS LIGHT. A play. By Patrick Hamilton. Apollo Theatre,
    Tuesday, January 31, 1939.

[*February* 5, 1939]

A hopeful group, misled by the success of the biographical play
Oscar Wilde, decided to try one of Mr Wilde's own comedies, *The
Importance of Being Earnest*. The sound of its creaking must
surely have been audible in London.
New York Correspondent.

BUT *of course* the play creaks, given the mentality which
in an Old Master can see nothing but the cracks in the
canvas! So to our spry manipulators of hot rhythm must
Beethoven lumber. "Pity it creaks!" said a bridge-
player recently of my Queen Anne card-table, and I could
have brained him! Whatever was perfect in its own day
remains perfect when that day is over. That's all that can
be said about creaking. "Even in a jocular play," wrote
Allan Monkhouse, "we expect the dramatist to steady himself occasionally and say something about the Union Jack
or the sanctity of home, and in Wilde this austerity of art
that never trifles with morals or realities, except in the
sense that it is all trifling, is disturbing to respectable
citizens." This is a further reason why *The Importance*
cannot be said to creak, which is only another word for
' dating.' The day may come when this country has de-
serted the Union Jack for a pair of crossed broomsticks, and
the sanctity of the home is held for an intolerable thing.
And if it does, how will Wilde be concerned? Not at all.
His masterpiece belongs to no time and no place.

The piece must be intensely difficult to act, largely because there is no model for an airy abstraction which had no forerunners and has not had successors. The players, as all the world knows, must act the piece with immense gravity and yet without seriousness. On this point Monkhouse—and it is a privilege to give honour where honour is greatly due—writes as follows : " Here are not lifelike traits, but comic extensions of them, and they bring to us a world in which nothing heavy can fall on us. Actors who are accustomed to big sentiments and the emphasis of common farce must part with something of their specific gravity in this atmosphere."

Let us bring the players in the present revival to this test. It shows some odd results. Mr Gielgud, rightly aiming at the humourlessness of John Worthing, conveys a sense of dudgeon, like a monarch at some unseemly Drawing-room, though the loyalty to his author is there whenever he lets the rage simmer down. Probably the part is unplayable, for how reconcile humourlessness with the invention of that brother? Mr Ronald Ward wholly fails to realise the Mercutio-like quality of Algernon, who should be fantasticated. But then probably this part could only be played by a Shakespearean actor who, for the nonce, had emptied himself of Shakespeare. The point about the young ladies in this play is that they are descendants, one living in town and the other in the country, of that brittle piece of nonsense Millamant, and, like her, " very strange and well-bred." Miss Joyce Carey's Gwendolen and Miss Angela Baddeley's Cecily have little that is strange about them. They are not more consciously inane or unconsciously dewy than any other ingénues in any other comedy, and they do not abash us with over-breeding.

In the other half of the cast the players must have more specific gravity than human nature has ever carried. Mr David Horne fails because his Chasuble is a recognisable

221

country rector. He should boom, and after each sentence pause, and not strike again until clangour has died away. Mr Horne's realistic manner would be admirable in a serious comedy for trivial people. But not here! And now let me say that the farce comes to full flowering in the persons of Miss Margaret Rutherford's Prism and Miss Evans's Lady Bracknell. Of Miss Rutherford I must be content to say that she could not miss perfection if she aimed wide of it, while to do Miss Evans anything approaching justice would require a whole essay. You feel that in the presence of this dragonhood the most august of Mrs Kendal's matrons would have seemed pert and forward. As long as Miss Evans is on the stage one has no doubt about anything except the relative grandeur of Lady Bracknell's upholstery, and those two hats in one of which swans nest while in the other all the fowls of Rostand's *Chantecler* come to roost.

The fact that Ibsen's *A Doll's House*—I entirely decline to call the play *Nora!*—is also being revived this week suggests that we should make up our minds once and for all where we stand in the matter of plays dating. There is a school which holds that with the emancipation of women this great play " lost much of its sting and tang." I do not agree, if only for the reason that the burning agitation over Women's Rights never, so far as I was concerned, gave it any sting or tang! You see, I am of the school which holds that there is a very good case to be made for Helmer, that Nora is a born dunce, a natural liar, and an incorrigible cheat, and that the world is no place for canaries to gad about in. That, in short, the proper place for a song-bird is its cage.

But it would be monstrously uncritical if dissension from everything Ibsen preached in this play should prevent one from realising that it is, among prose dramas, the entire and perfect chrysolite. Being perfect in its day, it cannot date now. I am much more worried about another matter which concerns the nineteen-thirties, and moreover this particular year and this particular month. It has been maintained until one is blue in the face that the saving of the theatre in this country lies with the people who can afford only the cheaper seats. There are over a hundred pit seats at the Duke of York's, and on Friday night only four of these were occupied. This is disgraceful. I am ashamed of and for our pittites. It is useless for the elderly and middle-aged to plead that they have had their fill of *A Doll's House*; they ought to want to see a new Nora, just as concert-goers ought and do want to hear a new reading of a symphony which they know by heart. As for the juniors, I just do not believe that every young person in London, excepting four, has seen this masterpiece. They cannot have done so, because it is fourteen years since it was put on for a run.

It is not as though this production were frowsty, routine, hugger-mugger, and dull, and just yet one more perfunctory effort of some notoriously tired and effete management. This is a *new* management horribly let down at its first venture. Mr Marius Goring has produced, in my view, excitingly. There are some things to disagree with, beginning with the amazing architecture of Torvald's summer palace, which appears to be on the ground floor of Park Lane's latest and most luxurious block of flats. I think Mr Austin Trevor's Torvald looms too large and makes too much noise. Torvald may be a windbag, but he should be a windbag of charm. I think that Miss Lucie Mannheim's Nora should not be allowed to let off shrieks and whistles which suggest a railway-engine in hysteria. I think the lighting at the end is wrong, that Nora should turn up the gas before having it out with Torvald, who should not be left standing in a reddish glare like the hero in a drama by Hall Caine.

But there objections end. What an extremely clever actress Miss Mannheim is when she does not act too much!

And how great is her variety! She does not sit about, as English actresses do, waiting for something to happen; she is always making something happen. A great deal of her Nora is exceedingly touching, and the end of the second act is very nearly the best I have seen. Which is some compensation for the end of the third act, which is very nearly the worst. How refreshing it is to see Mr Trevor away from Balkan inanity and pursuing his avocation as an actor! How good are Miss Marian Spencer's Mrs Linden and Mr Harold Scott's Krogstad! It has been suggested that the author ought to have written a play on what afterwards happened to Nora. But Ibsen was a wily old bird. He probably realised that such a play must include the Linden-Krogstad nuptials, and that before the spectacle of that joylessness even he must draw the line! Dr Rank is an actor-proof part, which does not mean that any actor must necessarily be so good as Mr John Abbott. We shall probably never be told to whom in this production should be given the credit for Rank's final and astonishing exit. The man is a little drunk. He has lit his last cigar. He is going to an undeserved death. And he stands in that doorway with his back to the audience, in gala costume, with confetti on his shoulders, and on his forehead a mask to which is attached a balloon, baleful and ridiculous. It is as though Ibsen, foreseeing Strindberg and wishful to take the wind out of his sails, had thrown in an entire Strindberg play as a mere decoration.

Gas Light, the extremely effective little piece now promoted from Richmond, still does not quite fit. For horror as masterly as this we feel that the author should have contrived a skeleton of events less clumsy. Because a man is required to pace an attic for hours together in order to frighten his wife below, it is supposed that jewels are hidden there, whereas they might equally well be hidden in any other part of the house. The villain is a mental sadist. Then why confound him with a man who murders an old lady for her rubies? He might possibly be both? Alas! you cannot build good plays on ' might be ' suppositions.   But then, I cannot believe in any of this play's mechanics. I feel that Mr Hamilton should have retained everything of his play excepting the plot. Nevertheless, and in spite of all objections, there is no doubt that as a study in terror and suspense this is the best play we have had for a very long time. It is frighteningly well acted by Miss Gwen Ffrangcon-Davies, Mr Dennis Arundell, and Mr Milton Rosmer.

A Flood at Kew

THE MOTHER. A play. By Karel Capek; English version
by Paul Selver and Miles Malleson. " Q " Theatre,
Monday, February 13, 1939.

THE DOCTOR'S DILEMMA. Revival of Bernard Shaw's play.
Westminster Theatre, Friday, February 17, 1939.

[*February* 19, 1939]

THE first thing in an argument is to decide what it is that
you are arguing about. The other day I listened to an
angry debate as to the greatness of a modern dictator who
shall be nameless. Intervening, I told the two debaters
that discussion between them was useless, since one took
John Wesley as his idea of greatness and the other
Napoleon. Similarly it would be absurd to argue whether
The Mother is or is not a good play unless you first make
it clear what in your opinion constitutes a good play.

The dilemma is an old one. Writing nearly forty years
ago, the late A. B. Walkley said : " It is better not to enter
into so dangerously controversial a subject as the value of
Mr Shaw's criticism of life; nor is there any need, seeing
that he fails to express it in terms of drama. The essential
law of the theatre is thought *through emotion*. No
character exhibits real emotion in those fascinating exercises in dialectic which Mr Shaw miscalls plays." Now let
us reverse this. I can imagine Walkley writing about
Capek's play : " In this fascinating drama which Capek
miscalls an exercise in dialectic no character exhibits any
power of thought. The essential law of melodrama is
emotion without thought. Since in this play Capek completely succeeds in fulfilling this law, it is needless to
inquire into the value of his play as a criticism of life."

I will put it another way and say that I agree with Mr

226

E. P. Montgomery, who wrote: " I can only record that *The Mother* affected me more deeply and more powerfully than any play I have seen since *Journey's End*," and disagree with Mr Charles Morgan, who said: " The resultant of Capek's many and unhappy moods is not dramatically communicated." On the night I attended at Kew the house was more moved than in any theatre at any time within recent recollection. Sniffings abounded. Here and there were frank tears. And after each act-drop people kept their seats for an appreciable time without moving. Immediately behind me sat a well-known actor, who, at the end of the play, was so overcome that he could not speak. Then, pulling himself partially together, he said: " Tell me, dear boy [*sob*], is it [*bellow*] dramatically communicated [*howl*] ? "

Now let us see what the emotion is all about. Seventeen years before the play opens the Mother has lost her husband, an army major compelled to throw away his life in deference to the stupidity of his colonel. But in her mind he is not dead, and in his study he has continued to walk and talk with her. A year or two before the curtain goes up the Mother has lost her eldest-born, a doctor who gave his life for science. He too has continued to keep his mother company. She has four other sons—George the airman, Christopher the Fascist, Peter the Communist, and Tony, whose bent is music and poetry. One by one these sons pass from the living state to the near-living. George throws away his life in order that bombs may be dropped from a greater height than ever before. Civil war breaks out; Peter, who has been taken as a hostage, is executed, while Christopher dies for the other side.

Up to this point it is difficult to see what Capek is aiming at, and I doubt if in the theatre the play would be more effective if you did. Death plays all, levels all, and in the end obliterates all. I speak only as I feel, but when these sons come into the room and recognise their dead

father and brothers and talk to them—which recognition
and talk announce to the Mother that she is again be-
reaved before ever the news has been physically communicated to her—why then it is nonsense to ask me to bother
about the brand of adventure or politics or harum-scarum-
hood which brought about these deaths! You might as
well ask me on seeing a child run over in the street to
debate whether the motorist was or was not exceeding the
speed-limit.

I see an immense power of emotion in this play, but not
any approach to thought, except possibly in the last act.
It is now supposed that the country in which all this has
been taking place is set upon by a foreign power seeking
to take advantage of the disruption of civil war. Now
something in Tony's blood draws him away from music
and poetry and precipitates him into the struggle, that
something being the spirit which has already brought so
much calamity upon the Mother. Must she let the boy go,
or mustn't she? The family shades say Yes. Honour,
glory, patriotism, duty, self-sacrifice—these things may
be so abused that the very names for them become meaningless. But if life is never lost on their behalf the virtues
themselves and not the names cease to have any meaning
at all. Finally the Mother's father—a Maeterlinckian Plus
Vieil Aveugle!—puts in his appearance. His contribution
is that there wasn't any fighting in his day, and he
wouldn't have been much of a one for soldiering. But he
thinks that Tony ought to feel as he does, and that he
himself missed something in life for never having felt that
way. But even now the Mother is convinced less by
Grandpapa's argument than by the fact that children are
being destroyed. To put an end to this, or rather in the
slender hope of putting an end to it, she consents that her
last remaining child shall be destroyed also.

So far as I can see this play contains nothing to argue
about. This being so, I will only say that the playgoer who

remained master of himself throughout would be a scoundrel, and that of all the pieces now running in London this is one for which, as ordinary playgoer, I would soonest pay entertainment tax. It is played with extraordinary reticence by Messrs Raymond Lovell, Anthony Hawtrey, Alan Judd, Michael Kingsley, Nigel Stock, Henry Hepworth, and Eliot Makeham, and Miss Louise Hampton shows the finest possible sense of the play's quality by allowing it to speak for itself. This stroke of abnegation-cum-shrewdness receives instant reward in that she remains the only dry-eyed person in a house of Niobes.

No equivocation is called for, or is even permissible, in the case of Mr Shaw's masterpiece which, with one or two others, notably *Candida* and *Androcles*, shows how near its author has come to being a playwright. Capek's fault in his last play is that the assault on the emotions blinds you to everything else. In the normal Shavian drama the assault on the intellect achieves the same thing. But in this rampageous piece of sheer theatricality Mr Shaw for once in a way forgot himself.

The central thesis raises a point so moot, as Mr Gordon Harker would say, that æons hence bright schoolboys will still be arguing how great a painter, say, a Manet would have to be to entitle him to behave like a Landru. The sub-plot about the doctors with their phagocytes and their nuciform sacs is obviously going to wear well and is already a good deal better than a lot of Shakespeare's clowning. Dubedat's death scene is always going to give people plenty to praise and abuse, cry over and deplore. (Walkley called it " cheap and nasty.") All these are things of the theatre, though I have the sneaking suspicion that Mr Shaw attached far more importance to the love of Ridgeon for Jennifer, a piece of aridity which isn't of the theatre at all. Whether the epilogue wears well or ill it is not possible for me to say. Once bitten, shy not only twice but ever after !

The revival at the Westminster is beautifully and expressively done. Dubedat is to every sensitive, fine-grained young actor what your Schubert-Liszt-Tausig confection is to your insensitive, coarse-grained old pianist! Neither can fail in either. I confess to becoming a little anxious about Mr Stephen Haggard, who does this sort of thing so well that there is a danger that he will never be allowed to play anything else. Will the Old Vic please rescue him, *à tour de revanche* of course? Which is French for rescuing the Old Vic! The doctors are a good team, even if Mr Barry Jones, who leads them, is the last in a long line which has failed to persuade me that Ridgeon can be acted at all. Or, better, that there is any part to act. Mr Max Adrian buffoons " B.B." to the top of his bent, and even further. This is a clever actor giving a clever performance, and a shade conscious of it. Whereas " B.B." should see no more in his own booming than Big Ben himself. Mr Hugh Miller should really try to radiate a little less distinction; Cutler Walpole should be a bustling, rather common, wholly expert little man, ready to cut anything out of anybody at a minute's notice, and reminding us that surgery was once the *succursale* to hairdressing. Nigel Playfair used to be admirable here. Perhaps the most successful portrait of all is Mr Stephen Murray's Sir Patrick Cullen, frosty but kindly. This performance is so good that for a long time I thought Mr Cecil Trouncer was the actor! Miss Ruth Lodge is the Jennifer, and I shall not attempt at this hour of the day to disturb Mr Shaw's illusions as to what the wives of unthrifty artists are really like. The revival was listened to with great attention by a very large audience. If anybody living can write a new play as good as this old one, will he now please come forward?

Bees on Charon's Boat-deck

JOHNSON OVER JORDAN. A play. By J. B. Priestley.
New Theatre, Wednesday, February 22, 1939.

AN ENEMY OF THE PEOPLE. Revival of Ibsen's play. Old
Vic Theatre, Friday, February 24, 1939.

[*February* 26, 1939]

I can see no magnificent meanin' jumping out of that!
SEAN O'CASEY, *The Silver Tassie*

AUTHORS approaching middle age are often exercised
about death; it is sometimes the only exercise they get.
This play shows that Mr Priestley has been thinking a
great deal about his and everybody else's approaching dis-
solution. Unfortunately he has not been thinking very
freshly, for though I listened hard on Wednesday evening
I could gather no hint of any new thought on the subject.
" Take away but the pomps of death, the disguises, and
solemn bugbears, and the actings by candlelight, and
proper and fantastic ceremonies, the minstrels and the
noise-makers, the women and the weepers, the swoonings
and the shriekings, the nurses and the physicians, the
dark room and the ministers, the kindred and the watches,
and then to die is easy, ready, and quitted from its
troublesome circumstances." Anybody who knows his
Jeremy Taylor knows what a funeral at the Johnsons' is
like.

Then why, if the way of thinking must be old, choose
one of the bad old ways and ignore the good? Mr
Priestley's peppering of the play with the Burial Service
—it happened at the beginning of every act—was piling
up agony for agony's sake, except that the second *reprise*
made for titters rather than jitters. Then why harp upon
physical corruption, of which no man is conscious? Even

231

death itself ceases to exist once he who is to suffer it realises that, as the old writer said, " either it has happened, or it is not yet." That, as Lady Bracknell would remark, is all there is to be said about death. And even if it isn't, has Mr Priestley forgotten the pronouncement of Feeble, the tailor in Shakespeare's *Henry IV* : " We owe God a death : I'll ne'er bear a base mind " ? *Johnson over Jordan* is base in the sense that it shows a debtor who would, if he could, get out of paying his debt.

Come, come, my dear Jack ! If I were your schoolmaster I should make you write out Browning's *Prospice* ten times. As I am only your greatest admirer when you are at your best, the limit of my severity is to permit myself this Epigram on a Dramatist Aiming High but Wide :

> His aim was noble; let us shake his hand,
> That arrow's gold which scorns to find the target.
> All Golden Arrow trippers understand
> 'Tis better to miss Naples than hit Margate.

But this, after all, is the theatre. And, it may be argued, if you are not going to think about your theme in a striking way, how about making the audience sit up in the matter of presentation ? In this, the most old-fashioned piece he has yet contrived, our author has gone back to the Expressionism of the nineteen-twenties as practised by Messrs Toller, Kaiser, Molnar, and Elmer Rice, and dead almost before it was alive. You know the kind of thing. A business magnate wants to write a letter, whereupon twelve typists appear joggling twelve imaginary typewriters while twelve office-boys lick twelve imaginary stamps. The whole of Mr Priestley's first act is a wilderness of dusty antics of this sort. It shows the soul of Johnson repairing to a spiritual clearing-house where he is put through a lot of questions. Has he gone in for regular exercise ? Has he looked after his teeth ? Did he ever take the trouble to find out what the letters

T.U.C. stand for, and what is meant by Proportional Representation? All of which is expressed in terms of ballet.

Then comes a great deal of skimble-skamble stuff about Johnson's money. But by this time fog, for me, had set in, and it did not lift when an incinerator, horribly suggesting the crematorium, turned out to be the door of a night-club. Here the characters wore masks, and the point of the lugubrious orgy seemed to be the pet proposition of the a-sensualists, that commercialised pleasure is dull. Hereabouts one glimpsed the tremulous approach to an idea, the notion that no human being can exist to be the toy of another human being. In other words, that the meanest drab has had a mother somewhere. But even here I think that, if I were put to it, I could find a Victorian music-hall ditty with the same burden!

The third act relapsed into sentimentalities *à la* Mr Chips. It seems that for a short time after a man has left this world he is accompanied by the praiseworthy things in his life—affection for helpmate, children, the county cricketer who was his schoolboy hero, the clown at his first pantomime, the characters in his story-books, his favourite quotations. But is this anything except Everyman's Good Deeds sentimentalised? And then that Celestial Floorwalker, without whom the outward-bound drama cannot happen and who had hovered at Johnson's elbow throughout, put in a last appearance. This suave young man now told Johnson that his time was up and that he must begin his journey. Naturally Johnson wanted to know where to and how far. But the Floorwalker did not know, and for the very good reason that Mr Priestley didn't, and that no character even in Expressionist dramas can be wiser than his playwright.

I do not accuse my old friend of having consciously bamboozled us; I suggest that he has unconsciously and with complete sincerity bamboozled himself. I sat through all but the last four minutes of his play dry-eyed, un-amazed, and unexcited, and as I am honest I must hold that any play, whether about death or anything else, is a failure if it does not move me emotionally, intellectually, or theatrically. Only in the last four minutes was that plane attained on which the whole thing should have been conceived and executed. Here Mr Ralph Richardson, who up to this point could only pull against the current, sud-denly felt the tide go with him, and the effect was tremen-dous. Alas, that all that went before was merely a whimper that life does not last for ever!

Let me be more than fair. The world is divided into two classes—those who, like Dr Johnson, find it impos-sible to think for long about any subject except death, and those who never give death a thought. Similarly playgoers may be divided into two classes—those whom Expressionism bored to hysteria even when it was fresh, and those whom it is spoofing for the first time. It follows that people in the second category in each case will prob-ably take *Johnson over Jordan* for a masterpiece. And so it may be, for them.

Enormous care has gone to the production, lighting, and music, much of the last being by Mr Benjamin Britten, at his most ingenious. But where on earth did Mr Basil Dean get the notion that in 1910 or thereabouts we bowed to our partners at every half-dozen bars of the Valse Bleue? Can he have been confusing this lovely old waltz with the Veleta?

Even to the faithful Ibsen's play was always minor and unexciting. It was precious little use telling us, as in the early years of this century we sat shivering in unwarmed provincial theatres, that the first thing to note about this Public Baths drama was its place in the canon. What did it help us to know that the next play was *The Wild Duck*, which nobody had seen, and that the previous one had been *Ghosts*, which again none of us had seen? Unless, of

course, our provincial town was Manchester, when, with
luck, we might have been present ten years earlier at one
of those historic five performances given in the lecture
theatre at the Athenæum in Princess Street. A young man
engaged in peddling calico at a salary of thirty shillings a
week, less sixpence laid out on the *Saturday Review*, was so
greatly excited by some articles signed G.B.S. on the plays
of one Ibsen that he determined to do something about it.
He made inquiries, and discovered the existence of a troupe
of Ibsenite players, headed by Charles Charrington, Janet
Achurch, and Courtenay Thorpe, which traipsed the
country with baggage consisting of a single dress-basket
and Helmer's front door, complete with letter-box.

Our young man decided to intercept the company,
which had slithered from a mission-hall in Darlington to a
drill-hall in Dover, and was hoisting itself up to Dingwall
at the invitation of the Institute for Deep Sea Fishermen.
They were met at some hole in the Midlands, the young
man having collected £90, in cash, *not* promises, from the
wealthy German Jews to whom he sold his calico, *no
Aryan contributing a penny*. The result was that performance of which Montague wrote: "Tragedy burned
up the lamp that had held it, and flamed like a star, un-
conditioned and absolute."

Now *An Enemy of the People*, the panjandrums said,
was conditioned and relative. But relative to what? In
1882 that which lay behind this play was Ibsen's quarrel
over *Ghosts*. What lies behind it in 1939? Why, Democracy's quarrel with Dictatorship, or, rather, Dictatorship's
low opinion of Democracy. "Democracy is the right of
imbeciles to govern themselves," said a speaker at a recent
debate at the Oxford Union. And, so saying, unwillingly
condensed the whole of Dr Stockman's great speech in
Act IV. Yes, this play, and its revival, are miraculously
apt to the times, and I fancy that not only Nazis and
Communists, but famished tigers and pet lambs, will have

to do a lot of lying down together amicably before it is seen for what it is—a rather dreary parable about a lot of pump-water. In the meantime it makes an intensely exciting evening.

The Old Vic company acts it very well. The Doctor is the difficulty, and Mr Roger Livesey gets out of it by steering a middle course between the adroit and lavish insincerities of Beerbohm Tree and the muddled grandeurs of Henry Austin. The part is one for a great actor who is careful not to let any of his great acting show. Mr Livesey does not carry quite enough guns, though he is correct in keeping the waterproof covers on such guns as he does carry. Stockman is a cruiser cruising, and not a battleship giving battle. Mr Edward Chapman's Peter Stockman is a brilliant and most amusing bit of character-drawing, Mr Jonathan Field as the young man in the printer's office knocks up something out of nothing, Mr Frederick Bennett wittily makes up Morten Kiil to look like Ibsen himself in the mood to rout the entire hedge-crawling brood. For this was the period when the old porcupine's bristles were at their prickliest. Or if you prefer the badger simile, the period when he did not wait to be drawn, but adjusted his glasses, sharpened his nose, bared his teeth, and came out into the open uninvited.

La Comédie Française

[*March* 5, 1939]

That the House of Molière must start with a play by
Molière is a self-evident proposition. But a proposition
attended with some danger, since it too often means *Le
Misanthrope*, which inaugurated the famous visit of 1879,
and of which Sarcey wrote: "Il était à craindre que le
Misanthrope n'ennuyât quelque peu son monde. Dame!
entre nous, le *Misanthrope*, même à Paris, n'est pas toujours régalant; on l'écoute avec respect, mais sans trans-
port." Joseph Knight, dealing with the same visit and
the same play, has the following:

> *Le Misanthrope* is a difficult play wherewith to please
> an English audience. Without either action or situa-
> tion, it seeks to interest by purely psychological pro-
> cesses, and exposes to vulgar gaze a nature which
> vulgar perceptions can never penetrate. It is painful,
> if edifying, to watch the efforts to force into drollery
> the biting phrases of Alceste, out of regard for a public
> which, hearing of Molière as a comic writer, waits for
> comic scenes.

But the scenes in *L'École des Maris*, now preferred by
our visitors, *are* comic. They expose to English gaze that
which English perception has no difficulty in penetrating.
Sganarelle, the eternal *niais*, is universal in the sense that

237

Sancho Panza and Aguecheek, to whom he is first and second cousin, are universal; it is only their manners which they wear with a difference. Every drama in the world has had its gallant, Valère; our own Shakespeare found it convenient to unite wideawake heroine and knowing serving-maid in the person of Maria; and the valet, Ergaste, is our old friend Figaro all over again. Only the presentation is French, and here Hazlitt . . .

"Pest upon the fellow!" I can hear the reader saying. "Why can't he tell us what he thinks and not what other people have thought?" The point is that I cannot, and perhaps will not, divorce myself from what better men have thought and better expressed on this great subject. Hazlitt said of *L'École des Maris* :

> The plot is charming, and the style is profuse of sense and wit; but there is this remark to be made here, as of other of Molière's plays, that however elegant, ingenious, or natural, the scene must be laid in France, that the whole passes under that empire of words, which is confined to her airy limits, and that there is a credulous and unqualified assent to verbal professions necessary to carry on the plot, which can be found nowhere but in France.

The piece was deliciously presented and, as far as one knows, traditionally, except that in Ergaste Molière appeared to have foreseen the Russian Ballet, the actor in this case, M. Robert Manuel, contributing a literally skipping wit which added greatly to the visual excitement of the piece. Gorgeously caparisoned, M. Jean Weber raised the clowning of Valère, if that be not too gross a word, to heights independent of language. In the short part of Léonor Mlle Irène Brillant showed how galleons move; and as Isabelle Mlle Lise Delamare was a little rogue in samite. But the keystone of the play must always be the Sganarelle, and here M. Max Lafon's performance struck us as the perfect piece of engineering, holding the plot together and meeting its strains and stresses with perfect understanding and imperturbable good humour.

Musset's *Le Chandelier* was for an English audience much more difficult. For here the passion of love is exposed to our gaze in an aspect of which until recently English sense has by no means approved. Truth insists that for ' love ' in the foregoing sentence one should read ' adultery.' Now this was the period in which Musset was most in thrall to Byron—indeed his detractors dubbed him " Byronet " and even " Mademoiselle Byron "—that enslaver of reason whose system of ethics, compounded, according to Macaulay, of misanthropy and voluptuousness, knew only two commandments, to hate your neighbour and to love your neighbour's wife. But it is not Musset's immorality, if you pass the word, in this play which affrights the modern English sense : our own Mr Coward has given us a wholly French courage. The point is Musset's brand of melancholy, which is still alien to the English temperament. To quote Macaulay again :

> We know very few persons engaged in active life, who, even if they were to procure stools to be melancholy upon, would be able to enjoy much of what somebody calls the " ecstasy of woe."

But Musset's Fortunio is just such an ecstatic ; he does nothing but weep, and the English sense cannot wholly sympathise with this overflowing urn. We feel that Fortunio belongs to that part of Dickens's world which contains Job Trotter and the Rev. Stiggins, and that his name is Dick Sniveller.

Our visitors did their gracious best to put this play across not only the footlights but the Channel. M. Gaston Baty's production and the décor of M. Marty were both sentimental and effective, to the point when looking at this play was like listening to a Chopin ballade by candlelight. Jacqueline was given a quite unimaginable finesse by Mlle Madeleine Renaud, who made her a ' keepsake ' of the period and look all the virtues she does not possess. So much for the first evening.

The second was more understandable and altogether jollier, though not so Britannically jolly that the programme was entitled to declare Musset's *A Quoi Rêvent les Jeunes Filles* to be in prose! It isn't. It is in verse, and verse in which the wit and sensibility, equally matched, are so much part of each other that you think of the result as a compound rather than a mixture. If it were possible to cavil at the acting of this company during the week it would be at M. Denis d'Ines's ' throwing away ' of the exquisite soliloquy beginning :

> Mon Dieu! tu m'as béni.—Tu m'as donné deux filles;
> Autour de mon trésor je n'ai jamais veillé. . . .

and ending :

> Je te livre, ô mon Dieu! ces deux herbes tremblantes.
> Donne-leur le bonheur, si je l'ai mérité.

But this is dangerous ground; it is possible that what is sentiment to us may be sentimentality to a nation whose peculiar genius it is to know in any art exactly how much to put into any scale at any moment. It is all very well for the programme to prattle of music by Debussy and Delibes. The décor of Marie Laurencin, the faintly balletic charm of Mlles Mony Dalmès and Françoise Delille, M. Pierre Bertin's stressing but not over-stressing of the extravagances of *le fat*, Irus, and the grave charm of M. Julien Bertheau's Silvio—all of these combined to keep the comedy in its Chopinesque dimension, the music in our ears being, I do not hesitate to affirm, the Valse in C sharp minor.

Regnard's great farce of *Le Légataire Universel* brings us back to the battleground of argument where we make the surprising discovery that our neighbours are capable of flirting with that to which the Englishman is wedded—the moral justification of his pleasures. We all remember how Charles Lamb provided Restoration comedy with a moral coating when, of course, he should have said : " Vice is its own reward—see Restoration comedy ! " The editor of my Regnard actually seeks to justify the insensibilities of a piece which makes a mock at a dying man !

> Et voici le prestigieux tour d'adresse : c'est d'un sujet funèbre que jaillit ce rire intarissable, d'un spectacle en soi propre à faire naître la pitié et l'horreur. Géronte, cet affligeant exemplaire de l'humaine misère, est gourmandé, rudoyé à plaisir par trois gredins qui exploitent sa crédulité et son agonie. Le spectateur devrait, semble-t-il, compatir et s'indigner. Comment l'artiste s'y est-il pris pour éviter le drame qui est au fond des choses, et même le moindre commencement d'émotion douloureuse ? Il a éloigné de la victime la sympathie et l'estime. Au physique et au moral, Géronte est répugnant, à la fois tout à fait ridicule et tout à fait odieux. . . .

And so on and so forth. But why not be content with the ridiculous part of the business and never mind about the odious ? The piece is hateful only if Punch-and-Judy is hateful. It is a monstrous, quasi-medieval guffaw at the major catastrophes. Here are the body and mind of an old man falling apart like a worn-out typewriter, and the spectacle is very, very funny. At least it is when there is a great French comedian to make it so. M. Fernand Ledoux is such a comedian. What cackling proceeded from his bosom when bronchial derangement permitted anything to proceed at all ! Did ever human legs so vacillate ? Except perhaps Grandfather Smallweed, was ever anybody so laid out in his chair by those hoping to lay him out in his coffin ?

The spring of mischief was the Crispin of M. Pierre Dux, who in this part contrived to run the entire gamut of the *cocasse* without respect to clime or time. Some such span as in our own country might begin with Ben Jonson's Mosca and end at a pantomime dame by Mr Douglas Byng. This was the perfection of acting, and one might remark about both players not only their intellectual and artistic but their physical fitness. The very pores of their skin seemed to act, and in this piece they had to. I have no space left to pay more than formal but sincere compliments to Mlle Béatrice Bretty and the other players. It would be improper to let our visitors depart without an expression of admiration for the enormous technical skill which has brought these four elaborate productions on an unfamiliar stage to a complete and hitchless success. Every seat throughout the week was taken, and the audiences were as discriminating as they were enthusiastic. The second because of the first.

In any other week one might perhaps seriously consider Mr Levy's unhappy little misfit. Reeling from the effects of true professional playwriting, what am I to say of a piece which in a fourth act and the neighbourhood of eleven o'clock turns into a dissertation on singleness of will after beginning with the foibles of ornithologists and wandering *via* a Saturday afternoon cricket match, a marshful of the will-o'-the-wisps of marital infidelity, and a complete slough of conscientious objection, to a world war in which nobody believes? In some other week I might take Mr Levy seriously to task for that many-paged letter expounding a whole philosophy of life which is supposed to have been written by a soldier in the trenches. I should tell him that his character only writes this letter because it is what he, the dramatist, wants to say. I should tell him that relatives about to break the news to a wife that her husband has been killed are just not going to let her say " Listen, folks ! " and then indulge in a ten minutes' reading aloud from his last letter. *Pace* the spirit of Arthur Hugh Clough, I shall insist on saying that on the present occasion the struggle of the players naught availeth.

The Eumenides at Home: Audience at Sea

THE FAMILY REUNION. A play in verse. By T. S. Eliot.
Westminster Theatre, Tuesday, March 21, 1939.

THE MAN IN HALF MOON STREET. A play. By Barré
Lyndon. New Theatre, Wednesday, March 22, 1939.

THE DANCING YEARS. A musical play. By Ivor Novello.
Music by Ivor Novello. Drury Lane Theatre, Friday,
March 24, 1939.

[*March* 26, 1939]

I T does not worry me that this verse has three stresses,
Why shouldn't it since the glass in my car is triplex?
One must move with the times,
As the old maid said in the musical comedy
On meeting a young gent Oxonianly debagged.
Nor does it worry me that this verse does not tinkle.
I do not expect modern art to sound nice,
Or even to look nice.
I am not alarmed because a horse by Chirico bears no resem-
blance to one by Solario.
Or perturbed when Hindemith sounds like somebody shoot-
ing coals.
Or distressed when a block of luxury flats looks like a ship
or a warehouse.
That the pretty-pretty should give place to the ferro-
concrete
Is just the age expressing itself.
What does worry me about this play is something altogether
different—
The sneaking suspicion that I may not be intellectually up
to it.
" *Il est si facile,*" said Balzac, " *de nier ce que l'on ne
comprend pas.*"

243

Meaning that the fool sees not the same tree that the wise
    man sees.
Perhaps it might be easier if I had the Eumenides nearer my
    finger-tips,
In which case I should know whether moaning becomes
    Agatha as mourning became Electra.

Before it all opened the Dowager Lady Amy lost her
    husband,
A good easy man, who bred pigs and took
Prizes and even championships at the local shows,
But had a kink, which was to do his lady in.
(Pass the expression : *Pygmalion* uses it.)
And in his nefarious design would have succeeded
But that his sister-in-law, the aforesaid Agatha,
Rumbled him.
Quoth Aggie to herself :
" Amy's with child ; otherwise 'twere quate all reaight ! "
And used her power of veto.
The child was born, called Harry, grew up, married,
And every evening plotted wife-deletion. One day
On a cruise convenient for the purpose, the moon for
    lanthorn,
And nobody on deck but just the two of them,
He did as he had planned, pleaded accident, and then
Repaired to the ancestral home,
To talk the matter over with Aunt Agatha, who—
Here out of bag comes cat—
Wished that her nephew had been her son,
And that, it seems, is exactly what was biting her,
Though what was biting him it was very hard to tell,
Except that whatever it was it wasn't murder.
Something, perhaps, about the truth of opposites,
How sleeping's waking, event not happening (or vice versa),
Nothing is change except the *status quo*, and a lot more
Of Mr Polly's Sesquippledan Verboojuice !

CHORUS

Twice two are four
But twice three are not five
Cows neigh in the byre
Herb-o'-grace looks for Sunday
Octaves wilt
Fifths grow consecutive
Moon and green cheese
Have come to terms
Fog horns summon
The household to supper
The bones of the majordomo
Rap out curses
Methylated spirits
Wait round the corner.

By the way, I nearly forgot to mention
Harry's two brothers, John and Arthur,
Neither of whom appears because of motor trouble.
One is in a smash, and Harry says :
   " A minor trouble like concussion
   Cannot make very much difference to John.
   A brief vacation from the kind of consciousness
   That John enjoys can't make very much difference
   To him or anyone else."

From which you glean
How much difference exists
Between this play's elegant verse and my pastiche,
Except that every now and then
Our author slips in a line or two just to prove
That when he wants he can do the straight stuff, like
    Picasso.
And here, of course, the reader's all agog to know
Is this a good play, and will he enjoy it ?

All I can say is it depends on
Whether he feels
That English tubs stand best on these antique bottoms
Ponderous buskinage, club-footed sockery
Having to do with expiation,
Innocents repaying guilty debts,
And elaborate curses that went out with Sheridan
Knowles. For Wishwood House,
Whose name reminds us of a mental hospital,
Is still the sport of gods plentifully back-numbered
Long, long before
Harvey proclaimed the blood goes round and round,
And retribution like W. S. Gilbert's poisèd hawk
Swooped. But to the point !
My chief complaint about this play
Is vagueness, a confluence of sublimations.
Unparsable, people going nowhither to do nowhat.
Will some one, for example, tell me exactly where
Harry is going to when he puts on John's overcoat.
Is he for the police-station to give himself up,
Or lankly starting on an introspective, cis-Jordanian trek ?
Where, where, where, where, where, where ?
And as the author didn't know,
Nor Æschylus, nor even the Libraries,
We in the audience must pretend to be wabe-conscious,
Some gyred, others gimbled. I did neither.
But nothing could stop foyer-cluttered Bloomsbury
From explaining *en deux mots* what the play was all about.
It baffled me, but did not in the least baffle them,
To read a B.C. crossword by an A.D. light.
Yet, try as I would, I, a modern Englishman, could not see
   why
Because a man's aunt ought to have been his mother
He must push his wife overboard
And I just could not accept the explanation
That it was all because Harry's soul

Had got mixed up with the Wishwood drains.
And here I have to say quite firmly
That what was good enough for Æschylus is by no means
Good enough for me !

About the playing there cannot be
Any two opinions. Michael Redgrave
Spoke cloudy words with clear-cut superiority
As of a B.B.C. announcer. Helen Haye, the dowager,
Back-chatting with her sister,
Proved what an actress should be, while
Aunt Agatha, grandly sustained by Catherine Lacey,
Looked incommunicable things and, the broadcast over,
Implied that the station was closing down.

Mr Lyndon's preposterous but highly exciting nonsense
is all about a man of ninety who, in order to prolong the
appearance of youth, buys the organs of poor men and swops
them for his own. He may be said to exchange kidneys to
save his bacon. As healthy young men require from time to
time sums like £24,000, he procures these by robbing bank
cashiers and dissolving the bodies in a bath of acid, which
is then run off in the usual way. Mr Leslie Banks and Mr
Malcolm Keen enact all this with terrific sincerity—if they
didn't they must surely fall into hysterics ! Mr Morland
Graham, Mr Leslie Dwyer, Mr George Butler, and Mr
Michael Shepley are more credibly amusing. Mr Marcus
Barron, bereft of any part except for an occasional hum
followed by a periodical ha, proves himself to be still very
nearly the best actor in England. This play cannot run a
day short of two years, and I invite readers to decide for
themselves how long they think *The Macropulos Secret*,
Capek's first-class play on the same subject, would run if
put on commercially.

General opinion insists that the latest is the best to date
of all the Tales from the Novello Woods. So be it ! It is

certainly an excellent example of that form of entertainment which should be called Magnoperetta—meaning the filling of the vast Drury Lane stage and the still vaster British bosom with the grand passion's small change. Mr Novello is the usual velveteen hobbledehoy who pursues, or is pursued by, Miss Mary Ellis's wayward warbler. Always in the same waltz-time, and I suspect to the same waltz. The scenery is pretty enough to eat, the chorus is agile, there is a pleasant newcomer in Miss Roma Beaumont, there is no wit, and there is, thank heaven, no humour !

California Gate-crashes: Crashing Success at the Gate

OF MICE AND MEN. A play. By John Steinbeck. Gate Theatre, Wednesday, April 12, 1939.

A WOMAN'S PRIVILEGE. A play. By Margaret Branford. Kingsway Theatre, Thursday, April 13, 1939.

[*April* 16, 1939]

WHEN I was in New York two years ago I called at Brentano's and asked them to give me the book most representative of what young America was thinking. Brentano's handed me not *Gone with Aurora Borealis* or other spinsterish guff running to 1072 pages, but a book the length of a long short-story by Joseph Conrad and called *Of Mice and Men.* I gave this novel immense praise in the columns of the *Sunday Times*, and then persuaded an English newspaper to serialise it. The next step in the book's history was its dramatisation in New York, where the play ran for nearly two years. That the big film studios would studiously ignore it was obvious. For the story is what in the 'nineties we were calling a slice of life, meaning something raw and bleeding, whereas what Hollywood means by a slice of life is a cream puff drenched with Chanel No. 6.

Again, the film public would not stand for such a story without drastic alteration. For it is a law of cinema that in a film in which a platinum cutie and a tousled husky have a broken neck between them, the neck must be that of the husky and broken while accomplishing some act of obeisance to femininity. And in Mr Steinbeck's story it is the neck of, if you please, the cutie which gets broken, just as a mouse and a puppy-dog have already had their necks broken by the simpleton husky who does not know how strong he is.

249

Is this an appalling tragedy? Yes. But it is not the girl's, since we are no more concerned for her than we are for that mouse and that puppy. The tragedy is that of Lennie the husky, and even more of his friend George, who has nursed and fenced in Lennie throughout his horribly precarious existence, and must now shoot him to avoid his inevitable lynching at the hands of the cutie's husband and the other ranchers. Obviously there is not a scenario-monger living who would touch such a plot. His kind realises that what the film-goer wants to see is a Norma or a Loretta extravagantly alive and not expensively dead. Also that in the eyes of the one-and-ninepennies the Georges and the Lennies are pure thugs, to be kept in their place, which is the edge of a picture and not the centre. However, it is early days, and I have no doubt that we shall presently be given a film entitled *Of Mice and Women* in which the batting order will be the lynching of Lennie, the discovery that the cutie's neck was only bruised, the dispensing with the cutie's husband, her marriage with George, who until then has not, as they say, spoken, the further discovery that George is not a rancher at all but the son of Mervyn T. Huggermugger, the Brooklyn Chewing-Gum King, and the revelation that the cutie is not a cutie at all but a blonde who was platinum at birth !

In the meantime the production of the play in London has been left to one of the coterie theatres. This is odd because there is nothing spruce, affected, or, as Shakespeare's Holofernes would say, peregrinate about it, despite the fact that Lennie and George are, strictly speaking, peregrinators. In other words, they are Californian hoboes or tramps, whereas by all the coterie-laws they should be ghosts, or souls of mummies, or other-selves, or characters out of lost plays of Æschylus. But George and Lennie are none of these things. They are just a pair of ordinary, dirty, unsavoury tramps, chained to the pettifoggery of three-dimensional existence. And what do the pair stand for? The poetry of earth? The prose of humanity ? The redemption of capital through the sweat of labour ? Aw, shucks !

Here is a passage which continually recurs like a litany, showing how far removed is the earthly paradise of George and Lennie from the signs and symbols of the metaphysical dramatist. This is what they look forward to :

> Got a little win'mill. Got a little shack on it, an' a chicken run. Little fat iron stove, an' in the winter we'd keep a fire goin' in it. It ain't enough land so we'd have to work too hard. Maybe six, seven hours a day. An' we'd keep a few pigeons to go flyin' around the win'mill. An' it'd be our own, an' nobody could can us. If we don't like a guy we can say, ' Get the hell out,' and by God he's got to do it. An' if a fren' come along, why we'd have an extra bunk, an' we'd say : ' Why don't you spen' the night,' an' by God he would. An' if a circus or a ball game came to town we'd just go to her. We wouldn't ask nobody if we could. Jus' say : ' We'll go to her,' an' we would.

This is something which has been in the mind of man since the first delver—a handspan of land on which he shall be his own master, of earth fertilised by the sweat of his brow and the rain from heaven.

The play is the oldest and most intelligible of poems, mercifully free from the newest and least intelligible of poetry. It is grandly acted. As the dumb giant Mr Niall MacGinnis, who has hitherto been merely feeling his way as an actor, arrives at something that is very close to power ; Lennie's inarticulacy is the most articulate thing this young and promising player has yet done. As George Mr John Mills provides the most explicit and direct of foils. Here is another young actor on whose previous admirable work this performance of shrewdness, subtlety, and pathos sets a seal. I warn him, however, not to expect the highbrows to cotton to him on the strength of a commonplace young man with a penchant for pigeons flying round a windmill. A Greek

reincarnation absorbed in the wheeling flight of his ancestors' spotted souls would be another matter !

Miss Claire Luce handles the cutie with all possible discretion, cleverly making us feel that the girl is neither wholly
bad nor wholly good, and that it is merely a matter of cir-
cumstance that she has found her way to the barley-fields.
Another turn of the wheel and she might have adorned a
heavyweight champion's two-seater or a film magnate's
limousine. Wholly authentic, as I judge, and well diversi-
fied performances are given by Messrs Sydney Benson,
Edward Wallace, Nicholas Stuart, Robert Berkeley,
Richard Rudi, Jefferson Searles, and Conway Palmer, and
it is all nonsense that this piece is not playing at a bigger
and public theatre. In the meantime all honour to the little
Gate Theatre.

Mrs Branford's is not a good or even a goodish play. But
I take off my hat to the author for having done something
almost unique on the modern English stage, and which
would be quite unique were it not for a similar achievement
by Mr H. F. Maltby in a play called *Three Birds*. In that
bitter comedy Mr Maltby took three women regarded as
' nice,' and revealed them as possessive, predatory harpies
without a redeeming virtue between them. The noise of
this play's flop was as though somebody had dropped Mount
Everest into the Womb of Time. Now comes Mrs Branford
with the heroine of a hundred successes, the most popular
and perhaps the only kind of heroine the English stage has
known since the War, and shows her to be an odious, mean,
greedy, common baggage. And when the curtain fell one's
inward ear heard a noise as though all the chandeliers at
Versailles had fallen. There is something glassy about the
shattering of illusions.

The story of the play is told in a few words. Dora Spen-
low and Agnes Wickfield are sisters, except that Dora is a
hard-faced schemer and liar as well as doll. First she tries
to inveigle Traddles because Traddles's aunt is going to leave

him money. Then she has a go at Steerforth, who sees through her and takes to Agnes instead. Then back to Traddles, whose aunt dies leaving poor Traddles a mere pittance. This should be the end of Dora were it not for a millionaire American Mr Dick, whose King Charles's head is reverence for woman combined with maximum gullibility. This is the weakest point in the play, for it is not credible that *that* could have remained un-nobbled in his own country. Nevertheless, Mrs Branford has the makings of a playwright. Only a playwright could have made Agnes go to the door and, with her head in the hall, shout to her sister upstairs : " Dora, Traddles is on the 'phone to say his aunt's dead ! "

The piece is well acted. Dora is vigorously played by Miss Phyllis Calvert, who comes from the Coventry Repertory Theatre, and has, I hope, another range of parts up her sleeve. On Thursday next we are to see the American play, *The Women*, in which all but one of the forty characters is this play's heroine at some stage of her development, and it is in my mind that a glut may prove enough. Miss Rosemary Scott, who plays Agnes, possesses a quality which has almost disappeared from the English stage, that of being able to stand, sit, walk, talk, look, and listen like a lady. And it is one of this play's merits that it contains a lady. Traddles is very well done by Mr John Penrose, and it is another of this play's merits that Traddles does not use a pocket comb, or blow smoke down his nose, or cheek women, or adopt any of the loutish behaviour of drawing-room comedy *à la mode*. Indeed, both Mrs Branford and Mr Penrose between them give us a Traddles who is not a counter-jumper. If this play fails it will not be because the heroine is insufficiently nasty, but because it contains a young lady *and* a young gentleman. And, of course, no West End audience is going to stand for that !

Storm over New York: Kensington Runs for Shelter

THE WOMEN. A play. By Clare Boothe. Lyric Theatre, Thursday, April 20, 1939.
LITTLE REVUE. By Herbert Farjeon. Music by Walter Leigh. Little Theatre, Friday, April 21, 1939.

[*April* 23, 1939]

Miss BOOTHE would have done well to take a leaf out of another book and issue as *First Aid to the English Dramatic Critics* her admirable preface to the printed version of her play. Had she done so we might have been spared a humiliating display of muddled thinking on the part of that critical fraternity which Mr Max Beerbohm once described as " a fine body of men, like the Metropolitan Police."

" A crude, coarse narrative of the sexual jungle . . . beauty parlours, exercise salons, bedrooms, bathrooms, and jaded, arid dialogue by grim women about men and money and money and men," sniffs Distinguished Colleague A. This is like complaining that Ibsen's *Ghosts* is a crude, coarse play about transmitted disease, with grim, unpoetical dialogue between a hidebound pastor and a woman who didn't have the sense to leave her husband. Surely A has fallen into the old critical trap of misliking a play through dislike of its subject-matter ?

Eminent Colleague B thinks that the play is " pretty horrible " and goes on : " This is a satire which in New York bites home. Here, it is not true and fails to bite." Again I rub my eyes. Why should a play which is about a restricted New York coterie be supposed to apply to the women who do their shopping in Kensington ? And what does B's second sentence mean ? Will he hold that because

254

the plays of, say, Tchehov are not true to English character, they must fail to bite when performed over here ? One might as justly complain that the remedy for African beri-beri is no cure for a whooping-cough in Bayswater.

Cherished and Revered Critic C is of the opinion that Miss Boothe's picture is " grossly inaccurate," and for the reason that " no capital in the world could contain in one area such a collection of tedious harridans . . . a very *common* play." So Sheridan's Mr Sneer on the morning after the first performance of *The School for Scandal* might be imagined as saying : " A very common play, egad, and vastly inaccurate. Where in Mayfair will you encounter these Candours, Sneerwells, and Teazles? I vow they are but Mr Sheridan's foppery ! "

Now let us find out how much of all this Miss Boothe foresaw. Her preface begins with the categorical statement : " *The Women* is a satirical play about a numerically small group of ladies native to the Park Avenues of America. It was clearly so conceived and patently so executed. The title, which embraces half the human species, is therefore rather too roomy. . . . The play is a clinical study of a more or less isolated group, projected, perhaps, in bad temper, but in good faith." From which it surely appears that the play is not to be judged as a study of women in Kensington or Kidderminster, Kenya or Kamchatka, or anywhere except a tiny, highly circumscribed area of America's capital cities.

Miss Boothe, still in her categorical vein, asks : " Is this play ' a crime against the spirit ' ? Does it ' degrade the whole human race ' ? " She goes on : " A good misogynist would quote Mr Burke as the ungallant author of the brute statement : ' A woman is an animal, and an animal not of the highest order.' Strindberg, Schopenhauer, Ibsen, and a great horde of other bilious misogynists, including St Paul, could then be called upon to uphold speciously, no doubt, but brilliantly that loutish definition. But I have no heart for the easy game of woman-baiting. . . . I truly, heartily, and thankfully echo the cry of all who have been revolted by the *specific* bitterness of *The Women* that ' *All* women are not like that ! ' '' From which it would seem fairly obvious that Miss Boothe does not intend *The Women* to be a portrait of all women.

Now is the play true to *any* women ? Miss Boothe says : '' Whether or not this play is a good *play* is any man's business to say. But whether or not it is a portait of *such* women is a matter which no man can adequately judge, for the good reason that all their actions and emotions are shown forth in places and times which no man has ever witnessed.'' Is the behaviour of these women condoned, which would certainly make this a bad play ? Or are they held to execration, which does not necessarily make it a good play, but keeps the door open ? Read Miss Boothe : '' The women who inspired this play deserved to be smacked across the head with a meat-axe. And that, I flatter myself, is exactly what I smacked them with. They are vulgar and dirty-minded, and alien to grace, and I would not if I could gloss their obscenities with a wit which is foreign to them, and gild their futilities with a glamour which by birth and breeding and performance they do not possess. Everything they say and do is in deplorable taste, because everything I have ever heard such women say and do *is* in deplorable taste.''

Is the play poor considered as a piece of plot-making ? Miss Boothe has her answer : '' The plot is deliberately a commonplace squirrel-cage, full of holes, getting nowhere, serving only the purpose of further emphasising the minuscule, foolish, whirligig activities of a few cancerous little squirrels, whose little cheeks bulge with rotten little nuts, which in their civilised little cage they have neither the wit, nor the grace, to hide.'' And then comes the final challenge to the playgoer : '' That the antics of these women do strike most audiences as funny, instead of dull or nauseating, is a very happy accident for me at the box-office.'' And just to make assurance doubly sure Miss Boothe winds up her case by saying : " But indeed, if one is not susceptible to these women's ludicrousness, tickled by their gargantuan absurdities, one is quite justified in being either bored or appalled by them."

So there you have it ! If you are bereft of logic and/or a sense of fun, if you hold the Coventry Patmore or " Angel in the House " view of women, if you stamp indignantly about the foyer, as I saw one man do, barking : " Thank heaven, our Englishwomen are not like that ! "—why then, this play, which in my opinion is the wittiest in ten years, is not for you. For once in a way I range myself with the younger school of critics. With Mr Lionel Hale, who described it as a play about Cressida written by Thersites. With Mr Alan Dent, who makes no bones about calling it a " scathing, shocking, searing, sizzling, and almost unbelievably witty play." I have no doubt that I shall presently resume quarrelling with this Blest Pair of Sirens. But for the moment the alliance stands firm. Having seen the play in New York, where it ran for two years, I firmly decline to say anything about the way it is acted over here. My dislike of second elevens would make me unfair to a performance which anyhow is plenty good enough. All that remains for me is to thank Miss Boothe for having written my notice for me !

Mr Farjeon mixes his revues in the same way in which John Opie was said to mix his paints, and his brains are of the best quality. I am not going to say that this revue, which runs to some thirty-five numbers, is an entire and perfect chrysolite. No revue that was ever written could be ; this one is as near as makes no matter. Since the show is to begin at nine, it is at present half an hour too long, and I suggest that the items to be cut should be the burlesques of Tchehov and Ella Wheeler Wilcox and *Hamlet*, and the scenes on the beach and in the girls' dormitory. In the matter of preferences among the riches which remain, I shall merely say that the piece is like a race in which all the runners should consist of Derby winners. My own choice, even if it offends Mr Farjeon, would be the two contributions written, devised, and acted by Miss Joyce Grenfell. These monologues are the best thing in their kind since Miss Ruth Draper, the difference between the two being that Miss Draper's have sometimes been too long and that Miss Grenfell's are too short. I have the greatest possible admiration for Mr Farjeon, not to mention Miss Hermione Baddeley, for allowing Miss Grenfell to come within a thousand miles of this theatre!

Perhaps Miss Baddeley realises that she can afford to be generous. Conscious or not, her generosity gives her breathing-space in a tireless, cataclysmic succession of triumphs. Indeed, at one time I got the impression that Miss Baddeley just sat still while they shoved all these triumphs under her. Here again the choice is nice, and I personally elect for a tottering ballerina and an invalid wintering at Torquay. But let me call a halt! The more sparkling the revue, the more dismal the inventory of that revue's bubbles. Enough to say that the dry toast of Mr Farjeon's wit is thickly buttered throughout by Mr Cyril Ritchard and Mr George Benson, by Miss Charlotte Leigh and Miss Betty Ann Davies, and by Messrs Eric Anderson, Gordon Little, Michael Anthony, and Ronald Waters in a host of lesser parts. The revue has two little sketches in the minor which are of great value to it. These are a study of the backward girl oppressed by her homework, and a sinister aspect of the Lambeth Walk entitled " Daisy Goes Out With Bert." This last is, I say with conviction, the best thing in a show which has at least six or seven best things. I am, however, surprised, shocked, and even pained that Mr Farjeon's good taste should in one item have permitted him to poke fun at Glyndebourne!

Shavian Phonetics

PYGMALION. Revival of Bernard Shaw's play. Haymarket
Theatre, Tuesday, June 13, 1939.

BRIDGE OF SIGHS. A play. By A. de Grunwald. St
Martin's Theatre, Wednesday, June 14, 1939.

[*June* 18, 1939]

THE best that can be said about Mr Shaw's phonetics is
that they are phoney! Take that passage in which Mrs
Eynsford Hill asks Eliza how she knows her son's name
is Freddy. Eliza answers:

> Ow, eez ye-ooa san, is e? Wal, fewd dan y' de-ooty
> bawmz a mather should, eed now bettern to spawl a
> pore gel's flahrzn than ran awy athaht pyin.

I have some practice in this matter; for example, I know
English as she is spoke by Viennese actresses. But I pored
for twenty minutes over this passage in the printed version
of the play before I could translate: "Fewd dan y'
de-ooty bawmz a mather should" into: "If you had done
your duty by him as a mother should." Mr Shaw apologises
for his failure to represent Eliza's dialect without a phonetic
alphabet, " the absence of which makes it unintelligible outside London." But the author of the following needed no
phonetic alphabet to make him magnificently intelligible
wherever any kind of English is spoken. I cut this out of a
newspaper article by Mr Thomas Burke some four or five
years ago:

> The Cockney gamin actually does not talk in words.
> He talks in sounds. He does not say: "Wot erbaht
> going aht fer ther dye," or anything so clipped and
> definite as that. He slurs it to "Wodda buht go nuht
> f'th'daey."

Here is a genuine eclogue, overheard on a 'bus between Putney and Fulham :

" Lo, Bert. Wodger do Saddy ? "
" Din do nuthen. Wodjoo do ? "
" Bidda gardnin. Wenna pigchers."
" Wodgersee ? "
" O, silly muck. . . . Owzerni ? "
" Ernizallright. Gottarise."
" Gottarise. A ? Cor ! Nomenny rises baht nah."
" Naow. Biddaluck frim. Ecun do wivit."
" Beteecan. Well, seeya seevnin'."

And here is a phonetic riddle which, I believe, the Post Office solved only last week without the assistance of any phonetic alphabet. It was an address which ran :

Captain David Jones,
Saucy Sally,
ARIJABA

Cockney lingo is an intricate subject which Chesterton managed better than Mr Shaw. In his preface to some Dickens novel G.K.C. relates how he drove in a hansom cab down a lane which ended in a cul-de-sac. G.K.C. said : " This is no good ! " Whereas the cab-driver said : " This is a bit of orl right ! " Compare that passage in *Pygmalion* in which Pickering asks the transmogrified Doolittle whether his daughter Eliza has been buying him new clothes. Doolittle answers : " Eliza ! not she. Not half. Why would she buy me clothes ? " Obviously Mr Shaw has never grasped the fact that the Cockney " not 'arf " is the emphatic affirmative, and must mean that *of course* Eliza has bought her father clothes ! What Mr Shaw was looking for was the emphatic negative, for which Doolittle's phrase would be " like 'ell she 'as ! " The point of Cockney slang is *irony*, cabman and dustman alike making their point by stating the direct opposite. But the whole line is riddled with inaccuracies. Doolittle would not say " not she "; he would say " not 'er." He would not say both " not she "

and " not half." And " Why would she buy me clothes ? "
never came out of a dustman's mouth. The passage, if it is
to be true to life, should run as follows :

> PICKERING. Has Eliza been buying you clothes ?
> DOOLITTLE. Eliza ! Like 'ell she 'as ! Wot for would
> she be buyin' *me* clothes ?

And talking of clothes, how comes Mr Shaw to imagine
that Doolittle would call on Higgins ' in his dirt,' and with
that coalman's contraption on his head ? He would wait till
the evening, spruce himself up, and call strategically late
after screwing his courage to the sticking-place at the Red
Lion.

All this would be pernickety if it were not that class
distinction is the very marrow of the play. The point is
not and never was whether fine words can turn a dustman's daughter into a lady, but whether they can provide
the necessary veneer. And it is just this which makes the
play so irretrievably out of date. For ladies are out of
fashion. The younger generation has no idea what you
mean when you tell them that some indigent gentlewoman
is a lady, and that some blonde enchantress, ermine-
swathed from perm to sandals, isn't. We must, I suppose,
move with the times. Even before *Pygmalion* was written
Rudyard Kipling was telling us that the Colonel's lady
and Judy O'Grady are sisters under their skins. Now that
they both daub their skins with the same messes, differentiation is over. Innateness has ceased to be.

On the other hand, Mr Shaw is quite right when he says
in his preface : " The English have no respect for their
language, and will not teach their children to speak it."
To the Frenchman the flowers of speech are as essential as
to the cultivated person are flowers in a room. To our
neighbours good speech is a part of good manners. An
excellent example of this was provided recently in the
film called *Quai des Brumes*. A quite ordinary French-

man, being held up by thugs, told them what he thought
about them. An Englishman of breeding would have said :
" You're a pack of scoundrels ! " An Englishman without breeding : " You're a lot of dirty swine ! " In such a
matter all Frenchmen are of one breeding, and the Frenchman in the film said : " *Vous êtes des gens mal élevés !* "
Elsewhere in his preface Mr Shaw says that there is too
much sham English spoken in our theatres and too little
of the noble English of Forbes-Robertson. My ear tells me
that the English spoken on the stage to-day is too often
not that of gentlemen but of gentlemen's gentlemen. The
misflavour may be slight, but it is unmistakable, like that
of bread cut with an onion knife. The offenders cannot
hear the way they speak and there is nobody to tell them,
for the good reason that nobody considers that their
speech is bad. Does it matter in the present state of the
world ? I think it does. Let us, if the pressure of the time
compel it, do away with our arts. Let us dispense with
drama, poetry, painting, music. Let the lids of pianos be
shut. Let the virtuosi put their fiddles back in their cases.
But while they hold them to their chins, let them play in
tune. While there is speech on the stage, let it be well-bred
speech. I have wandered some distance from Mr Shaw's
play, and perhaps not unintentionally. For I have always
regarded *Pygmalion* as all my eye and Eliza Doolittle.

Mesdames Margaret Rawlings, Helen Haye, and Dora
Gregory, and Messrs Basil Sydney and George Merritt
enjoy themselves hugely, though the performance I like
best is that of Mr Lewis Casson, who makes of Colonel
Pickering the best, by far the best, Dr Watson I have ever
seen ! And now it remains to say that the answer to the
Post Office riddle is—Harwich Harbour.

An Empress in *Bridge of Sighs* thought that some in-
significant chit was conspiring against her. So she sent a
trusty count to secure Chit's person. He found her playing
a guitar, and by telling Chit that she was to be crowned

in the Empress's stead persuaded her to come with him to the court. Arrived back, the count told the Empress that Chit was quite a nice little thing and couldn't conspire for toffee, and could he marry her, please? The Empress was thinking this over when the river burst its banks and drowned Chit in the kind of cell which, if this had been an opera, she would have shared with Azucena. Actually it was all supposed to be happening at the Court of Catherine the Great. What Messrs Reginald Tate, Neil Porter, and James Raglan thought about the evening I cannot imagine. Miss Judy Kelly as Catherine put up a bit of a fight, and in the matter of Chit I shall certainly not blast a newcomer's career seeing what, as Eliza Doolittle might say, she was up against!

Visit of the Royal Greek Theatre

HAMLET. Revival of Shakespeare's tragedy. His Majesty's
Theatre, Tuesday, June 20, 1939.

ELECTRA. Revival of Sophocles' tragedy. His Majesty's
Theatre, Wednesday, June 21, 1939.

AFTER THE DANCE. A play. By Terence Rattigan. St
James's Theatre, Thursday, June 22, 1939.

[*June* 25, 1939]

WHILE ready enough to express opinions on things I
think I know a little about—this readiness is part of the
outfit of a critic—I have always had an invincible repug-
nance to airing opinions where I am without knowledge.
The performance of plays in unknown tongues falls and
fits perfectly into this category. How is it possible to
estimate the justice of some player's emotion when you
have not the vaguest idea what emotion he is purporting
to convey ? " There's always the synopsis," objects somebody. There is, and it is like being stranded at Leatherhead
and told to find Bisley with the aid of a single signpost !
" That doesn't apply to *Hamlet*," pursues the tireless one.
" You know *Hamlet* like the back of your hand, and ought
to be able to tell where you are in it in any language."
The gentleman is wrong. I know, like the back of my
hand, all that part of London which lies between Camden
Town and Swiss Cottage. Can I find my way about it in
a fog ? No ! Can it be that I don't know the play of
Hamlet ? I hardly like to think so. Yet when I see it in a
foreign language I am at once lost, my only landmarks
being bits of business which come surprisingly into view
as in a fog does some remembered pillar-box or shop-
window. I know the soliloquies by heart, and can I at a
performance in English keep one line ahead of the actor ?

Yes. But when I listen to an actor in an unknown tongue
I find that I am not one, or six, but an indeterminate
number of lines behind him. When all is said and done,
Hamlet in any tongue remains a known masterpiece,
and to have an opinion about a foreign Hamlet is not
wholly overweening. The *Electra* of Sophocles is, I submit, a horse of another colour. That, in brief, is the
reason why on the first night on Monday I avoided the
first performance of the Royal Greek Theatre in that play.
Modesty forbade.

" Drop everything and come ! " telephoned, in the ever-
delightful *Mariage de Mlle Beulemans*, the grocer's wife to
her spouse on receiving the unwelcome advances of the
commercial traveller from Marseilles. " *Lache tout et
viengi!* " was as near as I can remember and spell the
Provençal. At lunch on Wednesday a political leader-
writer came up to me at my club and said sepulchrally :
" Drop everything and go to His Majesty's to-night ! "
And he added the words : " I conjure you ! You will see
a great actress." Now it is rare indeed in these inelegant
days to be conjured, and it is rarer still to see an actress who
can be called a *great* actress. That Mme Catina Paxinou
was a very fine actress I had realised the previous evening
when, at the beginning of *Hamlet*, she first turned her eyes
from Claudius to her son. And again when, in the closet
scene, she played with her back to the audience and gave
Hamlet the stage for fear of playing him off it into the wings
to join the ghost and the body of Polonius. But a *great*
actress ? At that most critical of all adjectives the Cerberus
in me bares his fangs. And so I went to the *Electra*.

The first thing to be said about Mme Paxinou is that
she is an actress of full stature. This, for some reason or
other, has gone out of fashion, most modern tragic
actresses being either chits or elves. " O, cleave, my sides !
Heart, once be stronger than thy continent. Crack thy
frail case ! " said Antony. But that was a Roman warrior

preparing to die, and not a teacher of dramatic art preparing young ladies to become tragic actresses. The first business of such a teacher is the gymnasium of the body rather than the mind; a *great* actress must have the bosom to carry passion, the limbs to sustain gait, and enough of the physical stamina to support the wear and tear of greatness.

It was said of Mrs Siddons in her famous entrance in Franklin's *The Earl of Warwick* that she did nothing except stop suddenly within the extensive archway *and fill it*. Only an actress of physical means can do this; all that your merely intellectual actress can accomplish is to lessen the size of the archway and reduce it to her own scale. In the *Electra* Mme Paxinou must fill the archway of heaven not with resounding joy and triumph but with low-toned grief. Remember, too, that this is a classical and not a romantic rôle, the unhurried tide and not the restless cataract, the solemn flow of Gluck and not the rushing spate of Richard Strauss. Does Mme Paxinou prance like some maddened horse as did Mme Rose Pauly in the opera last year? No, and it would be wrong if she did. Does Electra at Orestes' disclosure of himself leap towards him with the felinity of Bernhardt's: " *Armand, ce n'est pas possible que Dieu soit si bon!* " No, and again it would be wrong. There is here a sublimity, an extrasensual quality of sister and brother which unseals the spectator's heart and mind. And what extraordinary subtlety is in that playing which tells us even at this moment of rapture that rapture is irrelevant, and that before the pair there is yet that which is to do, the high duty of vengeance upon Clytemnestra and Ægisthus!

And now let it be realised that all this had to be conveyed to at least one spectator by tone and gesture only, since of literal meaning there could be none, the words either of Sophocles or of M. Gryparis, his modern translator, being equally Greek to him! For such a spectator the part is reduced to an opera for the voice, a dance for the arms, and a masque for the lineaments; it is a performance in audible show. I cannot believe that one would have come away from the theatre on Wednesday evening filled with the Sophoclean sense if one had not been in the presence of a great actress.

Only, let the word be sparingly used. Of the rest of the *Electra* I most gratefully remember the quite rightly Dumasian Clytemnestra of Mme Hélène Papadakis; the competent Orestes of M. Cotsopoulos; the extraordinary dignity of M. Rozan's Guardian; the intense emotion of an almost motionless chorus which, if they were to see it, would make the wilting corybants of Kensington desist for ever; the music of M. Mitropoulos recalling the brassy cymbals of *Salammbô*, and the staggering decorum of the whole. One must not conclude without word of the imagination and technical virtuosity of the *Hamlet* production; the bloat grandeur of M. Emile Veakis's King; the pathos of Mme Manolidou's Ophelia; a general grasp of the temperamentals of acting which distinguished nearly all the minor characters and indeed made one wonder whether minor were the word; and the Oresteian Hamlet of M. Alex Minotis. One will not easily be able to forget the way in which the actor threw himself on the Player King and felt with his hands whether or not he had tears in's eyes.

Mr Rattigan is the author of the most successful farce of modern times. Presumably it would have been easy for him to continue to provoke what Goldsmith so unkindly calls the loud laugh that speaks the vacant mind. But Mr Rattigan's mind is by no means vacant. His present piece is largely a re-arrangement of old spots in a new pattern. We are now to see what happens to his Young Things when the bright day declines. At least that is what is proposed to us, though what is unfolded is something different —nothing less than the fact that David Scott-Fowler and his wife Joan have never been at heart, but have only pretended to be, dyed-in-the-wool hedonists. David is a drunk-ard heading for cirrhosis; Joan is only not a drunkard be-cause that is not a term one applies to ladies who live in expensive flats in Mayfair. As the play goes on we learn that David is an author who, knowing his books to be third-rate, still persists in the writing of them because they help him to keep a hold on decency. We learn, too, that Joan was never really a willing gadabout, and that her twelve years of throwing parties and being thrown out of them have really been a valiant attempt to turn herself into the kind of wife who would not prove boring to David.

Now I see nothing here that is not praiseworthy. Mr Rattigan has at least perceived that people are not neces-sarily all of a piece. The difficulty is that a tragedy—and this is intended to be a tragedy—must be all of a piece whether the characters are or are not. We come now to Helen, the young girl who is engaged to Peter, David's young brother who acts as his secretary. Helen is the most unlikeable young woman one has encountered in a year's march from one theatre to another. So be it! I see no reason to assume that the race of female prigs is extinct, and again one must be grateful to Mr Rattigan for giving us an ingénue who is unsympathetic enough to be interesting. Helen, in the cant phrase, falls for David, whom she desires to reform and then marry. Being a humourless prig, she tells Joan that she and David are soul-mates and that Joan is in duty bound to divorce David with maximum speed and minimum fuss.

Now this might be all very well if David and Joan were heartily sick of each other and only continued to share the same flat because one apartment is cheaper than two. But there is a scene towards the end of the second act in which the pair are shown to be dependent upon each other. A demoded Victorian poet has described married life as

> Beautiful friendship tried by sun and wind,
> Durable from the daily dust of life.

And the fact that there is very little of the open air and far too much dust about comradeship in our couple does not prevent that comradeship from being real. The little scene at the piano proves it. This being so, we reject with some finality the notion that David, who is a man of the world and not a callow youth, would fall for Helen to the extent of wanting to marry her, and we entirely reject the notion that Joan would obligingly throw herself out of the window. The third act shows David resigning Helen to Peter for Helen's sake. Does not Mr Rattigan perceive that six months of priggishness would have made David extricate himself for his own sake?

The muddle is complicated by a singular perversity in the casting. Despite the brilliance of their playing, I am not to be persuaded that the spiritual homes of Mr Robert Harris and Miss Catherine Lacey are within a thousand miles of Shepherd Market. Miss Anne Firth, on the other hand, seems to me to be dead right as Helen. So too is the secretary of Mr Hubert Gregg. I should say the same of Mr Martin Walker's crapulous and witty *raisonneur* if it were not that on the night I attended this excellent actor threw away three-quarters of his lines while the remainder were difficult to hear. Nevertheless, and for the reasons given, I suggest that this play is worthy of respect.

The Nature of Hamlet

HAMLET. Revival of Shakespeare's tragedy. Lyceum
Theatre, Wednesday, June 28, 1939.

THE PLOUGH AND THE STARS. Revival of Sean O'Casey's
play. " Q " Theatre, Monday, June 26, 1939.

[*July* 2, 1939]

G. H. LEWES never saw Garrick's Hamlet. But, basing
himself on Fielding's description, he deduced that the
great actor " tried to be natural, without duly considering
the kind of nature that was to be represented." And,
possibly, without considering his own. For in the delineation of natural passion there are two natures to be considered, that of the character, *and that of the actor.*
Every dramatic critic knows this, because it is exactly
this which every day of the week puts him into his most
familiar difficulty. Mr X proposes to play Hamlet, un-
deterred by a mean expression, a common voice, an awkward station, and an uncouth gait. In these days of
emasculated criticism can the critic say that Mr X, because
of these defects, is debarred from playing Hamlet ? No !
That is why you will see an otherwise honest critic stoop to
the dishonesty of praising Mr X for his ingenuity in discovering that Hamlet, though a prince, was not a gentleman !

There is this to be said straightway for Mr Gielgud's
new Hamlet, that the actor has all the physical attributes
required to make that prince princely. The more important question to ask is whether this gay and gracious
prince can be deemed to be Shakespeare's Hamlet.
" Gay ? " queries the reader, and I repeat, " Gay." The
English stage at the present moment boasts two tragedians
only among our younger actors—Mr Gielgud, whose
nature is sunny, and Mr Olivier, whose nature is sple-

270

netic. " How far," comes a second query, " should the
critic be influenced by the personality of an actor, since
the essence of the business is for the actor to cloak
his identity and to pretend to be somebody else ? "
The answer is that the finest pretending in the world
cannot wholly override personality, and that in the
classic rôles it is on his personality that the actor rides
to success.

Lewes wrote : " I never saw Kean's Hamlet. He must
have been puzzled what to do with many of the long
speeches and quiet scenes, and could have had no sympathy with the character." Now if it is legitimate to say :
" I saw Kean and know he could not have played
Hamlet," it is surely legitimate to say : " I saw Irving
and know that his Hamlet must have been the ideal
representation of Shakespeare's character." Are we going
to write of Mr Gielgud's Hamlet, as Montague wrote to
Francis Dodd of Irving's, that it was " all over faults but
a regular globe of passion and romance with huge sub-
terranean caverns and flames of fire inside it " ? I think
not, and for a reason to be found in Montague's definition
of the play as a " monstrous Gothic castle of a poem, with
its baffled half-lights and glooms." You felt that when
Irving had discarded Hamlet the actor himself remained a
vast Gothic cathedral of a man in whom Hamlet's
thoughts might have welled up naturally. That they
would not is not to the point ; even if the Shavian interpretation of Irving as ignoramus doubled by mountebank
had been correct, the *envelope* remained. And in acting
the envelope is three-quarters of the letter. When a
' natural ' Hamlet is playing the melancholy is settled and
the gaiety assumed. With Mr Gielgud it is the other way
about, and probably this is the reason that my impression
of this brilliant performance does not outlast the moment
of its brilliance. It is cometary. That was Hamlet, that
was ! And the sky is empty again.

Now let us take the performance in detail. Mr Morgan has perciepiently observed that the first soliloquy, " O that this too too solid flesh would melt," was a little forced. I agree. One feels that, with the knowledge of all that is to come, the actor can afford, and is indeed under the obligation, to play himself in. The trouble is Shakespeare, who, with an eye like Bradman, is so confident of the century he is about to score that he can open his shoulders at the first ball. The recent Greek Hamlet spoke this soliloquy with his head against a pillar, so that it was a study in lassitude and distaste, making it the empty soil of Hamlet's mind in which the flowers and weeds are to grow in such profusion. But it is probable that any first-class Hamlet—and Mr Gielgud's is in the first class—must be a give-and-take affair, that if the actor decides to avail himself of this, he must renounce that. For example, Mr Gielgud treats the long scene with the ghost as an occasion for heartrending pathos, and I have certainly never seen anguish more movingly presented. But is anguish the point? What about that metaphysical awe on which Lewes is so insistent here? Does not this Hamlet run counter to his own advice? What about setting on some quantity of thoughtful spectators to cry, though in the meantime some necessary question of the play be then to be considered? It is a law of Lewes's *optique du théâtre* that the spectator cannot listen to A properly if he is busy looking at B. Besides, a piece should always be played as though the audience were hearing it for the first time, if only for the reason that there is always somebody in the audience hearing it for the first time. The spectator's mind at this point should be with the ghost on the other side of the grave and not with Hamlet on this side. Forbes-Robertson at this point had the stage darkened so as to be himself almost invisible. Mr Gielgud might be well advised to draw up a profit-and-loss account as to what should be retained and what thrown away at this point. Forbes-Robertson was marvellously effective after the ghost had gone because he had done nothing before. Mr Gielgud is comparatively ineffective because he has done so much.

In the second act (Shakespeare's) Mr Gielgud is for a long time at his best. "What a piece of work is a man!" is like a jewel hung on the air, the reception of the players is charming, and the second major soliloquy, "O, what a rogue and peasant slave am I!" is given the honours of maximum virtuosity. Some grand playing is forthcoming too in Shakespeare's third act. "To be, or not to be" is introspection's very self; a definite one of the many possible meanings has been selected for the scene with Ophelia; and the advice to the players is easy and urbane.

Then suddenly, and some may think unaccountably, the performance dries up in the play scene. But I think not unaccountably, holding the fault to be not that of Mr Gielgud the actor but of Mr Gielgud the producer. What is the sense of setting the King and Queen with their backs to the audience when the interest now centres in their faces? Take away the royal target, and however well Hamlet aims interest must go out of the marksmanship. And if bad begins, worse remains behind. My colleague Mr Darlington praises the actress entrusted with the Queen for making her "a woman with senses but no mind, luscious as a lollipop and shallow as a puddle." I have nothing with this criticism. I make nothing of a Gertrude who is the double of the Comtesse de Lage in *The Women*, expatiating on "l'amour, but not lopsided l'amour"! But the point is not what any critic can make of such a character, but what Hamlet can make of it, and I say that he can make nothing. Like Lamb's Old Actor, Hamlet in the absence of any sentient partner in the closet scene is reduced to fighting with his own shadow, to "seeing ghosts," and it so happens that in this particular play Shakespeare indicates with extreme precision when Hamlet should be seeing a ghost and when not!

The actor fails too, and fails handsomely, in the third scene of Shakespeare's fourth act. The sinister itch, the spleen that finds its images in the sun breeding maggots in a dead dog, and its most exquisite sensation in the doom of all loving flesh—" and now my Lady Worm's "—this instinct for rottenness and death—" your worm is your only emperor for diet "—is as much a part of Hamlet, whether we like it or not, as the most urbane of his philosophy, the most flowerlike of his chivalry, the last of his tenderness. Here Hamlet should show himself as much intrigued by putrescence, material and moral, as any Baudelaire that was to come after; the terrible quality of his gusto at this point is something far beyond that pert scoring off his uncle which is all that Mr Gielgud gives. But after this scene the actor makes magnificent recovery, sending us into the foyer in good fettle with his delivery, at once superb and passionate, of the fourth major soliloquy, " How all occasions do inform against me! " Back in the theatre it is disconcerting to find the graveyard scene strangely ineffective, and short, as it were, of specific gravity. But the subsequent mouthing and ranting are well done, and there is a remarkable death-scene in which the man really dies as distinct from the star actor who desists.

Now let it be said that all these are personal reactions—they cannot be anything else!—to a performance of great intelligence, abounding interest, increasing vigour. It is an immense advance upon the performance of five years ago, and in the process of advancement has shed nothing of its nobility and poetry. But although I admire this Hamlet greatly, I think it must not be called a great Hamlet until one defect is remedied. " The world is out of joint," cries Hamlet. " O cursèd spite, that ever I was born to set it right! " The mark of the great Hamlet is to make the spectator feel that the finger of the casting director, if not of Fate, has known exactly what it was about, and that here and nowhere else is the actor to set Hamlet's world right. When this Hamlet tells us that he is " dreadfully attended " we do not believe him. Perhaps with the years Mr Gielgud will acquire that moodiness which sat so naturally on Irving. But then Irving had no need of years. He was destined to play Hamlet from the cradle.

What is the matter with English playgoing that a revival of *The Plough and the Stars*, one of the greatest plays of our time, can be produced on the outskirts of London, draw crammed houses, and yet not be deemed a paying proposition for the West End ? The word masterpiece should be sparingly used. This play is more. It is a blazing masterpiece. And it is superbly acted. Nothing need be said at this time of day about the performances of Miss Sara Allgood and Miss Maire O'Neill. All I have to do is to announce a new and magnificent Fluther Good in the presence of Mr Brefni O'Rorke, and a brilliant rendering by Mr Cyril Cusack of the false, fleeting, prating Young Covey. The English are an odd nation, and never odder than when, with this example of West End indifference staring them in the face, they go gaily on babbling about a National Theatre.

Magic Keyboards and Perilous Platforms

ALIEN CORN. A play. By Sidney Howard. Wyndham's
Theatre, Wednesday, July 5, 1939.

THE GENTLE PEOPLE. A play. By Irwin Shaw. Strand
Theatre, Thursday, July 6, 1939.

[*July* 9, 1939]

ONLY those whose youth, as Stevenson said, has been
" depressed by exceptionally aesthetic surroundings " will
fail to recognise in this play a ranting, roaring *succès de
théâtre*. The chief figure is a music-teacher who believes
herself to be a potential concert-pianist of the first order,
and the play invites us to consider to what extent the pre-
monition of genius justifies its victim in immolating herself
and other people. Now it will not be contested that a certain John Ruskin was a pretty good second to Ecclesiastes
in recognising Work as a thing both wholesome and ennobling. But you could not fool J.R. into believing that all
work is equally ennobling, or that there is as much spiritual
value in carrying bricks as in composing sonatas, always
given—and I can point to the passage in which careful
John makes the proviso—that the sonatas are good
sonatas. But let us have J.R.'s own words, slightly
abbreviated :

> Rough work, honourable or not, takes the life out of
> us ; and the man who has been heaving clay out of a ditch
> all day is not the same man at the end of his day as one
> who has been sitting in a quiet room reading books or
> painting pictures. If it is any comfort to you to be told
> that the rough work is the more honourable of the two,
> I should be sorry to take that much of consolation from
> you. When both kinds are equally well and worthily
> done the head's is the noble work, and the hand's the
> ignoble.

There is a character in Mr Howard's play who admirably illustrates Ruskin's point. This is the piano-tuner. Let Mr Tuner be the very genius of tuning he cannot do more than tune. But a concert-pianist is a horse of another colour. There are, of course, the mere virtuosi, the miraculous twiddling of whose fingers no more amounts to musical thought or makes their possessor a Busoni than the leger-demain of a card-manipulator amounts to a bridge sense and makes its possessor a Culbertson. But this play is concerned with more than virtuosity, with nothing less, if you please, than the soul of an artist. Good! Then we have to argue that if you deprive the musician of his soul he ceases to exist, whereas if you take other people's pianos from the tuner he looks about for another way of making his living.

At this point the reader may say: " Agreed, my dear critic. But do artists in real life unpack their souls in quite so many nerve-storms as does Miss Elsa in this play? Is not art emotion recollected in tranquillity, and is not the artist the tranquil recollector?" The answer is: No, my dear reader. Not all art is necessarily anything of the sort, and turmoil is the breath of their nostrils to nine-tenths of interpretative artists. Are not Busoni's letters full of tub-thumping about the artist's lofty mission? Did not Bernhardt, after her first failure, hysterically contemplate suicide?

> Je n'eus ni succès, ni insuccès; je passai inaperçue. Et, le soir, maman me dit : " Ma pauvre enfant, tu étais ridicule, dans ta princesse russe ! Et tu m'as fait un profond chagrin." Je ne répondis pas un mot; mais j'eus très réellement le désir de me tuer. Je dormis mal et je m'en fus vers six heures du matin chez Mme Guérard. Je lui demandai du laudanum. . . .[1]

Why, then, does an eminent colleague ask : " Ought there to be quite so much excitement, so many moments of exalta-tion and hysteria, so much shrieking, and brandy, and

---

[1] *Mémoires de Sarah Bernhardt*, p. 145.

suicide, before Elsa can count the world well lost ? " ? He goes on : " Perhaps that is how pianists feel . . ." Of course that is how some pianists feel ! *A fortiori* it is how all pianists must feel who, as the heroines of splurgy, draw-ing-room melodrama, are under the obligation to drama-tise their emotion and make it visible and audible.

But we have not done with the subject yet. Say that we have established the proposition that to the non-artist work is a harmless, necessary nightmare, whereas to the artist all that is not his work is an irrelevant dream. What follows ? Mr Howard's play is the answer, since it is nothing less than a debate as to the morality, or if you prefer it the expedience, of such dreaming. Is Elsa Brandt entitled to regard as of dream-account only the comfort of her crippled father in his exile and declining years, her financial obliga-tion to her would-be lover, her own genuine affection for this married man who would help her, the necessary mean-ness of her conduct towards the wife who takes the helping out of her husband's hands ? The case is argued with in-genuity and even subtlety. The non-artistry of the married man, Conway, is stressed, and in the recent theatre we have heard fewer honester declarations than this :

> Watkins says you're a genius. I wouldn't know. It puts you pretty far off my street. I mean I wouldn't buy stock in a company I didn't know from the ground up ! And you're asking me to invest my money in something I can't even make a guess about.

And since the play is Pinerotic rather than Ibsenite, it follows that Elsa is given bouts of spectacular piano-playing, the lover has occasion to declare his passion in jodhpurs, his wife as a pretentious musical amateur is in-vited to provide the comic relief, Elsa's old father is allowed the red herring of Viennese homesickness, while obeisance is paid to current fashion in a setting reminiscent of Mr Odets's *Paradise Lost*.

Mention of that playwright brings me to the character of Julian, an earlier lover of Elsa who, that she may follow her career, shoots himself in the stomach. How so? The answer is, in the manner of Eilert Lövborg! For there are parts of this astute play which remind one not only of Mr Odets but of Ibsen himself. Which brings me to the suggestion that what is undoubtedly a good play might easily have been a better one. The Grim Old Man of Norway would, I submit, have shown an Elsa winning her battle with herself and losing it with her public. There are times, said Ibsen, when truth should not prevail. Must he not have made the point here that the artist is a fool who throws away the substance before he or she has made sure of the shadow?

Nevertheless the piece makes excellent entertainment, and it is grandly acted. The scene remains alive throughout, largely, perhaps, because of the pace maintained throughout. The fact that Elsa is a Viennese pianist and a show part for a fine actress is presumably the reason that none of our Viennese actresses has looked at a play which has been around and in print for six years! Miss Margaretta Scott, stepping into the breach, plays Elsa with exactly the right kind of bravura, and perhaps something more. Miss Marian Spencer, adding Mrs Conway to her Mrs Linden in *A Doll's House* and her governess in *Asmodée*, now declares herself as an actress of dangerous versatility; Mr Fritz Valk, by speaking from the stage at Wyndham's in a voice which doubtless penetrates to the auditorium at the New, gives English actors a much-needed German lesson; Mr John Clements brings remarkable tact and discretion to the American Eilert, a part which one false step could make ridiculous; Mr Edmon Ryan as a newspaper editor destroys the notion that in America only the women can act; Mr Henry Hewitt contributes an admirable picture of pedagogic absurdity; and Mr Noel Howlett, Mr Miles Otway, and Miss Barbara Everest fill in with great cleverness. Last there is **Mr Hartley Power**. In the part of Conway this good actor portrays a man of slow mind moving with much uncertainty but complete integrity among forces which he feels to be real, but of which he has little understanding. There is a deliberate understatement in this piece of finely controlled acting which is most effective.

In *The Gentle People* Jonah, an elderly Jewish chef, and Philip, his Greek chum, are victimised by Goff, a Brooklyn gangster. Their hobby is fishing from a motor-boat, and all fishermen who own motor-boats must pay for " protection." As surplusage in meanness, Goff proclaims his intention of debauching Jonah's daughter, Stella. Presently the pair revolt and Jonah calls the police. Whereupon a night court magistrate whitewashes Goff. Half-an-hour later Goff gives Jonah half-a-dozen with a piece of india-rubber tubing, after which with an odd solicitude he recommends the old man to take his hurts and stiffness to a Russian bath. Why a Russian bath? In order that the author can let off some sociological steam. Anyhow, the pair find the place not too public to plot a murder in. Next night down by the wharf the couple pay their tribute, after which Jonah says to Goff : " My daughter wants you to keep a date with her, a piece of a way down the river. What about a lift ? " Goff falls for this, and when in midstream the motor breaks down he consents to lower his head to a position in which he can be knocked out. After which the pair tip him into the river.

A week later Jonah is conning the contents of Goff's easily identifiable note-cum-cigar case. Enter a G-man, who proceeds to search the pair. On Philip he finds nothing, and nothing likewise on Jonah, who, while his friend is being searched, has baited his hook with the incriminating wallet. Exit G-man saying he has nothing on our friends. Whereupon Jonah hauls in his line and retrieves the dripping wallet. Then enter Stella. Within ten minutes of losing her gangster she decides to settle down with the honest boy who throughout the play has pursued her with diligence. Exit audience.

Is there anything in the play besides this? A little, perhaps. There is an attempt to humanise Jonah, and a sincere passage in which he tells his common little daughter that she is no different from ten thousand other screen-struck ninnies. A non-Jewish Jonah and his friend would be another Bouvard and Pécuchet; Jewish, they must be Potash and Perlmutter. But, alas, Mr Abraham Sofaer, from the rise of the curtain, sees Jonah not as a bewildered Potash, but as an offended Patriarch, and the part will not bear him out! If, in the result, the piece ever attains even a fleeting convincingness it is because of Mr Clement McCallin's gangster. There is a slipping gaiety about the fellow that is truly dreadful. The glittering smile, the dandiacal grooming, the soft, workless hands for ever being gloved and ungloved, all that charm which harks back to the scamps of Molière except that those were Hyperions to this Satyr, the reluctance to put the whole foot to the ground, a tip-toed station making a quicker get-away—all this is perfect Runyon, Damonic but also dæmonic. Does the over-elaborate setting harm the play? I see it in a tiny theatre with a trestle and a yard of oilcloth to represent Bridge and River, and a pair of actors who shall endow Jonah and Philip with the awful veracity of George and Lennie in that other American play.

Do Novels Make Plays?

CAPTAIN NICHOLAS. A play. By Leslie Burgess. Adapted from the novel by Sir Hugh Walpole. Richmond Theatre, Monday, July 10, 1939.

PRINTER'S DEVIL. A play. By R. F. Delderfield. " Q " Theatre, Tuesday, July 11, 1939.

[*July* 16, 1939]

ONE of the attributes of the good critic is that he shall know where to find the perfect expression of whatever it is for which he himself happens to be fumbling. I have often been reproached with possessing this quality, and moreover with impressing it into the service of this column. I am quite impenitent and shall continue in the habit whenever it seems to me to be to the reader's advantage. Originality is the thief of more things than time, and I hold that a critic is not justified in enhancing his little ego at the expense of the reader's greater enjoyment.

Coming home from Richmond the other night, I had an idea that what I felt impelled to say about *Captain Nicholas* had been said once and for all by a great master of criticism. It might be Mr Shaw or Walkley, but something told me first to look in the works of Sir Max Beerbohm. And there it was :

> Some novels, as being merely melodramatic, deserve no better fate than being foisted upon the stage. Others, as containing no melodrama at all and being, therefore, unlikely to attract the public, are allowed to rest within their covers; but, if they were dramatised, at any rate they would not be degraded so unspeakably as is *Tess*. For *Tess*, as a book, is full of melodrama. The melodrama in it is made beautiful by the charm of Mr Hardy's temperament. One sees it softened and ennobled through a haze of poetry. One would vow, in reading it, that it was sublime tragedy. But come the

adapter, however reverent, and how fearfully one's eyes
are opened ! A seduction, a deception, an intercepted
letter, a confession, a parting, a broker in the house, a
relapse into impropriety, a taunt, a murder, a reunion,
a death scene—that is all that *Tess* is when it is
translated to the stage. A wronged heroine, a villain, a
prig, some comic rustics—these, and nothing more !

All the novels of Sir Hugh Walpole contain melodrama.
But it is melodrama made delectable by the generosity of
Sir Hugh's temperament. One sees it softened and ennobled
through a haze of understanding. One would vow in reading
these melodramas that they are dramas. But come Monday
night's adapter, whose reverence one did not doubt, and
how fearfully were the eyes opened of one who had never
peeped between the covers of *Captain Nicholas* ! And now
perhaps I ought to stop hauling myself along by Max's
apron-strings. What exactly did I see ? I saw a mischief-
maker and petty pilferer introducing himself into the house
of his married sister. To be the principal figure of one of Sir
Hugh's sinister canvases the Captain must surely be an
adumbration of Evil. What evil in the play did the Captain
achieve ?

But before answering this let me enumerate the people
upon whom that evil could be wrought. There was, first of
all, the Captain's sister, Fanny Carlisle. Then Fanny's
sister, Grace. Next Fanny's children, Romney and Nell.
Last came Fanny's husband, Charles, and her brother
Matthew. Six ' subjects,' so to speak. Of these subjects evil
was wrought on the stage—and that is where in the theatre
such an operation must take place—upon only two, the impact of the Captain upon the remaining four being either
beneficent or negative !

Those who came off badly were Fanny and Grace. The
Captain, having found an old love-letter in the pocket of
Charles's dressing-gown, showed it to Fanny, thus awaking
her from her fool's paradise of marital fidelity. Fanny going

off into the hysterics normal among deceived wives of the middle classes, I bent forward hoping to hear Charles say : " My love, you were perfectly happy all the time I was deceiving you. What is the sense of pretending to be unhappy now that I have stopped deceiving you ? " But nothing of the sort happened. And what did happen could only take place on the supposition that Mr Dunne's Time Theory is not yet a practicable proposition. If it were, Mr Leslie Burgess must have deleted this scene on the ground of a sentence in *The Women*—a sentence which for all time has knocked the bottom out of this particular marital argument. I quote from memory : " The man who can think out an answer to that one about the husband who loves his wife while carrying on with another woman is going to win that prize they're always giving out in Sweden ! "

However, let it be granted that the Captain did definite harm to Fanny. The hurt to Grace was, I suggest, worse. For an elderly spinster to write love-letters to herself is unusual if not new. It was the *clou*, as I remember, of a beautiful novel called *Une Ame Obscure* written some thirty years ago by Jean de Ferrière. To laugh the poor woman out of her one hold upon life was really wicked, the heinousness being greater than in the case of Fanny, who was merely being apprised of a situation before being told to compose herself to it. And there the mischief ended. Romney, who was becoming uneasy about a romantic friendship, was bluntly told to cultivate golf and chorusgirls. Nell, who was spiritually attracted to a man of fine nature encumbered by a vulgar wife, was told the true state of her feelings, whereby an unhappy trio was turned into two happy people with an alimony-contented third !

Since the good done to Romney and Nell perfectly balanced the harm done to Fanny and Grace, it follows that the play's significance at this point, arithmetically considered, was exactly nothing. But how about Charles and

Matthew ? We were told at the beginning that Matthew had ' got ' religion badly, and at the end that the Captain had destroyed his faith. Then why of the destruction were we vouchsafed neither sign nor word ? Worse still, there was a great moment in the second act when Matthew threatened to get Nicholas thrown out of the house. This also came to nothing ; it was as though the composer of a symphony should usher in some tremendous theme and then forget all about it.

Last it seemed to me that to Charles nothing whatever happened. Now Sir Hugh is above all things a craftsman, and unlikely to tell the story of a household and have nothing to say about its head. With this in mind, before writing this notice I took a keek at the novel. There I found that what Nicholas was up to here was Charles's intellectual disintegration. The Captain was not content that Charles, good, easy, and stupid man, should remain settled in his goodness, ease, and stupidity. He must be shaken out of it to his detriment, and the Captain's way of shaking was to get Charles's children to unsettle him. First Nell gave her father a novel by D. H. Lawrence, which he found " depressing and disgusting," and then Romney gave him a " gay story " called *Stomach Pump* by one Essex Waters, a writer *à la mode*. In the novel I found Charles's reaction described as follows :

> I've read fifty pages and I don't know *what* it's about. They are all staying in the country together. They slide down the stairs on tea-trays. Someone's going to have a baby. There's an awful description of some disease someone's got. There's a pet dog called Ramsay MacDonald. And that's *all* I've understood. What's the matter with me ? Have I gone potty ?

To return to our arithmetic. If Matthew's apostasy and Charles's disintegration had been dramatically presented, then I suppose Captain Nicholas might be, on balance, considered evil. Actually, with the exception of the theft of

eighteen-and-sixpence and a gold snuff-box, there seemed
to be not enough in the scales to account for the big speech
in which the Captain put forth his justification, the essence
of that justification being that Gregers Werle was right and
Ibsen wrong. If this was the play's message what, I must
now ask, was supposed to be conveyed by the Italian black-
mailer with gold earrings who breathed fire in the first act,
slaughter in the second, and in the third was reduced to
being helpful at the other end of the telephone?

Mr Stephen Murray as the Captain lacked both dash and
dæmonism, and the rest of the playing was moderate.
Always with the exception of Miss Renee Ascherson, who,
as the Captain's fourteen-year-old daughter, astonishingly
held together what there was of a play. Here, if I mistake
not, is an actress in the making. That is, if the power to sit
and stand still, say nothing and yet speak volumes, constitutes acting.

Printer's Devil is good repertory Ibsen, and so is Ibsen!
It tells the story of the editor of a small newspaper in a
coast town in the South of England. The paper badly needs
advertising support, and can only get it if the editor is
willing to back up a scheme for building council houses in
the middle of an unhealthy swamp. If the author has never
read or seen *An Enemy of the People*, then this is a good
play. If he has, then it is a less good play. I am inclined to
think that he has not. Otherwise he would show us his
mass-meeting in the Town Hall, instead of merely letting
us hear what happens at it. There is one respect in which
this play and Ibsen's are as alike as two peas: there is no
place for the women in either of them. With this difference,
that Ibsen took care to leave sentiment out, whereas Mr
Delderfield drags it in by the ears, and not too logically.
In the first act the editor's fiancée will marry him if he
pulls himself out of the local rut. When, in the second
act, he won't, she flounces off to London. When, in the
third act, he is in trouble, she flounces back again to make

that speech at the Town Hall which turns the tide in the editor's favour.

Miss Curigwen Lewis does well in a part in which there would be every excuse for doing ill. But the whole play is well acted, is at least about something, and quite good enough to be an instantaneous failure in the West End.

Faust in the Haymarket

THE DEVIL TO PAY. A play. By Dorothy L. Sayers. His
Majesty's Theatre, Thursday, July 20, 1939.

[*July* 23, 1939]

In the forefront of the printed version of her play Miss
Sayers has placed John Donne's:

> What Tophet is not Paradise, what Brimstone is not
> Amber, what gnashing is not a comfort, what gnawing
> of the worme is not a tickling, what torment is not a
> marriage bed to this damnation, to be secluded eternally,
> eternally, eternally, from the sight of God?

This is taken from a sermon preached to the Earl of Carlisle,
and one wonders whether the great divine was not trying
his patron a bit too high! An easy trap for the critic would
be to say of Miss Sayers, or any other writer who should
tackle the Faust legend: " Mr Blank or Miss Dash will
obviously not lay claim to Goethe's intellect or Marlowe's
poetry. Why, then, not leave the legend alone? Are there
no other fish in the dramatic ocean? " Miss Sayers forestalls
this in her preface: " To endeavour to do again what
greater poets have already magnificently done would be
folly as well as presumption, and I have tried to offer a new
presentment of Faustus." As to this I can only say that I
cannot find, with the possible exception of ' underground '
and ' all-in terms ' used in the modern connotation, any
reason why this play should not have been written by a
medieval monk, say Thomas à Kempis, with a third act
supplied later on by Machiavelli.

Of all plays else I had avoided this one. Miss Sayers,
turning a powerful eye upon the critics assembled at His
Majesty's Theatre, might have singled out the unworthy

288

author of this column and exclaimed, with Macbeth and
greater justification : " Of all men else I had avoided thee ! "
For assuredly immersion in medieval legend is not my cup
of tea. This play is not up any street of which I inhabit
cellar or garret. It is trying me above my capacity. It has
me at a mystico-metaphysical disadvantage. The reason
why I must be a bad critic of this doubtless good drama is
that I cannot, and perhaps will not, think like a medieval
monk. I believe that metaphysics is one thing and mysticism another, and that while it is difficult to keep steady
with both feet in either camp, it is impossible to retain one's
balance if one has a foot in each ! Incidentally, the difference between the metaphysician and the mystic is that the
former will always agree, if you press him, that he may be
utterly wrong, whereas the latter, however pressed, will
always insist that he is utterly right. And again, I am in
the habit of keeping my intelligence and my emotions in
separate compartments. That I should intensely admire
the architecture of some mosque would not make me a
Moslem, any more than the tin walls of a mission-house
would make me reject the tenets of that mission.

But mystics, when they venture into metaphysics, have
no such scruples. They permeate argument with the un-
arguable. They will establish an inquiry into the existence
of a Higher Power and then call that Higher Power as their
first witness ! The advertisements to the present play
contain the phrase : " There must be some meaning in
this tormented universe." There *mustn't* be anything of
the sort. If there were we should leap into our graves like
beds. But that is your mystic all over ! Mystics insist upon
reconciling mutually destructive worlds. As a dabbler in
metaphysics I distrust this play's mysticism. Were I a
dabbler in mysticism I should equally distrust its metaphysics. I fail to see how one can make the best of two
worlds when the essence of each is the denial of the other.

Take that age-long confounding of moral evil with

lighting-up time which runs all through this play. Says Mephistopheles :

> I am the price that all things pay for being,
> The shadow on the world, thrown by the world
> Standing in its own light, which light God is.
> So first, when matter was, I was called Change,
> And next, when life began, I was called Pain,
> And last, when knowledge was, I was called Evil.

I take this to be excellent mysticism but poor metaphysics. Darkness is no more than absence of light; evil is much more than absence of good. The opposite of " chair " is not sofa, but non-chair. The opposite of standing is not sitting, but non-standing. This is something never to be understood by your mystic, who insists that the opposite of something of which he disapproves must be something of which he approves.

In her preface Miss Sayers says : " Time has been exercising the minds of many writers of late. . . . The Church has always carefully distinguished time from eternity." " Many writers " clearly means Ouspensky and Mr Dunne and Mr Priestley. What standing, I cannot help asking, had the medieval Church or any other non-metaphysical body in such an argument ? The medieval Church knew about time only in the mystical and not in the metaphysical sense ; its concern was with the curve of a crozier and not the curvature of space-time. In this matter I am wholly consistent. Were the debate one between churchmen as to the efficacy of faith I should equally disallow some rationalist objection that the removal of mountains contravenes the parallelogram of forces.

Last reason why I am impatient with Miss Sayers' play is that the author will not accept the limitations of the finite mind. Hear her Mephistopheles :

> Look at the world He made, and ask yourself, what is
> He like that made it ? Would you not say it was the work
> of a mad brain, cruel and blind and stupid—this world

where the thorn chokes the flower, where the fox slays the fowl and the kite the fox, where the cat torments the mouse for pastime before she kills it for sport ?

And so on. Well, it's an old riddle. How can God, being good and omnipotent, permit evil ? In my view the argument is unpursuable, since it stands outside the limits of finite intelligence. Why, then, pursue it ?

But suppose, say you, being an argumentative reader, suppose the attempt to solve the unsolvable makes good theatre ? Suppose the unfeasible turns out to be the excuse for stirring dramatic happenings and lashings of poetry ? Well, let's suppose it ! What excitement does the spectator who shuts off his metaphysical mind get out of this play ? I cannot help thinking—very little. Doubtless it would have been great fun to a citizen of Canterbury living in the Middle Ages. But I am not a citizen of Canterbury living in the Middle Ages. I suggest that this is a play for mystics who confound, and are comforted in confounding, plainsong with plain thinking.

The last scene of Shavian quibbling, while tedious to listen to, is undeniably good to look at, and the play throughout is full of the legend's emotional appeal. I have no doubt that if it had been the work of an actual fourteenth-century monk I should have been enormously impressed. As it is, the play has sincerity, and a perfect and measured dignity. It is, in places, even noble. Better still, it is, as craftsmanship, nowhere amateurish. But as contemporary argument it has for me no validity. I see it rather as the libretto to an oratorio by Elgar in his *Gerontius* vein, with Mephistopheles worked out in the mood of " Cockaigne," the Devil's action in wiping the Judge's chair with his tail providing the perfect excuse for a twiddly bit on the clarinet ! At the same time and in my view, Berlioz and Gounod were correct in holding that *ce qui est trop mystique pour être discuté on le chante*. And that is why they were rightly beforehand with Miss Sayers and turned *The Devil to Pay* into the rocking diabolo of *Faust* and the rocketing diablerie of the *Damnation*.

Miss Sayers is a sufficiently good poet to have trusted herself more and leaned on her echoes less. Were I writing a poetic drama on this subject—which heaven forbid!— I should turn ten thousand corners to avoid any allusion to Marlowe's ships and towers. When I must refer to wantonness I should consult my Roget's *Thesaurus*, and blue would not be permitted in my stage décor. Thus would I prevent my Muse from being blasted out of the theatre by comparison with

> In wanton Arethusa's azured arms.

Has Miss Sayers any of this discretion? Nary a bit! I entered the theatre repeating to myself:

> *O lente, lente, currite noctis equi !*
> The stars move still, time runs, the clock will strike,
> The Devil will come, and Faustus must be damned.
> O, I'll leap up to my God! Who pulls me down?
> See, see where Christ's blood streams in the firmament!

and vowing in fairness to Miss Sayers to put all such recollection out of mind till her play was over. How could I still that echo when I saw the new Faustus prick his arm and heard him say:

> See how the red stream runs upon the table like letters written in fire. *Homo fuge*—Flee, O man. What, shall I turn back now?

Later, quite horrifically, I must listen to a description of Helen by Mephistopheles which went like this:

> Gaze on her face, for men have died for her,
> Great cities perished, gallant ships gone down.

At this point I was moved to whisper to my neighbour: " All is dross that is not Christopher! "

The piece should be acted in one of two ways—either by rank amateurs or by blazing geniuses. What it will not stand is professional competence, and perhaps at His

Majesty's it does not get very much more. Mr Harcourt Williams's high-pitched querulousness becomes in the long run monotonous, and I suggest that the comparative ineffectiveness of his performance of Faustus may be due to the labours of production. When will leading actors realise that they should not produce as well, if only for the reason that they cannot tell themselves when they are being inadequate ? Any other producer could have told Mr Williams that Faustus, on fire for his tremendous experiment, should show greater excitement than a spiritualist medium preparing for an afternoon séance in Kensal Rise.

Mr Frank Napier has been greatly praised for his Mephistopheles. Doubtless this actor's performance is a good one in so far as it carries out the hint in the play's preface that this character is the Merry Devil of the medieval theatre. But personally, if ever I am visited by the Devil, I shall expect him to radiate at least one little whiff of sulphur. The Mephistopheles of Thursday evening was no more frightening than the tame bailiff who twice a year distrains for the rates, while at any moment I expected him to sing " Rocked in the Cradle of the Deep," that ineluctable choice of Demon Kings of the *basso profundo* persuasion. As for the ladies, they seemed to me to be less redolent of Wittenberg and Ilium than of topless Hampstead and lengthless Cromwell Road. The player most in his period seemed to me to be Mr David Phethean, who played Wagner. As the Judge Mr Raf de la Torre looked impressive and spoke sonorously. But here, I think, was a case for a mask if ever there can be a case. The Judge should have lineaments of an unearthly radiance far beyond the competence of the human face. And the shop for this is, of course, Mr Oliver Messel !

Index